THE CONTEMPORARY WRITER

THE

INTERVIEWS WITH SIXTEEN NOVELISTS AND POETS

CONTEMPORARY

EDITED BY L. S. DEMBO AND CYRENA N. PONDROM

WRITER

THE UNIVERSITY OF WISCONSIN PRESS

PUBLISHED 1972
THE UNIVERSITY OF WISCONSIN PRESS
BOX 1379, MADISON, WISCONSIN 53701

THE UNIVERSITY OF WISCONSIN PRESS, LTD.
70 GREAT RUSSELL STREET, LONDON

COPYRIGHT © 1972
THE REGENTS OF THE UNIVERSITY OF WISCONSIN SYSTEM
ALL RIGHTS RESERVED

FIRST PRINTING

PRINTED IN THE UNITED STATES OF AMERICA
ISBN 0-299-06141-8 CLOTH, 0-299-06144-2 PAPER
LC 71-176410

The interviews in this volume originally appeared in Contemporary Literature
(*see page* 281).

To Norman Holmes Pearson

ACKNOWLEDGMENTS

The editors acknowledge with appreciation the invaluable assistance of Mr. Robert Weber in preparing the index and Mrs. Nancy Pell-mann in typing some parts of the manuscript. We also wish to thank Mr. George Stavros, whose actions as managing editor of *Contemporary Literature* during first publication of most of these interviews did much to guarantee their editorial consistency and accuracy. Finally, we express our sincere gratitude to the Wisconsin Foundation for grants to the journal which made it possible for us to obtain five of the sixteen interviews.

L. S. D.
C. N. P.

CONTENTS

INTRODUCTION

In his introduction to interviews collected from *The Paris Review*, Malcolm Cowley said, in effect, that the [genre] had finally come of age in English. Concerned chiefly with the craft of fiction, these interviews tell us "what fiction writers are as persons, where they got their materials, how they work from day to day, and what they dream of writing." John J. Enck had similar ideals when he interviewed four leading novelists (John Barth, Mark Harris, John Hawkes, and Saul Bellow) for *Wisconsin Studies in Contemporary Literature* in 1965. But in doing later interviews for the same journal (now titled *Contemporary Literature*) we felt that the medium had an even greater potential. We believed that whatever its appeal to a general readership, questioning a writer on the technicalities of his craft, his work habits, his models, and his extempore opinions of the state of letters could interest but not wholly satisfy a scholarly audience. In short, we believed that it was desirable for the interviewer to come to grips with the specific philosophic, ethical, and aesthetic issues raised in the work of his subject. We were aware that this approach, like others, had its dangers for the insensitive inquirer, who might fall into pretention and pedantry. We also knew, however, that we stood to gain a document that was unique in its intellectual value.

There was also a danger that our questions would suppress the writer rather than stimulate him, and we were gratified to discover that, far from wielding the clichés by which authors are expected to defend themselves against solemn students of their work, many of the persons interviewed were delighted to talk about their writing conceptually and at length. This is not to say that we felt the interview had to be uniformly intense and devoid of personality. We often asked biographical questions "for the record" and if the writer was moved to reveal personal details, so much the better. Furthermore, we knew that not all the authors would respond with equal warmth to philosophic questions. Borges, for example, said at the outset that he was not a "thinker" but only a man "very pleasantly puzzled by life and things"—and he maintained that position throughout the interview. At any rate, we kept in mind that all writers are writers and not necessarily thinkers.

But we were encouraged by our first efforts, which began with Kenneth Rexroth and I. B. Singer in the spring of 1968. Actually, Mr. Dembo had had his first experience the year before in a long, taped session with Robert Duncan, most of it on the poetics and philosophy of the Black Mountain School, but for his own reasons, Duncan didn't want to put it into print. Mrs. Pondrom volunteered to interview Rexroth and Singer; she had been teaching the work of both and had been doing special research on the latter. We discussed at length the possibilities of the "analytical interview" and she subsequently drew up her questions. We nonetheless had misgivings that Rexroth might balk at the terminology or reject the analytical turn of the formulations. A needless fear! Rexroth accepted the analytic approach with enthusiasm and bedazzled us all afternoon.

The following week, Singer, a subtle man who relishes the guise of simplicity, was even more responsive. Much of the three-hour discussion was stimulated by The Magician of Lublin and encompassed Singer's philosophy of art, religion, and life in general. Both Rexroth and Singer felt they had more to say after the allotted time had elapsed and additional sessions were scheduled.

It was also in the spring of 1968 that we had the extreme good fortune of bringing to the Madison campus, separately, the so-called "Objectivist" poets, Louis Zukofsky, George Oppen, Carl Rakosi, and Charles Reznikoff, each enjoying not so much a revival as a re-efflorescence. A serial interview of these writers would, we surmised, clarify an important trend in the history of modern poetry and still give each the opportunity to expound his own views. As it happened, all four were articulate, energetic men quite prepared to discuss their work and its context before an audience of students and faculty familiar with both.

With the Swedish writers (May, 1969) the interviewer's knowledge was limited to books in English translations. These interviews were designed to present the Swedes to an audience largely unacquainted with their work and we were satisfied that the results justified the effort. With the Barker interview, which Mrs. Pondrom conducted

during a trip to England in the summer of 1970, we were virtually
back on native ground.

The journal was also fortunate to acquire an interview with
Nabokov held by Alfred Appel, Jr. (September, 1966), who was one
of Nabokov's students at Cornell and who had a thorough knowledge
of Nabokov's fiction. James Merrill was interviewed in the spring of
1967 by Donald Sheehan, then managing editor of *Wisconsin Studies*
and a friend of the poet; and Gwendolyn Brooks was interviewed in
the spring of 1969 by George Stavros, who as managing editor of
Contemporary Literature was completely familiar with the style we
were developing.

These interviews speak for themselves, testimonies to the individuality of each writer, but in addition there are correlations among them
that point toward some of the important philosophic and aesthetic
concerns of contemporary literature. For example, the question "What
is knowledge?" occupies writers so divergent as Rexroth, Oppen, Zukofsky, Singer, and Sundman. And, frequently, the answers have a
common denominator. Rexroth, influenced, as he tells us, by Buddhist
thought and the mysticism of Richard of St. Victor, quotes these
central lines from his recent volume, *The Heart's Garden:*

> He who lives without grasping
> Lives always in experience
> Of the immediate as the
> Ultimate. The solution
> Of the problem of knowing
> And being is ethical.
> Epistemology is moral.

"Experience of the immediate as the Ultimate" is recorded in Rexroth's many wilderness poems, in which precise observation is concur-
rent with mystical awareness. Alternatively, "grasping knowledge,"
immoral epistemology, is represented by "the blood-drenched civi-
lized/Abstractions of the rascals/Who live by killing you and me"—
lines reminiscent of Ezra Pound. Elsewhere Rexroth expresses one of
the main principles of the whole neo-Bergsonian trend in modern
poetics: the poem "possesses an intense specificity—the intense specificity of *direct* contact and direct communication."

The interviews with the "Objectivist" poets make clear that they
were working in the same tradition, though they really did not share
Rexroth's mysticism. Approaching epistemology and poetics from an

"existential" viewpoint, Oppen, for instance, was no less sceptical than Rexroth about the efficacy of abstractions in rendering a true knowledge of things. Ideal perception for him was provided by the "lyric valuable," the "emotion" that causes one to "see." The purely aesthetic vision of nature, devoid of sentiment and ratiocination, was the one power available to the poet. Again like Rexroth, Oppen believed that epistemology was moral: ideally, the poet expressed only what he knew and he knew only what he could see. In the realm of feelings, this precept translated into the view that the poet was a "reporter" who related with objectivity only those emotions he sincerely experienced. Any elaboration or distortion of them for ethical (or unethical) or intellectual purposes violated "sincerity." Such a violation of sincerity was as much a departure from genuine knowledge as what Rexroth might call grasping.

This kind of neo-realism similarly appears in Rakosi's comments: "When you write about something as though it were a principle or a concept or a generalization, you have in that moment evaded it, its specificity, its earthly life. You are talking about something else. Really a different order of reality." And Reznikoff likewise defines the term "objectivist": "[It applies to a poet] who does not write directly about his feelings but about what he sees and hears; who is restricted almost to the testimony of a witness in a court of law; and who expresses his feelings indirectly by the selection of his subject-matter and, if he writes in verse, by its music."

For Zukofsky, almost certainly the most esoteric poet of his generation, the objectivist was concerned with "living with things as they exist." Zukofsky denies any interest in the ontological status of things: he says it is unimportant whether one believes that objects are "outside you, even if you disappear, or if they exist only because you think of them." But he does clearly assume the givenness of things, and while the idea of a thing is a part of its existence, the thought must be faithful to the object-as-it-is: "I come into a room and I see a table. Obviously, I can't make it eat grass." (But that is not true, a surrealist might reply.) The poet was on surest ground when he identified himself with his eyes—"I's (pronounced eyes)"—and dealt with "solids" or "liquids." Since ideas (the gaseous state) "existed," abstractions were not forbidden, but they required "a very clear mind."

Poets like James Merrill and George Barker speak from an entirely different attitude toward poetry and experience—one that eschews metaphysics and aesthetics as such. Still, Merrill's urbanity and casualness, evident throughout the interview, can be deceiving. His comments about Montale are a clue to some of the deeper aspects of his work:

Q. What is the feeling behind Montale's poems that struck you especially?
A. The emotional refinement, gloomy and strongly curbed. It's surprisingly permeable by quite ordinary objects—ladles, hens, pianos, half-read letters. To me he's the twentieth-century nature poet. Any word can lead you from the kitchen garden into really inhuman depths—if there are any of those left nowadays. The two natures were always one, but it takes an extraordinary poet to make us feel that, feel it in our spines.

Merrill's own version of "emotional refinement" shows a casualness, that, by its seeming inappropriateness to the situation described, carries the reader into the realm of the grotesque. "The Thousand and Second Night" begins:

> Istanbul. 21 March. I woke today
> With an absurd complaint. The whole right half
> Of my face refuses to move. I have to laugh
> Watching the rest of it reel about it in dismay
> . . . .
> I see no reason to be depressed;
> There are too many other things I haven't seen . . . .

One of the subtleties in this passage is that the very detachment of the speaker appears to be part of the malady, which is not merely physiological but psychological and spiritual (rigor vitae). Even after he has been cured, he still feels as though the "mirror" of his "soul" had been "cracked" and that part of him "has remained cold and withdrawn." The two natures that Merrill spoke of in regard to Montale seem to coexist within his persona, the one associated with Athens (the "humane splendor" of the Parthenon), the other with Istanbul (the Sancta Sophia, "now a flameless void"). The experience in Istanbul has been with "inhuman depths":

> It is like a dream,
> . . . .
> The "death-in-life and life-in-death" of Yeats'
> Byzantium; and, if so, by the same token,
> Alone in the sleepwalking scene, my flesh was woken
> And sailed for the fixed shore beyond the straits.

After which Athens could never be the same ("The day I went up to the Parthenon/Its humane splendor made me think *So what?*").

The fact that the poet experiences the inhuman, however, does not mean that he is godlike. Merrill praises Elizabeth Bishop for virtually the same reasons he praises Montale and criticizes Pound: "I like the way her whole oeuvre is on the scale of a human life; there is no oracular amplification, she doesn't go about on stilts to make her vision wider." For Merrill, the way to Byzantium and back again has to be through the kitchen garden.

Barker, like Merrill, turns only with reluctance to philosophical and aesthetic theories—"it's a terrible bore, you know, to talk about theories, but one has to construct some in order ... to maintain one's sanity about what one's doing." Nonetheless, he shares not only Merrill's awareness of the poem's possibility for revealing the human being's "inhuman depths," but also the objectivist's concern with the poem as a way of knowing. But for Barker, as for Rexroth, the knowledge the poem embodies transcends conscious categories. The poet is a "seer" and "poems say much more than the words in them." At its most fundamental, the poem becomes "an act of faith," "praise," an aspiration towards resolution of "all those oppositions ... in one's consciousness." But ultimately resolution escapes poem and poet, and the poet continues to write, defining his task much as Augustine "defined faith as the pursuit of faith."

Thus Barker, for all his difference from Zukofsky and Oppen, is also struggling to compel words into forms which convey insight beyond literal meanings. It is such an enterprise that lies behind Barker's fascination with puns and his recent use of constrained and very demanding metric forms. Language in its strictest literal meanings resists the poet's efforts to communicate. The poet necessarily speaks through a narrative mask, and "one doesn't know whether the mask is real or what it conceals is real. Or whether both things are real. Because here language ceases to have any true responsibility; it simply doesn't say the kind of things that the mind is saying." But the untrustworthiness of language does not lead Barker (as it perhaps does Zukofsky) to the shaping of the poem as a quasi-musical artifact. The combination of intellectual and musical qualities of words makes the art of poetry "superior to the art of music" and provides the basis for the poem's being as "an act of ravishment" of the reader.

As a whole, the novelists, with the exception of Singer, were less prone to pursue their ideas than poets like Rexroth and Zukofsky.

Nonetheless, sometimes by implication, sometimes by elaboration, they shed a great deal of light on their thought and work. Singer pointed to one of the most salient characteristics of his work when concluding his first interview session: "Everything to me, everything is a paradox. The very existence of things is a paradox." The truth of this statement was borne out, both implicitly and explicitly, in nearly all he had to say about himself, the universe, and his work. Identified as a writer steeped in Yiddish lore and traditions, he baldly states, "Yiddish culture and I are two different things"; he believes in the literal existence of supernatural powers that influence men's lives, but argues that he is also a sceptic ("I don't say to you there are so many powers and here they exist and this is what they are doing. No. If I call them names, it's only because from a literary point of view, it's good"). He believes that "we are living in a kind of dream, even when we are awake. The only difference is that this dream seems to have a certain consistency." Thus he can say, "What we call reality is the things to which we are accustomed." But having accepted these idealistic views, he espouses a hardheaded realism. Kafka, he asserts, was completely wrapped up in dreams and symbols; "his miracles are too arbitrary to create the kind of literature that could last forever." Like Rexroth and Merrill, in their own fashions, Singer believes that the Ultimate can be approached only through the immediate; again, Byzantium only through the kitchen garden:

I don't believe in distortion . . . . Be as real as possible. But if you want to tell about a miracle, about a mystical experience, bring it into the milieu of realism. If not, it becomes nothing.

Singer is no less sensitive to the dualisms of the ethical life. He is unequivocal in his disbelief in revelation:

We don't know what God wants from us and there is no chance ever to know. Revelation is always dubious; we don't know if God has ever revealed Himself, or if He has ever told a man how we should behave, or if revelation is the nature of God—we know nothing.

But Singer can also say, "I think that the Ten Commandments contain the greatest human wisdom":

How do I feel, this is what you want to ask me? I can tell you how I feel; I feel that if we break the Ten Commandments, we are really in great trouble.

For the realistic and sceptical Singer, the matter of the commandments is not simple, and he goes on to raise the dilemma that is at the moral center of his work: "the question is only how to keep them.... is it possible to keep them?" Passion is vital; it "speeds up human life, it gives it more content, more intensity." Similarly, a "man can love many women." But passion "is bad when it brings suffering to other people" and women suffer because they cannot understand men's desire for more than one woman. And more:

If a man says, "I am passionately in love with a woman," it means that he suffers, and sooner or later the woman will also suffer, one way or another. If he will not marry her ... she will suffer. If he marries her, he may be jealous, or he may cool off after a while, and get a passion for somebody else. Passion really is suffering.

Yet Singer is contemptuous of the man who has no passion:

He doesn't strive to do anything and he goes on living a monotonous life, so he may continue for eighty years or so, being bored to death and boring other people; then he dies.

It is fitting that Singer should insist on his detachment as an author from his work. He is really concerned with defining moral problems and probing the psychology of obsession and dilemma, not with expressing a dogma or making explicit judgments:

I don't tell people what is good and what is bad. This I keep to myself.... It's enough for me if I give [the character's] story and his point of view.

But it is also fitting that Singer should confirm the other side of the question and admit an identification with certain of his characters or with aspects of them. Paradoxically, his aesthetic distance can be all the more appreciated.

It is striking testimony to the existence of basic philosophic currents in twentieth-century literature that writers as different from Singer as Nabokov and Borges (Singer of Nabokov: "He's a good writer, but I would say he's not my writer") nonetheless share with him similar attitudes toward the relation of real and ideal in the work of art. All three place emphasis on the labyrinthine nature of the mind and the status of the work of art as the mind's imaginative creation. Nabokov goes so far as to describe the writer as a little god: "the design of my novel is fixed in my imagination and every character follows the course I imagine for him. I am the perfect dictator in that private world insofar as I alone am responsible for its stability and truth." But for Nabokov, as for Singer, it is the sensually evocative detail which the mind reworks, incorporates into its imaginative pattern, that vouchsafes the truth of the artist's achievement. He adds, "It is true, however, that even with the best of visions one must touch things to be quite sure of 'reality.' " The mind synthesizes ideal pattern with physical detail by means of memory:

I would say that imagination is a form of memory. . . . An image depends on the power of association, and association is supplied and prompted by memory. When we speak of a vivid individual recollection we are paying a compliment not to our capacity of retention but to Mnemosyne's mysterious foresight in having stored up this or that element which creative imagination may use when combining it with later recollections and inventions. In this sense, both memory and imagination are a negation of time.

The idea of negation of time (with its parallels in Bergson) is one which Nabokov elaborated obliquely in his discussion of his methods of composition. Not only does imagination "negate time" by its synthesis of details stored with "Mnemosyne's mysterious foresight"; the vision which orders the physical details from memory also comes to Nabokov as if from a realm outside of time. "I am afraid to get mixed up with Plato whom I do not care for," Nabokov notes, "but I do think that in my case it is true that the entire book, before it is written, seems to be ready ideally in some other, now transparent, now dimming, dimension, and my job is to take down as much of it as I can make out and as precisely as I am humanly able to."

It is in this view of art as idealistic vision—however highly qualified the references to Plato or Spinoza—that Singer, Nabokov, and Borges approach each other most closely. Just as Singer said "what we see here is only kind of an image, a picture, which is fitted to our power of conception," Borges mused about the equivalent reality of dream and table: "I wonder why a dream or an idea should be less real than this table, for example, or why Macbeth should be less real than today's newspaper. I cannot quite understand this." But, like Singer and Nabokov, Borges refuses to commit himself unequivocably to an overall philosophy. "I suppose if I had to define myself, I would define myself as an idealist, philosophically speaking," he continues; but he adds, "I'm not sure I have to define myself. I'd rather go on wondering and puzzling about things, for I find that very enjoyable." Dealing, as many of them do, with prodigious mental acts, ratiocination, and coherent dreams, Borges' *ficciones* present idealistic or sceptical views of knowledge, but an important aspect of these works is, as Borges says, as much wonder and intellectual "pleasure" as philosophic or ethical vision. Knowledge may be paltry and man may be in a labyrinth, beset by confusion and mystery; for Borges, however, despair need not follow:

I really enjoy that mystery. I not only feel the terror of it; I not only feel now and then the anguish, but also, well, the kind of pleasure you get, let's say, from a chess puzzle or from a good detective novel.

The same impulse, of course, lies behind much of Nabokov's fiction, and as with Borges it is often accompanied by an ambivalence of attitude toward his characters, who are themselves frequently involved in some intricate chess game with life. Both writers create worlds in which there are many signs but no revelation, many patterns but ultimately no definitive significance. In such a world the value is to enjoy the patterns. It is a value rescued from the world's lurking potential for terror, however. In a pair of Borges' poems a man wanders in labyrinthine corridors; in the first sonnet, "the minotaur, of course, wants to devour him." But, Borges continues, "In the second sonnet, I had a still more gruesome idea—the idea that there was no minotaur—that the man would go on endlessly wandering. . . . I mean, if anything is terrible, it is terrible because it is meaningless."

Not surprisingly then, the *ficciones* can be seen as the creation of forms which bring the meaningfulness of self-contained patterns to the elements of fiction—the ambiguous fragments of memory or dream reworked by imagination. Like Singer, Borges stresses the correlation between life as we perceive it, literature, and dream, and he also emphasizes the artist's intervention to direct the "dream" toward meaning or coherence:

I don't think of literature and dreams as being very different. Of course, life has been compared to a dream many times over. But I think that in the case where you're imagining a story, you are actually dreaming it; at the same time you're dreaming it in a rather self-conscious way. I mean, you're dreaming and you're trying to direct the dream, to give it an end.

And despite the fact that he shares with Nabokov a view of the creative imagination as a recreation of memories, Borges ends closer to Singer than to Nabokov in his attitude toward the independence of the writer who shapes dream or memory toward an aesthetic end: "I suppose a source can be found for every line I've written, or perhaps that's what we call inventing—mixing up memories. I don't think we're capable of creation in the way that God created the world."

Sundman is another novelist fascinated with the powers and weaknesses of the ratiocinative mind. Like Singer, Borges, and Nabokov, he has an aversion to explicit judgment of his characters, an aversion that stems, in his case, from a general principle:

I have an old program or thesis . . . . It says that people are generally rash at interpreting and judging other people. I have a weakness for those people who talk and judge little. But this program might be described as being one of humanist tolerance.

Elsewhere, however, after having expressed an interest in behaviorism, he asserts: "But remember I'm not a psychologist; I'm an author and a 'moralist.' That is, the behaviorists scrutinize and describe human behavior, but I draw moral conclusions from it. I'm not satisfied with mere description; I judge—though with great caution." This ambivalence is apparent in Sundman's characterization. Olle Stensson, for example, the hyperrational schoolteacher who narrates *Two Days, Two Nights*, proves to be without compassion. Sundman says of him: "It is true that Stensson, like me, has an obsession with detail, but that's the only similarity between us. Stensson represents a kind of human being that I consider to be evil." Obsession with detail put to good use appears in "The Negotiators," where government and labor officials haggle over a school budget ("The negotiators are humane people. And it stands to reason that social problems should, if possible, be solved by such discussion"). But Sir John, the planning genius and leader of *The Expedition*, turns out to be a tyrant.

As he suggests, Sundman is as obsessed with detail as any of his characters, and it is clear that he admires the planning mentality, even (to some extent) when it is embodied in a Stensson, a Sir John, or an S. A. Andrée, whose balloon flight to the Arctic ended in disaster. And this virtue is no doubt one of the reasons for his enthusiasm for Alfred Nobel, on whose life he is basing a long novel. The paradoxes in Sundman's work are perhaps less complex and less subtle than those in the other novelists we've been discussing but they pertain, nonetheless, to the general problem of knowledge—its efficacy or inefficacy—that has often concerned the modern writer.

In the Enck interviews Hawkes is the only one who talked at

length about his work, but Barth, beneath his whimsical replies, also reveals something about himself as a novelist. Barth is probably quite serious when he says, "I thought I had invented nihilism, in 1953, and when I found out I hadn't, I lost interest." Elsewhere, consistently, he denies the influence of Camus on *The Floating Opera* and concludes, "It's quite curious how perceptive people . . . will point out things to you about your books and the connection between them and other works that you simply didn't know about, and yet which, once you've seen them, you know that you're not ever going to make anybody believe you didn't have in mind when you wrote your book." It is appropriate that Barth should refuse to see himself as part of any intellectual tradition, including nihilism, while remaining one of the best comic-absurdists of his time. And there is more than whimsy in this statement: "One ought to know a lot about reality before one writes realistic novels. Since I don't know much about reality, it will have to be abolished. What the hell, reality is a nice place to visit but you wouldn't want to live there, and literature never did, very long." Hawkes would agree: "I take literally the idea that the imagination should always uncover new worlds for us—hence my 'mythic' England, Germany, Italy, American west, tropical island, and so on. I want to write about worlds that are fresh to me. But in his preface to *The Secret Agent*, Conrad speaks of the sights and sounds of London crowding in on him and inhibiting his imagination. And this danger of familiarity is something I have tried almost unthinkingly to avoid."

Barth and Hawkes emphasize the imaginative world, but their fiction often has a realistic point of departure; Sundman remains chiefly a realist; Singer emphasizes the real world but hints at a "miraculous" one beyond it; Nabokov and Borges are caught up in artifices and imaginative patterns. But Sara Lidman, influenced by a Marxist conception of literature, sees herself as the absolute realist, for whom it was necessary to abandon fiction entirely; choosing to become a reporter of social conditions (with *style*), she said, "I'll write stories if I have time, but my imagination really can't compete with today's reality. Why make up stories when life is so full of forceful and powerful events? . . . The true problem, for me, is finding the means of presenting social reality. . . ." She repudiates her early novels—which gave her her reputation—because they all deal "with the minds of people" and contain "no conception of society." And it is on these grounds that, reminiscent of Georg Lukács, she attacks the "existential" writers, especially Camus, whose work she believes portrays a metaphysical situation divorced from all social reality.

Like Sara Lidman, Gwendolyn Brooks is also concerned with presenting social reality and she frankly admits that she is uncomfortable with "art" as such: "Those of us who have not grown up with or to it perhaps squirm a little in its presence. We feel that something is required of us that perhaps we aren't altogether able to give. And it's just a way of saying, 'Art hurts.' " This is the attitude of the folk writer; whereas Lidman sees herself as a social reporter and polemicist, frequently investigating the conditions of groups that she is not really part of (Africans, Swedish miners, Vietnamese), Gwendolyn Brooks identifies herself specifically as a black poet. "I have not abandoned beauty, or lyricism," she says, "and I certainly don't consider myself a polemical poet. I'm just a black poet, and I write about what I see, what interests me, and I'm seeing new things." For Miss Brooks, who agrees with Ron Karenga, blackness "is our ultimate reality," and her aim is simply to write poems that will be meaningful to blacks ("it won't be Ezra Pound poetry, as you can imagine").

These comments have touched upon only some of the more general issues raised in the interviews. Many of the authors spoke about the details of single poems or novels and provided other information that would normally be difficult to come by. We know that the reader will make his own discoveries. Therein lies one of the great advantages of, and true justification for, the interview as a genre.

L. S. D.
C. N. P.

Madison
Fall, 1971

NOVELISTS

JOHN HAWKES

Q. For many critics, your books show, if not the direct influence of, then affinities with, European works—perhaps more so than do most American novels. This connection may be a tie to a kind of internationalism noticed in the twenties, thirties, and forties, but less common now. Do you think American writers can learn anything from European writers, or is that period over?

A. Your word "affinities" seems to me more to the point than "influences." Certainly it's true that in many ways my own fiction appears to be more European than American. But the fact is that I've never been influenced by European writing. The similarities between my work and European work—those qualities I may have in common with, say, Kafka and Robbe-Grillet and Günter Grass—come about purely because of some kind of imaginative underworld that must be shared by Americans and Europeans alike. I don't think writers actually learn from each other. But obviously we tend to appreciate in European writers what we sometimes fail to recognize in our own writers—that absolute need to create from the imagination a totally new and necessary fictional landscape or visionary world.

Q. You mentioned Céline earlier this morning.

A. Yes, Céline is an extraordinary writer, and his *Journey to the End of the Night* is a great novel. His comic appetite for invented calamities suggests the same truth we find in the comic brutalities of the early Spanish picaresque writers, which is where I locate the beginnings of the kind of fiction that interests me most.

Interview conducted by John J. Enck on March 20, 1964, in Madison, Wisconsin.

Q. Let's turn to the older writers in the United States. For example, James, Hemingway, Fitzgerald, or Faulkner. Do any of these writers seem particularly significant to you at the present time—do they seem more or less significant than they did in the past?

A. As a writer I'm concerned with innovation in the novel, and obviously I'm committed to nightmare, violence, meaningful distortion, to the whole panorama of dislocation and desolation in human experience. But as a man—as reader and teacher—I think of myself as conventional. I remember that after Faulkner's death, which followed so closely on the death of Hemingway, there was a kind of journalistic polling of critics and reviewers in an effort to assess our position and re-assess our writers in terms of influence and reputation. I think that at the time there was a general inclination to unseat the accepted great contemporary writers in America, to relegate Faulkner, Hemingway, and Fitzgerald to history, and instead to acclaim, say, Norman Mailer and James Baldwin. And we've also seen at least one recent effort to debunk the achievement and pertinency of Henry James. I myself deplore these efforts and judgments. James gave us all the beauties, delicacies, psychic complications of a kind of bestial sensibility; Fitzgerald's handling of dream and nightmare seems to me full of rare light and novelistic skill; Faulkner produced a kind of soaring arc of language and always gave us the enormous pleasure of confronting the impossible at the very moment it was turning into the probable. I think of all these achievements as the constants of great fictional ability. I think these writers will always survive shifts in literary taste and changing conditions in the country, and will always in a sense remain unequaled. Incidentally, after my reading last night a man asked me if there was anything of Faulkner or Faulkner's influence in my work. He was thinking of the passage from *Second Skin*, and I answered that I didn't see much Faulkner in that book. But as a matter of fact, while I was reading from *The Lime Twig* last night, I became quite conscious again of echoes of a Faulknerian use of inner consciousness and expanded prose rhythms. The echoes are undeniable, I think—Faulkner is still the American writer I most admire—though at this point I ought to insist again that in general my work is my own, and that my language, attitudes and conceptions are unique.

Q. Such a view, then, would link you to the experimental writers of the avant-garde. As you know, the "avant-garde" was a rather popular concept about twenty years ago, but seems to be less so now. Do you have any views on the writer as experimenter?

A. Of course I think of myself as an experimental writer. But it's unfortunate that the term "experimental" has been used so often by reviewers as a pejorative label intended to dismiss as eccentric or private or excessively difficult the work in question. My own fiction is not merely eccentric or private and is not nearly so difficult as it's been made out to be. I should think that every writer, no matter what kind of fiction writer he may be or may aspire to be, writes in order to create the future. Every fiction of any value has about it something new. At any rate, the function of the true innovator or specifically experimental writer is to keep prose alive and constantly to test in the sharpest way possible the range of our human sympathies and constantly to destroy mere surface morality. What else were we trying to get at?

Q. The concept of the avant-garde.

A. America has never had what we think of as the avant-garde. Gertrude Stein, Djuna Barnes, whose novel *Nightwood* I admire enormously, Henry Miller—no doubt these are experimental writers. But I don't think we've ever had in this country anything like the literary community of the French surrealists or the present day French anti-novelists. And I'm not sure such a community would be desirable. On the other hand, in the past few years we've probably heard more than ever before about an existing avant-garde in America— we've witnessed the initial community of Beat writers, we're witnessing now what we might call the secondary community of Beat writers, recently many of us have defended *The Tropic of Cancer*. But I confess I find no danger, no true sense of threat, no possibility of sharp artistic upheaval in this essentially topical and jargonistic rebellion. Henry Miller's view of experience is better than most, Edward Dahlberg is a remarkably gifted writer who has still not received full recognition, I for one appreciate Norman Mailer's pugilistic stance. But none of this has much to do with the novel, and so far Beat activity in general seems to me to have resulted in sentimentality or dead language. My own concept of "avant-garde" has to do with something constant which we find running through prose fiction from Quevedo, the Spanish picaresque writer, and Thomas Nashe at the beginnings of the English novel, down through Lautréamont, Céline, Nathanael West, Flannery O'Connor, James Purdy, Joseph Heller, myself. This constant is a quality of coldness, detachment, ruthless determination to face up to the enormities of ugliness and potential failure within ourselves and in the world around us, and to bring to this exposure a savage or saving comic spirit and the saving beauties of language. The need is to maintain the truth of the fractured picture; to expose, ridicule, attack, but always to create and to throw into new light our potential for violence and absurdity as well as for graceful action. I don't like soft, loose prose or fiction which tries to cope too directly with life itself or is based indulgently on personal experience. On the other hand, we ought to respect resistance to commonplace authority wherever we find it, and this attitude at least is evident in the Beat world. But I suppose I regret so much attention being spent on the essentially flatulent products of a popular cult. A writer who truly and greatly sustains us is Nabokov.

Q. I think many Beat writers have a kind of popularity. Whom do you think of as your audience, and what sort are you looking for?

A. The question of audience makes me uncomfortable. I write out of isolation, and struggle only with the problems of the work itself. I've never been able to look for an audience. And yet after a number of years spent in relative obscurity, I'm pleased that my books are gaining readers. I think that works of the imagination are particularly important now to younger readers, and I think it's clear that my fiction is being studied in colleges and universities. Apparently it's being read even by New York high school students. But at any rate I care about reaching all readers who are interested in the necessity and limitless possibilities of prose fiction, and I think there must be a good many of them. I'm trying to write about large issues of human torments and aspirations, and I'm convinced that considerable numbers of people in this country must have imaginative needs quite similar to mine.

Q. One kind of reader is the critic. At its best, do you find any particular kind of criticism helpful—criticism appearing in larger circulation magazines or in smaller magazines? Does criticism mean anything at all to you as a writer?

A. I think the critic's function is mainly in terms of the reader. The critic makes the work more accessible, meaningful, and hence essential to the reader. I happen not to share the contempt for literary or academic criticism which appears to be current now. The critical efforts of the magazine *Critique*, for instance, which devoted one of its special issues to John Barth's novels and mine, are enormously helpful and gratifying. Generally I think I've benefited from criticism, though over the years what I've gained specifically from the critical judgment of a friend like Albert Guerard is almost too great to mention. I won't pretend not to be affected by newspaper reviews—in this area I'm easily outraged and just as easily pleased—but despite some of the silences and some of the more imperceptive or hostile responses, I have the impression that reviewers and readers alike in America are becoming increasingly receptive to original work. Certainly I've fared far better in America than in England where in one of the few sympathetic notices of my work to appear in that country I was described as a "deadly hawk moth."

Q. What do you think of the Sunday New York Times book review section?

A. The problem is so old I'm tempted to call it one of our dead horses. But I don't read the New York Times book review section (or any other book review section for that matter), and I could be very wrong. I think the scene is changing momentarily—perhaps the New York Times book section will become serious one of these days and give the lie to us all. It would be a welcome irony. It may sound paradoxical, but if they ever gave my own work the attention it deserves I'd be deeply moved.

Q. An aspect of your work that I have always appreciated, which I think many other critics have not, is the comic element. You have referred several times to comic writing—would you like to say something more about what you regard as the importance of comedy in your work?

A. I'm grateful to you for viewing my fiction as comic. Men like Guerard have written about the wit and black humor in my novels, but I think you're right that reviewers in general have concentrated on the grotesque and nightmarish qualities of my work, have made me out to be a somber writer dealing only with pain, perversion, and despair. Comedy puts all this into a very different perspective, I think. Of course I don't mean to apologize for the disturbing nature of my fiction by calling it comic, and certainly don't mean to minimize the terror with which this writing confronts the reader—my aim has always been the opposite, never to let the reader (or myself) off the hook, so to speak, never to let him think that the picture is any less black than it is or that there is any easy way out of the nightmare of human existence. But though I'd be the first to admit to sadistic impulses in the creative process, I must say that my writing is not mere indulgence in violence or derangement, is hardly intended simply to shock. As I say, comedy, which is often closely related to poetic uses of language, is what makes the difference for me. I think that the comic method functions in several ways: on the one hand it serves to create sympathy, compassion, and on the other it's a means for judging human failings as severely as possible; it's a way of exposing evil (one of the pure words I mean to preserve) and of persuading the reader that even he may not be exempt from evil; and of course comic distortion tells us that anything is possible and hence expands the limits of our imaginations. Comic vision always suggests futurity, I think, always suggests a certain hope in the limitless energies of life itself. In *Second Skin* I tried consciously to write a novel that couldn't be mistaken for anything but a comic novel. I wanted to expose clearly what I thought was central to my fictional efforts but had been generally overlooked in *The Cannibal, The Lime Twig, The Beetle Leg.* Obviously Faulkner was one of the greatest of all comic writers— Nabokov is a living example of comic genius.

Q. Do you have any comments on Flannery O'Connor as a comic writer?

A. For pure, devastating, comic brilliance and originality she stands quite alone in America—except perhaps for Nathanael West. Both of these writers maintain incredible distance in their work, both explode the reality around us into meaningful new patterns, both treat disability and inadequacy and hypocrisy with brutal humor, both of them deal fiercely with paradox and use deceptively simple language in such a way as to achieve fantastic verbal surprise and remarkable poetic expression. No doubt Flannery O'Connor is a more ruthless writer than West. But in an essay of mine called "Flannery O'Connor's Devil," which appeared in *The Sewanee Review,* I tried to suggest some of these similarities and also mentioned that I first read West and Flannery O'Connor at the same time and from that moment on felt a sustaining involvement with both of them. About six years ago I visited Flannery O'Connor in Milledgeville, Georgia, and have been writing to her since then. She's an extraordinary woman with what I like to think of as a demonic sensibility. I've been trying to persuade Flannery O'Connor that as a writer she's on the devil's side. Her answer is that my idea of the devil corresponds to her idea of God. I must admit that I resist this equation. Certainly in her two great short stories, "A Good Man is Hard to Find," and "The Life You Save

May Be Your Own," as well as in her brilliant first novel, *Wise Blood*, it's the unwavering accuracy and diabolism of her satiric impulse that impresses me most. At any rate, her imaginative authority, her absolute originality of voice and language, her unflinching, unsparing treatment of the reader as well as her materials—all of this suggests the importance of her fictional gifts. I do think that Nathanael West is the only other American writer whose fictional spirit is comparable to hers.

Q. To continue with your opinions on contemporary American authors, would you comment on Carson McCullers? What do you think is her place in the literature of our time?

A. I admire her compassion and the fine warm mordant tones and slow cadences of her writing. It seems to me that Carson McCullers deals more directly and consistently with the materials of childhood fantasy than perhaps any other American writer, which might help to account for her power. It's as if she's telling stories about legendary children to other children who have already died. But the differences between Carson McCuller's humor and Flannery O'Connor's black wit, which is like a steel trap snapping shut on the reader's mind, make me aware again of the loss involved in grouping writers together under such terms as "Gothic." I'm sure we could go on at length about Saul Bellow and Bernard Malamud, but obviously these are two of our most important comic novelists. I think that *Henderson the Rain King*, which seems to have flowered enormously and wonderfully out of his perfect short novel *Seize the Day*, is Bellow's finest work. Malamud is one of the purest creators I know of.

Q.   There are some personal questions here about how you write and you may answer them or not as you like. The first is, do you outline your novels before you start writing?

A. I've never outlined a novel before starting to write it—at the outset I've never been aware of the story I was trying to handle except in the most general terms. The beginnings of my novels have always been mere flickerings in the imagination, though in each case the flickerings have been generated, clearly enough, by a kind of emotional ferment that had been in process for some time. I began *The Cannibal* after reading a brief notice in *Time* magazine about an actual cannibal discovered in Bremen, Germany (where I had been, coincidentally, during the war); I started *The Lime Twig* when I read a newspaper account of legalized gambling in England. My other novels were begun similarly with mere germs of ideas, and not with substantial narrative materials or even with particular characters. In each case what appealed to me was a landscape or world, and in each case I began with something immediately and intensely visual— a room, a few figures, an object, something prompted by the initial idea and then literally seen, like the visual images that come to us just before sleep. However, here I ought to stress that my fiction has nothing to do with automatic writing. Despite these vague originations and the dream-like quality of some of these envisioned worlds, my own writing process involves a constant effort to shape and control my materials as well as an effort to liberate fictional energy. *The Beetle Leg* and *The Lime Twig*, for instance, underwent extensive revision. I spent four years revising *The Lime Twig* which, as you know, is a short book. And I must say that once a first draft is finished I certainly do resort to outlines, sometimes to elaborate charts and diagrams. I suppose this writing method involves considerable waste motion. But since I'm compelled to work with poetic impulses there seems to be no alternative.

Q. Would you say something about your working conditions?

A. Like most people, I've written under a variety of conditions. I wrote my first novel in a writing class when I returned to college after the war; I wrote a short novel in the cab of a pick-up truck in Montana; I've written at night after work and in the early mornings before going to work; the first draft of *The Lime Twig* was written during my first academic summer after I began teaching; *Second Skin* was written last year on a kind of paradise island in the West Indies. In his book *Enemies of Promise*, Cyril Connolly said that one of the greatest obstacles to the young writer was the "perambulator in the hall." But I was married at a fairly early age and have always felt that the conditions of ordinary life, no matter how difficult they might prove to be, were the most desirable conditions for writing. My prose might be radical, but my habits are quite ordinary. On the other hand, I admit that I did have mixed feelings when a Guggenheim fellowship and several grants allowed me to take a year off from teaching at Brown—it was difficult to face the prospect of a year of ideal writing conditions without a certain amount of anxiety, especially since I had always resisted the notion of making special allowances for writers. However, I confess that now after those arcadian months in the West Indies—I worked on *Second Skin* every morning and spent the afternoon in the water washing away the filth of creative effort—I feel very differently about complete freedom and ideal writing conditions. *Second Skin* couldn't have taken the form it did without the time and locale made possible by the grants. I'm reminded that a few years ago Irving Howe gave a lecture at Brown in which he said that if Raskolnikhov tried to commit his murder today he'd receive a special delivery letter announcing that he'd been awarded a Guggenheim fellowship. It's an amusing and accurate comment on our own special artistic state of affairs and the risks existing today for the subsidized artist and subsidized culture. Subsidy seems absurdly contrary to the integrity of the writer's necessary anti-social stance. But personally I think foundation gifts are worth the risks involved. My own grants were unexpected boons which I look back on with nothing but considerable gratitude. I think that writers—and especially younger writers—should receive as much help and encouragement as possible.

Q. To a certain extent you anticipated a few moments ago my next question, but I'll ask it anyhow. To what degree are you worried about structure in your novels? Do you generally think of your novels in terms of a formal structure of the narrator, or do you discover structure as you write?

A. My novels are not highly plotted, but certainly they're elaborately structured. I began to write fiction on the assumption that the true enemies of the novel were plot, character, setting, and theme, and having once abandoned these familiar ways of thinking about fiction, totality of vision or structure was really all that remained. And structure—verbal and psychological coherence—is still my largest concern as a writer. Related or corresponding event, recurring image and recurring action, these constitute the essential substance or meaningful density of my writing. However, as I suggested before, this kind of structure can't be planned in advance but can only be discovered in the writing process itself. The success of the effort depends on the degree and quality of consciousness that can be brought to bear on fully liberated materials of the unconscious. I'm trying to hold in balance poetic and novelistic methods in order to make the novel a more valid and pleasurable experience. Of course it's obvious that from *The Cannibal* to *Second Skin* I've moved from nearly pure vision to a kind of work that appears to resemble much more closely the conventional novel. In a sense there was no other direction to take, but in part this shift came about, I think, from an increasing need to parody the conventional novel. As far as the first-person narrator goes, I've worked my way slowly toward that method by a series of semi-conscious impulses and sheer accidents. *The Cannibal* was written in the third person, but in revision I found myself (perversely or not) wishing to project myself into the fiction and to become identified with its most criminal and, in a conventional sense, least sympathetic spokesman, the neo-Nazi leader of the hallucinated uprising. I simply went through the manuscript and changed the pronouns from third to first person, so that the neo-Nazi Zizendorf became the teller of those absurd and violent events. The result was interesting, I think, not because *The Cannibal* became a genuine example of first-person fiction, but because its "narrator" naturally possessed an unusual omniscience, while the authorial consciousness was given specific definition, definition in terms of humor and "black" intelligence. When I finished *The Beetle Leg* (a third-person novel), I added a prologue spoken in the first person by a rather foolish and sadistic sheriff, and this was my first effort to render an actual human voice. Similarly, Hencher's first-person prologue in *The Lime Twig* (also a third-person novel) was an afterthought, but his was a fully created voice that dramatized a character conceived in a certain depth. This prologue led me directly to *Second Skin* which, as you know, is narrated throughout in the first person by Skipper who, as I say, had his basis in Hencher.

Q. On the matter of structure would you comment on the relationship of Sidney Slyter to the main action of *The Lime Twig*?

A. As soon as he read the manuscript of *The Lime Twig*, James Laughlin, the publisher of New Directions (who, by the way, has been a sustaining friend since I began to write), suggested that this novel might be more accessible if it had some kind of gloss or reader's guide. I believe that he even suggested the idea of a newspaper sportswriter as an appropriate kind of "chorus" to comment on the action of the novel. I don't know how I arrived at the sportswriter's name (I may have been trying to echo comically the common English term "blighter"), but at any rate that's how Sidney Slyter came into being, with his snake-like character embodied in the ugly sibilance of his name which was also related, of course, to Sybilline, the dark temptress in the novel. To me it's interesting that Sidney Slyter's column was in effect another afterthought, since actually his sleazy character and cheap column afforded me perhaps the best opportunity for dramatizing the evil inherent in the world of *The Lime Twig*. Slyter's curiosity, his callow optimisim, his lower middle class English ego, his tasteless rhetoric, his vaguely obscene excitement in the presence of violence—all this makes him one of the most degrading and perversely appealing figures in the novel. I would say that in reporting the criminal actions of the novel, Slyter carries degradation to its final end. I've been told that he's an authentic type, which pleases me since I've never known such a man and have only a passing interest in horse racing sheets. Perhaps Sidney Slyter is some indication of why *The Lime Twig* was overlooked or ridiculed in England.

Q. What is the relationship between William Hencher and Michael Banks? Is Hencher some sort of prologue for Michael Banks? One of the most shocking parts of the book is to find Hencher killed so early.

A. I thought his death was amusing. But given my need to parody the novel form, in this case to parody the soporific plot of the thriller, Hencher's death seems to me an appropriate violation of fictional expectation or fictional "rules." However, *The Lime Twig* begins and ends with Hencher; his early violent death is analogous, I think, to all that follows; and to me he reappears as Cowles (the murdered fat man) and as the constable. I meant the pseudo-mystery of his death to pervade the novel. On the thriller level, Hencher is literally a member of Larry's underworld gang, is an instrument of Michael's fatality. Like Michael Banks, Hencher—because of his need for love—is killed by the race horse; if we understand Michael's own story then we understand Hencher's death. But of course you're right that Hencher's introduction serves as a prologue to all the episodes of the novel in which Michael's fantasies become real. Michael and Margaret Banks were conceived as representing England's anonymous post-war youth (the borrowing of the hero's name from the Mary Poppins series has obvious significance), while I saw post-war England itself as the spiritless, degraded landscape of the modern world, in this case dominated by the destructive fatality of the gambling syndicate. But it seemed to me that the drab reality of contemporary England was a direct product of the war, and that Michael and Margaret were in a sense the innocent spawn of the war. However, since Michael and Margaret were mere children during the war, incapable even of recalling the bombing of London, the problem became one of dramatizing the past, of relating wartime England to post-war England, of providing a kind of historical consciousness for characters who had none of their own. Hencher served this function. He became the carrier of Michael and Margaret's past as well as of their future; I thought of him as the seedbed of their pathetic lives. To me Hencher is a thoroughly sympathetic character, though some readers would probably consider him (wrongly, I think) to be merely crippled, perverse, distasteful. My own feeling is that Hencher's innocence, like Michael and Margaret's, can only suffer destruction by ruthless victimizers in a time of impoverishment. But paradoxically, in *The Lime Twig* as in my other novels, even the victimizers have "their dreams of shocking purity," to quote Albert Guerard.

Q. Does teaching creative writing at Brown influence your own work in any way? Have you noticed any changes?

A. I think not. It may be that teaching has made clearer to me the possibilities for disrupting conventional forms of fiction, and no doubt I've benefited considerably from the imaginative exchange that occurs between teacher and student. There's a reassuring immediacy in students' needs and abilities. But it seems to me that the pleasures of teaching have to do with other people's writing and discoveries, rather than with your own. As you know, writing students are infinitely capable; the very variety of their work demands an appreciation from the teacher which forces him away from his own personal bias, and this, I think, is one of the most important aspects of academic life for the writer. There's a special value in a student's own work, and in his resistance as well as his enthusiastic response to the teacher.

Q. This anticipates, then, the next question, which is whether as a teacher you discern any trends among students as writers or whether you find all kinds and don't see any general patterns among them.

A. I've always tried not to generalize about students. Ten years ago the most exciting students were as unpredictable as they seem to me today. The trends and patterns that do appear to be developing among student writers strike me as superficial. As far as the undergraduate sexual revolution is concerned, I don't find it evident in student writing. That is, I've known unusually gifted and mature younger writers throughout my years of teaching.

Q. Are there any younger writers whom you think undervalued?

A. It seems to me that Grace Paley has not received the recognition she deserves. Three very different but promising first novels, *This Passing Night* by Clive Miller, *Seven Days of Mourning* by L. S. Simckes, and *Run River* by Joan Didion should have received more appreciation, I feel. On the other hand, William Melvin Kelley, who began to write in a class of mine at Harvard, wrote a first novel, A

Different Drummer, which received an award from the National
Institute of Arts and Letters—obviously a hopeful indication that
early encouragement is perhaps more prevalent now than it used to
be. And Susan Sontag's first novel, *The Benefactor*, has received
appropriate attention, though I must say I disagree with those reviews
that described the prose in this book as an easy imitation of French
style. Susan Sontag's writing is often pure, controlled, disturbing in
the best sense, and highly pleasurable. Her novel assumes a genuinely
significant attitude toward sexual experience, her use of a first-person
male narrator reveals an extraordinary kind of imaginative knowledge.

Q. We are back almost to where we came in with internationalism
and French influence.

A. I would still say that internationalism rather than influence is
the point. Malamud and Nabokov are international writers, but their
work really doesn't raise the question of influence. I think that a
younger writer like Susan Sontag is promising precisely because of
those moments in her novel where she's turning philosophical abstraction into concretely rendered life and is overcoming mere influence
through her own imaginative pressures.

Q. Would you want to say a few words about what you think is the
ideal relationship between the writer and the university where he
teaches?

A. It pleases me that Flannery O'Connor wrote her first novel in
the writing program at Iowa and that so many writers, including for
instance Malamud, Nabokov, and Susan Sontag, either are or have
been teachers. I suppose the university world is a good one for the
writer because it provides him with a literal experience in which he's
both involved and detached in terms of life materials and intellectual
and artistic effort. I think the writer, like other faculty members,
should teach with commitment and offer what he can to the life
around him; I think the university should encourage the writer's work
with time off. There's no question any more about the place of the
writer or artist within the university; the only question concerns the
extent to which the university is equipped to foster artistic activity.
Personally—and despite what I said earlier—I wouldn't give up
teaching entirely even if I could.

Q. I don't know quite how to phrase this, but it seems that in your
work one of the things that is unique, in comparison with other modern writers, is the setting of your novels in an alien situation, one

which you personally have never experienced as far as the actual milieu is concerned. You have never been in England, for instance, and the setting of *The Beetle Leg* and the others is far from literal. Is there any particular reason for this? Do you feel you are getting at important matters more effectively than you would have out of your own, more immediate world?

A.   I take literally rather than figuratively the cliché about breaking new ground. Or I take literally the idea that the imagination should always uncover new worlds for us—hence my "mythic" England, Germany, Italy, American west, tropical island, and so on. I want to write about worlds that are fresh to me. But in his preface to *The Secret Agent*, Conrad speaks of the sights and sounds of London crowding in on him and inhibiting his imagination. And this danger of familiarity is something I've tried almost unthinkingly to avoid. As I've said, my writing depends on absolute detachment, and the unfamiliar or invented landscape helps me to achieve and maintain this detachment. Such a landscape provides an initial and helpful challenge. I don't want to write autobiographical fiction, though I admire Agee's *A Death in the Family* or the ways in which Conrad or Ford Madox Ford transform elements of personal experience and elements of subjective life into fiction. I want to try to create a world, not represent it. And of course I believe that the creation ought to be more significant than the representation.

Q.   We can have a last question. In *The Lime Twig* you killed off Michael Banks and Margaret, the gang survive, at the end the detectives do not accomplish much. Despite what you've said about comedy, this novel doesn't appear to be very hopeful. Would you care to comment on this problem?

A.   For me the blackest fictions liberate the truest novelistic sympathy. When Michael is killed the whole world collapses with him, and comically—that is, the race track is littered with the bodies of the fallen jockeys and horses. And at the moment of Margaret's death, Larry, the head of the gang, is speaking comically about his hopes of journeying to a new world full of lime trees. (It's a journey which he won't be able to take of course, since his gigantic plan has failed.) But at any rate Michael has destroyed the "golden bowl" of earthly pleasure and destructive dream and has atoned for his betrayal of Margaret. This ending along with the novel's general pairing off of sensual and destructive experiences to me suggests a kind of hope.

The fictional rhythm itself is in a way hopeful. But I admit I'm reluctant to argue too strongly for the necessity of hope.

Q.   What about the detectives? Are they anything more than comic?

A.   The detectives represent law and order, or the baffled and banal mind at large. Specifically, and along with Sidney Slyter, they may be seen as images of the absurd and lonely author himself. Even the author is not exempt from judgment in my fiction. But at least the detectives, in trying to learn what the reader has presumably learned already (and it's clear, I think, that these obtuse men from Scotland Yard will never solve the "crime"), are attempting to complete the cycle of mysterious experience. At least they, like ourselves, will go on hunting for clues.

JOHN BARTH

Q. Some critics mention the emerging of a new kind of comic novel. Does this form hold any interest for you, and, if the answer is yes, what sort?

A. It holds interest for me because I thought I had invented it, and now it turns out that somebody else got there first. Rabelais. Machado. It depresses the Dickens out of me to think it is becoming a kind of novel, a genre; because if it becomes a genre, I'll have to start doing something else instead. Greek tragedies, maybe. I'm not sure what the novels are that these critics have in mind when they mention the new American novel.

Q. I suppose things like Heller's *Catch 22*, Donleavy's *The Ginger Man*, Hawkes' *Second Skin*. All these seem to have comic elements of a sort different from the novels of even the forties or fifties. Also, the so-called theater of the absurd probably belongs here.

A. What's pleasing about the ones I've read is a kind of wild inventiveness which you certainly don't find a decade or so previously. It's curious how these things spring up all at once. I honestly did think I had invented this genre, and that *The Sot-Weed Factor* was the first thing of its kind. If it wasn't, I don't know whether that's something to be discouraged about or pleased about.

Q. Who are some of the young writers whose work you feel is worthwhile but who, perhaps, have not received the critical attention they deserve?

A. The authors of the *Novellini* and the *Arabian Nights*, Boccaccio, Cervantes, Rabelais, Robert Musil, Laurence Sterne, also Machado de Assis. He is a brilliant fellow who wrote twenty or twenty-

Interview conducted by John J. Enck on April 17, 1964, in Madison, Wisconsin.

five novels around the turn of the century. Brilliant writer. They
sound as if they were written yesterday. Alas, nobody reads Portuguese.
They're just beginning to be translated. If you don't know them
already and you're interested in this new genre that I invented, you
should surely read Machado, because he invented it too. He writes
like the Sterne of *Tristram Shandy*, only solider than Sterne. I could
never finish *Tristram Shandy*. Machado is a simply brilliant writer.
Musil, who died a few years ago, did a book that I wish more of my
students would read: *The Man Without Qualities*. That book is one
of the giants that doesn't get spoken of when people are speaking of
Joyce, Kafka, and Mann. A real New American Novel.

Back to the question. I haven't read many of my contemporaries.
They haven't read me either, and so we are even. I can't speak ear-
nestly of young writers who aren't getting critical attention because I
haven't gotten it either. But I think it is a useful thing for young
people who are learning to write (like me) to spend a lot of time with
the old tales. The element of *story* — just sheer extraordinary, marvellous story — is not what we value Joyce for, for example, or Hemingway
or Faulkner, as a rule. I love those men very much, but it is refresh-
ing, it seems to me, for writers to become interested in yarns — elaborate lies. The *Arabian Nights* may be a better mentor for many than,
say, J. D. Salinger. There is a Hindu thing that I've always wanted
to go clear through. I believe it's Hindu. It's called *The Ocean of
Story*, and I keep seeing it on the shelf in the library. Four feet long.
Wouldn't it be wonderful to have written that?

Q. Do you have any further opinions on the following: Susan Sontag,
J. F. Powers, Joseph Heller, J. P. Donleavy?

A. Well, yes, but I don't know how much of this gossip is very interesting. I had never heard of Susan Sontag until her publisher sent me
her novel asking for a comment — *The Benefactor*, it was — I told the
publisher I didn't believe she existed. I didn't especially care for the
book. She writes like a middle-aged French roué. She writes like Carl
Jung dreaming he is Candide. That makes it sound exciting, doesn't
it? There's a picture of a good-looking chick on the back of the jacket,
and a note that she teaches philosophy and theology at Columbia.
Don't believe it. Susan Sontag does not exist.

Q. There is a lot of evidence that she does. Any other comments?

A. Joseph Heller was a predecessor of mine at Penn State. He
worked for twelve years on that book, *Catch 22*, and I kept hearing
about it while it was being worked on and then it was published and

after awhile I read it. I read things, I confess to you, with a sense of competition and jealousy. It puts me down when I read anything good by my contemporaries. Mostly I read student papers. But one day between terms I took out Heller's book, James Baldwin's last novel, and a collection of John Updike's stories — hoping, you know, that I would be cheered up by not having to like any of them—and I ended up liking them all. Well, almost all. I thought Heller's book was funny. I liked it much more than most of my friends did — whose judgment however is excellent. I thought it was funny. And Updike, too, whom I was really hoping I wouldn't have to like — it would have cheered me up — but, mercy, he writes well. Donleavy's book, *The Ginger Man*, was not only funny: it seems to me there was a technically interesting thing about it, though I am naïve about modern literature. I mean the almost complete homogenization of first and third person viewpoints: Sebastian speaks of himself sometimes in the first person and sometimes in the third. Like a number of finally useful artifices it's difficult to take at first, but by the third chapter you get with it, and then, Donleavy has the best of two worlds. It is a very clever thing to bring off.

Q.   This brings to mind the mixture of the first and third person in *Pale Fire*.

A.   *Pale Fire* is a joy.

Q.   The same thing happens there. One can't be sure whether it is the first or the third person or both.

A.   Nabokov's a real sport.

Q.   To move to another matter, in your view is the period of internationalism in the novel continuing or almost over?

A.   I didn't know really that it had begun.

Q.   You referred to Susan Sontag who seems to be more French than American.

A.   She *is* kind of French. *The Artificial Frenchman*. Or would be, if she existed. Oh well. The French — the *French* French — are of course the ones who are doing the curiousest things technically, and good for them, although the *nouveau roman* isn't just my cup of tea. They're all fighting Balzac, as I understand it, and I guess some of us are mad at Flaubert instead, in a friendly way. From what I know of Robbe-Grillet and his pals, their aesthetic is finally a more up-to-date kind of psychological realism: a higher fi to human consciousness and unconsciousness. Well, that's nice. A different way to come to terms with the discrepancy between art and the Real Thing is to affirm the artificial element in art (you can't get rid of it anyhow), and make the artifice part of your point instead of working for higher and higher fi with a lot of literary woofers and tweeters. That would be my way. Scheherazade's my *avant-gardiste*. But technical circus-tricks are good clean fun. Like that novel — Saporta's? — that was boxed instead of bound, with the pages assorted at random. Hot dog. Wouldn't it be fun to write a book with pop-up scenes, for instance, like kids' books used to have? Or print *Finnegans Wake* on a very long roller-towel?

At least you don't want to be a technical hick. If somebody built the Chartres cathedral now, it would be an embarrassing piece of real estate, wouldn't it? Unless he did it ironically. I couldn't read Baldwin's book because it seemed to me he was writing a kind of turn-of-the-century novel, technically, about mid-twentieth-century topics. So Baldwin cheered me up. What I liked about *Another Country* was that I didn't admire it.

Do you know what I think is interesting, by the way? (This has nothing at all to do with internationalism in the novel.) It's the spectacle of these enormous universities we have now, all over the place, teaching courses in *us!* These birds in your series, like me, who haven't even reached menopause yet, Notable Nobodies in the Novel, and already they're giving courses in us. Remarkable. Amusing. And I suppose it's admirable on the part of American universities. But I wonder what effect it will have on literature. For example, where I work there are 600 English majors — maybe 6,000, I don't know. Some can't read and write. But imagine 600 people in central Pennsylvania knowing and caring who Hawkes and Donleavy are—maybe before Hawkes and Donleavy find out themselves! Boggles the imagination. Now that means that a born loser like *The Sot-Weed Factor* might even be gotten away with, because 2,000 kids in northeast Nebraska or somewhere have to read it in a Modern Novel course. Alarming. Do you know we teach fiction-writing to about a hundred kids every term, just at Penn State? God knows what we're up to.

Q. To turn to some questions about how you write — if you don't mind talking about some of these things — do you outline your novel before writing?

A. That is the kind of question the answer to which is not going to do anybody any good. What difference does it make to anybody whether I outline my novel before writing? Yes, I do — very thoroughly as a matter of fact. I suppose you could start a short story without an outline, sort of see where it goes — not me, I don't write short stories. But frankly, I don't see how anybody starts a novel without knowing how it's going to end. I usually make detailed outlines: how many chapters it will be and so forth.

Q. How much difficulty did you have, writing *The Sot-Weed Factor*, in keeping to an eighteenth-century style?

A. The difficulty was just the opposite. It was to stop writing letters that way. It's an infectious style, and not very hard to do. Once you get in the spirit of writing in Hudibrastic couplets, say, then you start to think in Hudibrastic couplets and talk on the telephone in Hudibrastic couplets. Sometimes when I read and talk to people and fall into this vein, they begin to answer my letters in the same way. It's like syphilis.

Q. Do you usually begin with the concept or the fable?

A. One begins in different ways. The first novel I wrote, *The Floating Opera*, began with a photograph of an old show boat which used to go around the tidewater Maryland area. I remember seeing that boat when I was about seven. When I came across a photograph of that old show boat in 1954, I thought it would be a good idea to write a philosophical minstrel show. I wasn't going to write a novel at all; I was going to write a minstrel show, only it was going to be a work of literature. I started to do it and it ended up being a novel instead. *The Sot-Weed Factor* began with the title and, of course, Ebenezer Cooke's original poem. Those of you who haven't read the novel should be told that there is such a poem and there is such a man, although nobody knows much about him.

Q. To what extent do you worry about the structure of your novels?

A. I worry myself sick. I take the structure pretty seriously. When I started on *The Sot-Weed Factor*, for instance, I had two intentions. One was to write a large book, something that the publisher could print the title on across the spine, and I did, and then the publisher put the title on up-and-down anyhow. The other was to see if I couldn't make up a plot that was fancier than *Tom Jones*. *Tom Jones* is one of those novels that you don't want to end; you wish it could just keep going on and on. You feel that you're coming to your own end when you finish that book. And you can't meet anybody on the road who doesn't turn out to be your father! I like a flabbergasting plot. Nowadays, of course, you couldn't do it straight; it would have to be a formal farce.

Q. Along those lines of structure and such, you mentioned doing a philosophical minstrel show. Do you make any kind of correlation between the novel and philosophic methods?

A. I don't know anything about philosophy. I've never even studied it, much less learned it. But ontology and cosmology are funny subjects to improvise. If you are a novelist of a certain type of temperament, then what you really want to do is re-invent the world. God wasn't too bad a novelist, except he was a Realist. Some of the things he did are right nice: the idea that ontogeny recapitulates phylogeny is a master stroke; if you thought that up you'd be proud of yourself. But a certain kind of sensibility can be made very uncomfortable by the recognition of the arbitrariness of physical facts and the inability to accept their finality. Take France, for example: France is shaped like a tea pot, and Italy is shaped like a boot. Well, okay. But the idea that that's the only way it's ever going to be, that they'll never be shaped like anything else — that can get to you after a while. Robert Louis Stevenson could never get used to the fact that people had two ears, funny-looking things, and eye-balls in their heads; he said it's enough to make you scream. I agree. And it seems to me that this emotion, which is a kind of metaphysical emotion, goes almost to the heart of what art is, at least some kinds of art, and this impulse to imagine alternatives to the world can become a driving impulse for writers. I confess that it is for me. So that really what you want to do is re-invent philosophy and the rest — make up your own whole history of the world. Why should it just be Plato and Aristotle? They're nice fellows, but why can't we start over, for variety's sake, and be somebody else instead and have all history go differently? Now you wouldn't write like Phil Roth or James Baldwin with a bug like that in your head, but you might write some of these bizarre comic novels that we hear about. What I really wanted to write after The Sot-Weed Factor was a new Old Testament, a comic Old Testament. I guess that's what this new novel Giles Goat-Boy is going to be. A souped-up Bible. Its subtitle would be The Revised New Syllabus of George Giles our Grand Tutor.

Q. Do you find some such qualities in a neglected novel, William Gaddis' The Recognitions?

A. I know that book only by sight. 950 pages: longer than The Sot-Weed Factor. Somebody asked me to review the new reprint of it, but I said I couldn't think of anything worth saying in literature that can't be said in 806 pages.

Q. Do you ever, in the heat of writing, find yourself adopting a position you wouldn't consciously agree with? To what extent do your characters take charge?

A.   You know, I suspect that's a lot of baloney. You hear respectable writers, sensible people like Katherine Anne Porter, say the characters just take over. I'm not going to let those scoundrels take over. I am in charge. I like novels like Unamuno's in which the characters challenge the author and begin to argue with him, but in my book they don't take over. No, sir, my characters are going to do what I tell them. Really, I don't think you ought to pay very much attention — it wasn't Katherine Anne Porter, it was some silly woman who was being interviewed on the *Today Show* a few weeks ago; she had just finished a book and said that she hadn't wanted it to go the way it did, but the characters had just taken over. You shouldn't pay very much attention to anything writers say. They don't know why they do what they do. They're like good tennis players or good painters, who are just full of nonsense, pompous and embarrassing, or merely mistaken, when they open their mouths. All sports, for example, all knacks and skills, become close to second nature with experts. When writers speak of things like inspiration and characters taking over and space-time grids, it's usually because they don't know *why* they do the things they do. And, if you begin to think about it too much, I guess you might tie yourself in knots, like when you think consciously about tying your necktie or tying your shoes. At least I have never heard much that any writer has said about writing that didn't embarrass me, including the things I say about it.

Q. In what way does teaching, especially the teaching of creative writing, influence your own work?

A.   It delays its completion.

Q. What would seem the ideal relationship of the writer, the critic, and the scholar to the campus?

A.   This is a tiresome subject. Is it a good thing for our young writers to teach school or is it a bad thing? It's tiresome because, like so many questions of that sort, anybody who takes a serious position about it one way or the other, an indignant position one way or the other, is forgetting how many kinds of writing there are, and how varied are the backgrounds out of which good art comes. Any kind of life at all, it seems to me, can be shown to have produced work that you admire. You just can't make any prescriptions about that. The people who get upset, I think, by the fact that so many of the writers and poets teach school nowadays, are people from the thirties, when you were supposed to go around the country and get dusty and sleep in haystacks. You couldn't write Kafka's novels that way. A man who spends his time hopping physical freightcars — never mind spiritual ones — may write *The Grapes of Wrath*, but he isn't going to write *The Castle*, and he's not likely to write *The Magic Mountain*, and he is not likely to write *Finnegans Wake*. I'll take those over *U.S.A.* or *Tropic of Capricorn*. A university-type might not write *The Naked Lunch*, and I'm glad there are people like Burroughs to take the dope and all so *I* don't have to do it; on the other hand, I might write *Gargantua and Pantagruel*, and I'd settle for that. In any case, I have kids and am responsible though lazy. Professors don't work very hard, as you know. They get a lot of money and an awful lot of time off.

Q. As a teacher of fiction do you observe any notable trends among your students, or do trends appear with a discouraging frequency at the expense of individuality?

A. The only trend I notice among my fiction students is that the rascals aren't very arrogant. My memory is that as students we were all cocky as could be, and half a dozen of us were sure we were going to turn literature upside down. If a celebrity came through, we tried to shoot him down. I guess my students have more sense. They take their criticism like a man and they don't seem very conceited. I rather like to see a certain arrogance in talented students: an ornery self-confidence. It's a good thing to have for a new writer because it gets him over some awful long stretches, rough spots, where nobody is paying attention to him except to tell him to sell Buicks instead. It is not really moral resolution that keeps him writing anyhow, but a kind of innate stubbornness — or maybe an arrogant lack of alternatives! — and I miss this in my students. They may have it and just not show it because they're more grown up then we were at their age. I like cocky students.

Q. Would you comment on why you left off your projected series of short novels dealing with nihilism after completing *The Floating Opera* and *The End of the Road*? Was it your desire to work with more complex forms?

A. I will give a serious answer to that question. I thought that I had invented nihilism, in 1953, and when I found out I hadn't, I lost interest. That is a simple way to say something more complicated.

I didn't leave off that series, actually: *The Sot-Weed Factor* is in that series. I used to think — I was twenty-four or twenty-five, and, you know, one feels at that age that one is at the forefront of the culture and turning it any way one wishes — I thought I'd write a series of three nihilistic amusing novels. I thought I'd do it before I was twenty-six, but it took a little longer than that. And I did it: *The Floating Opera, The End of the Road,* and *The Sot-Weed Factor.* So the series isn't unfinished. What happened was, I had thought I was writing about values and it turned out I was writing about innocence, which I found to be a more agreeable subject anyway: "That field where we all wander, hand to brow." Now I'm tiring of writing about innocence and would prefer to write about experience. But I haven't got any.

Q. I don't quite see what you mean; *The Sot-Weed Factor* is very different from the other two.

A. The difference is simply that I didn't think after *The End of the Road* that I was interested in writing any more realistic fiction — fiction that deals with Characters From Our Time, who speak real dialogue. I never could write realistic dialogue very well anyhow, and so I decided it was a bad idea for writers to write realistic dialogue. One ought to know a lot about reality before one writes realistic novels. Since I don't know much about reality, it will have to be abolished. What the hell, reality is a nice place to visit but you wouldn't want to live there, and literature never did, very long. We may have to do our novels in iambic pentameter; I'll let you know. Reality is a drag.

Q. After the death of Rennie in *The End of the Road,* you imply that Jacob and Joe should feel responsibility. Is this possible in a world without absolute values?

A. I don't know. I used to burn with that particular question, but you must understand that although I enjoy those first two novels, *The Floating Opera* and *The End of the Road,* there is a sense in which everybody who isn't just standing still is decently embarrassed by everything he's ever done before in his work. It means that you're changing. Not necessarily that you're getting better. I would feel foolish trying to answer a question like that now, so I won't. Pity you didn't check with me when I was twenty-five; I could've straightened you out.

Q. Does Albert Camus' discussion of suicide in *The Myth of Sisy-*

phus color your treatment of Todd Andrews in *The Floating Opera?*
A.   There certainly may be similarities between them, but it didn't
color my work because I haven't read *The Myth of Sisyphus.* I believe
Camus says the first question that a thoughtful man has to ask himself is why he is going to go on, then make up his mind whether to
blow his brains out or not; at the end of *The Floating Opera* my man
decides he won't commit suicide because there's no more reason to stop
living than to persist in it. It's quite curious how perceptive people
— reviewers, critics, knowledgeable students — will point out things to
you about your books and the connection between them and other
works that you simply didn't know about, and yet which, once you've
seen them, you know that you're not ever going to make anybody believe you didn't have in mind when you wrote your book. Somebody
told me that obviously I must have had in mind Lord Raglan's twenty-
five prerequisites for ritual heroes when I created the character of
Ebenezer Cooke in *The Sot-Weed Factor.* I hadn't read Raglan,
so I bought *The Hero,* and Ebenezer scored on twenty-three of the
twenty-five, which is higher than anybody else except Oedipus. If I
hadn't lied about Ebenezer's grave, I would have scored twenty-four.
Nobody knows where the real chap is buried; I made up a grave for
Ebenezer because I wanted to write his epitaph. Well, subsequently
I got excited over Raglan and Joseph Campbell, who may be a crank
for all I know or care, and I really haven't been able to get that business off my mind — the tradition of the wandering hero. The only
way I could use it would be to make it comic, and there will be some
of that in *Giles Goat-Boy.* I make it a point not to learn *too* much
about these things, and so the minute I saw what Campbell had on
his mind, I stopped reading about mythology. It could hogtie you.
It's all right to learn things after you've written about them, but not
too much ahead of time. The hero of *The End of the Road,* Jacob
Horner, is supposed to remind you first of all of Little Jack Horner,
who also sits in a corner and rationalizes. Then a Horner is somebody
who puts horns on, who cuckolds, and this is what Jacob Horner does.
But a student told me that I had in mind a character in Wycherley's
play *The Country Wife,* which I read last month when the student
pointed it out to me. This eighteenth-century Horner does exactly
the same thing as mine, it turns out, but Wycherley did it first and
I didn't know it. I wish I were Homer and could say "rosy-fingered
dawn." That's a wonderful thing to say about the dawn. I'd say
"rosy-fingered dawn, rosy-fingered dawn," and nobody would have
beat me to it.

Q. When can we expect *Giles Goat-Boy* to be published?

A. *Giles Goat-Boy* isn't finished yet, and I have no idea when it will be, or whether any publisher will be interested when it is. There seems to be a streak of perversity in some writers that turns acceptance into a dare. I had not thought that anybody would publish *The Sot-Weed Factor*, it's so long and such tough sledding here and there. I wouldn't read a book that long unless I'd been assured it was a great novel, a *Gargantua.* But Doubleday swallowed hard and printed the thing. Now I wanted this one to stay lean and sharp and economical, but it's getting huge. And suppose they should publish it? Then I'll have to write *The Ocean of Story*, four feet long. A volume-size piece of *Giles Goat-Boy* is about done, and no publisher is going to do what it may turn out I want them to do: one of these multi-volume serials like they did in the eighteenth and nineteenth centuries. *Roderick Random* used to be always published in two or three volumes. If you're interested in Black Humor types, you ought to go read Smollett. He's a real Ace of Spades.

Q. Do you deliberately incorporate social criticism into your novels?

A. I can't in fiction get very interested in such things. My argument is with the facts of life, not the conditions of it. Of course, as a private citizen one worries about politics and civil rights and all that. And you can get to the bottom of the world through any door, you know — write a great novel that starts out as a tract for civil rights. But I find myself, for example in *The Sot-Weed Factor*, using stock figures, stereotype Jews and Negroes, just for fun, as they did in the eighteenth century — blackamoors and village Jews and so forth. I'm not very responsible in the Social Problems way, I guess.

Q. You seem in talking about the authors whom you like not to have much interest in the American writers of this century, for example, Hemingway and James and Faulkner. Doesn't their kind of work appeal to you?

A. I don't mean to sound disrespectful. It's just my own bias. One loves Hemingway, one loves Faulkner. But Kafka, Joyce and Mann seem to me to be in a different league entirely. It's not a point I'm interested in defending. If you challenge it I'll give up. It doesn't seem to me that I learned very much from my literary countrymen. On the other hand, Joyce's *Dubliners* stories are so good they make you want to turn in your union card, and that Kafka, I can't speak too highly of him. He not only astonishes me, he takes my breath away. He seems not to be able to make a mistake. I bet I've read pieces like A Hunger Artist a hundred times, and I'm still astonished every time. Perfect, perfect.

Q. You said that when you started to do The Sot-Weed Factor you thought you'd invented a new comic genre. What was your conception of the new comic novel? What was the difference between the new and the old?

A. Oh, well, you know, it did seem to me that when I was reading Salinger, whom I enjoy, or Bellow or Capote — any self-respecting writer has this feeling — it seemed to me that they were all on the wrong track, that this isn't what we want to do. It seemed to me that where I was going was right. I wouldn't be so uppity about it anymore. It doesn't seem to me that Donleavy and Pynchon and these other chaps are doing the same thing I'm doing, whatever that is, but I don't know their work well enough to insist, so I'll have to take Stanley Hyman's word for it. Some people — like Bellow, I guess — pay pretty close attention to what other people are doing. They read their contemporaries, and I don't, very much. This is not a stance or policy: there just isn't time. If I've got to choose between reading Franny and Zooey or Gil Blas I would rather read Gil Blas. It's a better risk. You only have a certain amount of time to read books, and there are so many of them.

Q. In The Sot-Weed Factor, did you find yourself aiming for a conscious moral allegory?

A. I'll try to answer that question clearly for you. I mentioned the word allegory to somebody off the cuff, and then they cheated and put it on the cover of the book, which embarrassed me. Maybe allegory's not the word I should have used. On the other hand, it may be an allegory; I wouldn't be surprised. I had some things in mind when I wrote it, and it is interesting and cheering to find out later that I had more in mind than I thought I had. I don't really say that facetiously — one works by hunch and guess and intuition, with some conscious patterns in mind, too, and one has a character do this instead of that because one feels this is appropriate. Maybe in the act of setting it down you say, "I know why he did that," but then you are looking at it as a college teacher. More often you read a piece years later by some bright fellow, interpreting your work, and you realize that while he's strictly left-field here and here, he's got your number in this other place here, in a way you recognize for the first time yourself. This is a rather upsetting, but pleasantly upsetting, experience: to be told by somebody else what you were up to, and recognize that he's right.

SAUL BELLOW

Q. Is the period of internationalism in the novel over or could writers in the United States learn anything from Europeans, particularly from the recent French and German writers?

A. Literature, like painting, is international today. It has in fact always been international—European. Now it is about to become universal. Every year we are offered more Japanese, Indian and African books, and those Japanese, Indian and African writers read us of course. It seems to me that recent French and German writers have taken more from the Americans than the Americans have been able to take from them.

Q. Could writers in the United States learn anything from Europeans, particularly from the recent French and German?

A. I take a dim view of recent French novels. Though some of them do show a large American influence. The French have always been drawn to our literature. At one time they were in love with Fenimore Cooper and Buffalo Bill; the surrealists were in ecstasies over Nick Carter and Gide loved Dashiell Hammett. Sartre swallowed a large dose of John Dos Passos. To my mind, the main fault of current French novels is that they are so cognitive. They lean so heavily on the history of philosophy or on ideologies of one sort or another. The mark of the école normale is stamped on many a brow. Often French novels take the form of logical demonstrations or work out postulates systematically. I prefer to get my philosophy from philosophers. This is not to say that I am opposed to ideas in fiction. It is a great defect of

---

Interview conducted by John J. Enck on April 24, 1964, in Madison, Wisconsin.

American novelists that they shun thinking. Sometimes they appear to take anti-intellectual attitudes in order to identify themselves with the mass of Americans and behave like untutored populists. Which they are not. Most of them are highly sophisticated.

Q. Do you outline your novels before writing?

A. I wish I were able to.

Q. To what extent do you worry about the structure of your novels?

A. They give me insomnia, but I seem helpless to do anything about it.

Q. Do you usually begin with a concept or a fable in your own work?

A. Fable is an Aristotelian word and I don't really feel strong enough to cope with it. I do, of course, have something that might be described as a concept—a working idea, a feeling, a sort of excitement.

Q. To what extent do you consider your fiction a method of problem solving?

A. There is a general feeling abroad that we cannot justify our existence. If I shared that feeling I shouldn't be writing novels.

Q. Do you ever, in the heat of writing, find yourself adopting a position you wouldn't consciously agree with?

A. Yes, very often, and I think this is the truest sign that I am doing well. If everything is going your way and you feel no challenge or strain, it is very likely that you are in the nutshell, king of infinite space.

Q. To what extent do your characters take charge?

A. If I burden them with flat or dead attitudes, they seem to resent it. The main reason for rewriting is not to achieve a smooth surface, but to discover the inner truth of your characters.

Q. In what way does teaching, especially the teaching of creative writing, influence your own work?

A. I don't teach creative writing. Not because I think it useless, but because it is very tedious and difficult. A man writes because he is a writer and not because he has taken courses. A writer is interesting because of his peculiar perspective. Can this perspective be taught? I think not. I know that the student longs for help, but what he develops in writing courses is generally a psychological dependency. He asks the teacher—perhaps even more important, the institution—to support him against an incredulous world which will not allow him to take things into his own hands and declare himself a writer. This is partly a problem of egalitarianism or levelling. A beginning writer hesitates to anoint himself, to make a declaration of his very special character. And so he seeks institutional support. He goes to the universities and gets a Ph.D. in creative writing and feels himself armed for the struggle. Like any other licensed professional. But this is social assistance rather than creativity.

Q. Could one argue that anyone who is going to teach literature ought to write a novel or at least try to write a novel?

A. I am often astonished at the ignorance of learned people. Even the best of teachers will sometimes fail to understand how a book is put together. I suppose that the maker of a thing, however clumsy he may be, acquires a sort of knowledge for which there is no substitute.

Q. Have you any opinions to express about contemporary writers?

A. I don't really like to discuss contemporary writers. Discussion of that sort generally turns into gossip, and while I am not absolutely opposed to gossip, what I like to avoid is the sort of gladiatorial combat with other writers which the public finds so marvelously entertaining. Let me say that I admire J. F. Powers greatly. I liked *Morte d'Urban* a lot, though I thought it had some faults. I rather enjoyed Mr. Donleavy's *The Ginger Man.* I thought it was very funny and free. I admire John Cheever and Wright Morris and Ralph Ellison and William Gaddis, and many more. I liked *The Ginger Man* more than I admired it. Here and there, its victories appeared a little easy. There is a tendency in modern literature to obtain a certain relief from throwing over the accumulated restraints of earlier generations. Samuel Butler, for instance, enjoys his liberation from Victorian attitudes and rhetoric. Anderson and Hemingway do it, too. Donleavy kicks free from the prevailing rules of good fiction as well as from responsibility, marriage, etc. Of course, he does murder some sitting ducks. Marriage, which everyone murders. Family, everyone's down on the family. It isn't too hard to be radical that way—when middle-class opinion is more than half on your side. Writers are not as radical as they would like to be. That is to say, they feel an active demand for extreme positions but the imagination fails to meet the demands. The world is far more sensational than their ideas. They cannot keep up with it, and this exasperates them.

Q. Do you think part of the role of the writer as a public figure is to enter into a comment on contemporary events, such as politics or civil rights or world affairs?

A. I have no objection to writers doing that, if they feel they should; but they must genuinely feel the obligation, or the need, not fake it. You are asking me about James Baldwin, I imagine. Is that the question?

Q. He was in the back of my mind.

A. Let's skip that.

Q. Very well. What are your views on modern criticism?

A. My feeling about most critical writing is that it is a rival form of imaginative literature. Formerly my attitude toward criticism was entirely hostile. Now it is beginning to change. From certain critics I have learned a great deal and I admire a rather odd assortment—Erich Auerbach, David Jones, Wyndham Lewis, Harold Rosenberg. I have never liked Leavis. He is too ideological. He makes literature too political, and I dislike his views.

The best of modern writers have a formidable theoretical apparatus—Joyce, Mann, Eliot, Yeats, Pound. Unfortunately, the modern writer is obliged to think about his situation, to make an effort to understand his historical condition. For it is a modern article of faith that one must not repeat what has already been done, and every vanguard artist dreads the superfluous and has a horror of vain gestures. It should be the function of criticism to free the imagination of writers from the burden of historical evaluation. If the critic met this obligation the imagination of the novelist might be liberated. Is this what we see when we look at critical journals?

Q. Present company always, I hope, excepted. Does this attitude of yours towards critics carry over to scholarship?

A. No, I don't have a similar prejudice against scholars, although I avoid mere antiquarianism.

Q. Would you elaborate on the way you write?

A. Every writer learns to do a number of things expertly, and he is frequently tempted to give an expert performance whenever he is in trouble. That is to say, when in doubt, he does what he knows best how to do. He trusts his skill as other professionals do. When this happens, he is no longer the free artist—he has failed. I don't say that there is a perfect freedom for every writer, but insofar as his vocation is real, he does yearn for freedom and struggle for it.

His life, like any other life, is so hedged about by duties, obligations, contractual relationships, that if, in his chosen sphere, he loses his freedom, his defeat as a human being is total. In literature, professionalism is slavery and our literature is drearily professional and narrow. It is not smoothness of performance or virtuosity that I object to, but you have only to listen to Paganini and then to Mozart to realize the difference between the virtuoso and the artist. Paganini is all very well, but except to professional fiddlers, he is very boring.

Q. What is your opinion on criticism of John Cheever?

A. I like him; he's a fine writer and his short stories are excellent. I admire *The Wapshot Chronicle*. He is, of course, a pro. Sometimes I wonder whether his connection with the *New Yorker* has been an unmixed blessing. It's a bad thing for any writer to wear the livery of a magazine and to become thoroughly identified with it.

Q. Have you comments on the relationship of writers and editors and about publishing in general?

A. Some writers like a good deal of help from their editors, others, like myself, reject it. Editors inhabit the publishing world, have lunch and cocktails together, and represent the opinions and attitudes of their class. Or its prejudices. Some writers want to imbibe these prejudices and feel them to be beneficial. The young writer is apt to feel helpless and dependent and opens his mouth like a young bird. The publishing industry feeds him a certain number of worms.

VLADIMIR NABOKOV

Q. For years bibliographers and literary journalists didn't know whether to group you under "Russian" or "American." Now that you're living in Switzerland there seems to be complete agreement that you're American. Do you find this kind of distinction at all important regarding your identity as a writer?

A. I have always maintained, even as a schoolboy in Russia, that the nationality of a worthwhile writer is of secondary importance. The more distinctive an insect's aspect, the less apt is the taxonomist to glance first of all at the locality label under the pinned specimen in order to decide which of several vaguely described races it should be assigned to. The writer's art is his real passport. His identity should be immediately recognized by a special pattern or unique coloration. His habitat may confirm the correctness of the determination but should not lead to it. Locality labels are known to

Interview conducted by Alfred Appel, Jr., on September 25, 27, 28, 29, 1966, at Montreux, Switzerland. Mr. Nabokov and his wife have for the last six years lived in an opulent hotel built in 1835, which still retains its nineteenth-century atmosphere. Their suite of rooms is on the sixth floor, overlooking Lake Geneva, and the sounds of the lake are audible through the open doors of their small balcony. Since Mr. Nabokov does not like to talk off the cuff (or "Off the Nabocuff," as he said) no tape recorder was used. Mr. Nabokov either wrote out his answers to the questions or dictated them to the interviewer; in some instances, notes from the conversation were later recast as formal questions and answers. The interviewer was Nabokov's student at Cornell University in 1954. The footnotes to the interview, except where indicated, are provided by the interviewer.

have been faked by unscrupulous insect dealers. Apart from these considerations I think of myself today as an American writer who has once been a Russian one.

Q. The Russian writers you have translated and written about all precede the so-called "age of realism," which is more celebrated by English and American readers than is the earlier period. Would you say something about your temperamental or artistic affinities with the great writers of the 1830–40 era of masterpieces. Do you see your own work falling under such general rubrics as a tradition of Russian humor?

A. The question of the affinities I may think I have or not have with nineteenth-century Russian writers is a classificational, not a confessional matter. There is hardly a single Russian major writer of the past whom pigeon-holers have not mentioned in connection with me. Pushkin's blood runs through the veins of modern Russian literature as inevitably as Shakespeare's through those of English literature.

Q. Many of the major Russian writers, such as Pushkin, Lermontov, and Bely, have distinguished themselves in both poetry and prose, an uncommon accomplishment in English and American literature. Does this signal fact have anything to do with the special nature of Russian literary culture, or are there technical or linguistic resources which make this kind of versatility more possible in Russian? And as a writer of both prose and poetry, what distinctions do you make between them?

A. On the other hand, neither Gogol nor Tolstoy nor Chekhov were distinguished versificators. Moreover, the dividing line between prose and poetry in some of the greatest English or American novels is not easy to draw. I suppose you should have used the term "rhymed poetry" in your question and then one might answer that Russian rhymes are incomparably more attractive and more abundant than English ones. No wonder a Russian prose writer frequents those beauties, especially in his youth.

Q. Who are the great American writers you most admire?

A. When I was young I liked Poe, and I still love Melville, whom I did not read as a boy. My feelings towards James are rather complicated. I really dislike him intensely but now and then the figure in the phrase, the turn of the epithet, the screw of an absurd adverb, cause me a kind of electric tingle, as if some current of his was also passing through my own blood. Hawthorne is a splendid writer. Emerson's poetry is delightful.

Q. You have often said that you "don't belong to any club or group," and I wonder if the historical examples of the ways Russian writers have allowed ideology to determine if not destroy their art, culminating in the Socialist Realism of our own time, have not gone a long way in shaping your own skepticism and aversion to didacticism of any kind. Which "historical examples" have you been most conscious of?

A. My aversion to groups is rather a matter of temperament than the fruit of information and thought. I was born that way and have despised ideological coercion instinctively all my life. Those "historical examples" by the way are not as clear-cut and obvious as you seem to imply. The mystical didacticism of Gogol or the utilitarian moralism of Tolstoy, or the reactionary journalism of Dostoevsky, are of their own poor making and in the long run nobody really takes them seriously.

Q. Would you say something about the controversy surrounding the Chernyshevski biography in The Gift? You have commented on this briefly before, but since its suppression in the thirties expresses such a transcendent irony and seems to justify the need for just such a parody, I think your readers would be most interested, especially since so little is known about the émigré communities, their magazines, and the role of intellectuals in these communities. If you would like to describe something of the writer's relationship to this world, please do.

A. Everything that can be profitably said about Count Godunov-Cherdyntsev's biography of Chernyshevski has been said by Koncheyev in The Gift. I can only add that I devoted as much honest labor to the task of gathering the material for the Chernyshevski chapter as I did to the composing of Shade's poem for him. As to the suppression of that chapter by the editors of Sovremennye Zapiski, it was indeed an unprecedented occurrence, quite out of keeping with their exceptional broadmindedness for, generally speaking, in their acceptance or rejection of literary works they were guided exclusively by artistic standards. As to the latter part of your question, the revised chapter fourteen in *Speak, Memory* will provide additional information.

Q. Do you have any opinions about the Russian anti-utopian tradition (if it can be called this) from Odoevsky's "The Last Suicide" and "A City Without a Name" in *Russian Nights* to Briusov's *The Republic of the Southern Cross* and Zamiatin's *We* (to name only a few)?

A. I am indifferent to those works.

Q. Is it fair to say that *Invitation to a Beheading* and *Bend Sinister* are cast as mock anti-utopian novels, with their ideological centers removed—the totalitarian state becoming an extreme and fantastic metaphor for the imprisonment of the mind, thus making consciousness, rather than politics, the subject of these novels?

A. Yes, possibly.

Q. Speaking of ideology, you have often expressed your hostility to Freud, most noticeably in the forewords to your translated novels. Some readers have wondered which of Freud's works or theories you were most offended by and why. The parodies of Freud in *Lolita* and *Pale Fire* suggest a wider familiarity with the good doctor than you have ever publicly granted. Would you comment on this?

A. Oh, I am not up to discussing again that figure of fun. He is not worthy of more attention than I have granted him in my novels and in *Speak, Memory*. Let the credulous and the vulgar continue to believe that all mental woes can be cured by a daily application of old Greek myths to their private parts. I really do not care.

Q. Your contempt for Freud's "standardized symbols" extends to the assumptions of a good many other theorizers. Do you think literary criticism is at all purposeful, and if so, what kind of criticism would you point to? *Pale Fire* makes it clear what sort you find gratuitous (at best).

A. My advice to a budding literary critic would be as follows. Learn to distinguish banality. Remember that mediocrity thrives on "ideas."

Beware of the modish message. Ask yourself if the symbol you have detected is not your own footprint. Ignore allegories. By all means place the "how" above the "what" but do not let it be confused with the "so what." Rely on the sudden erection of your small dorsal hairs. Do not drag in Freud at this point. All the rest depends on personal talent.

Q.   As a writer, have you ever found criticism instructive—not so much the reviews of your own books, but any general criticism? From your own experiences do you think that an academic and literary career nourish one another? Since many writers today know no other alternative than a life on campus I'd be very interested in your feelings about this. Do you think that your own work in America was at all shaped by your being part of an academic community?

A.   I find criticism most instructive when an expert proves to me that my facts or my grammar are wrong. An academic career is especially helpful to writers in two ways: 1) easy access to magnificent libraries and 2) long vacations. There is of course the business of teaching but old professors have young instructors to correct examination papers for them, and young instructors, authors in their own right, are followed by admiring glances along the corridors of Vanity Hall. Otherwise, our greatest rewards, such as the reverberations of our minds in such minds as vibrate responsively in later years, force novelist-teachers to nurse lucidity and honesty of style in their lectures.

Q.   What are the possibilities of literary biography?

A.   They are great fun to write, generally less fun to read. Sometimes the thing becomes a kind of double paper chase: first, the biographer pursues his quarry through letters and diaries, and across the bogs of conjecture, and then a rival authority pursues the muddy biographer.

Q.   Some critics may find the use of coincidence in a novel arch or contrived. I recall that you yourself at Cornell called Dostoevsky's usage of coincidence crude.

A.   But in "real" life they do happen. Last night you were telling us at dinner a very funny story about the use of the title "Doctor" in Germany, and the very next moment, as my loud laughter was subsiding, I heard a person at the next table saying to her neighbor in clear French tones coming through the tinkling and shuffling sounds of a restaurant —[turning to his wife] just as you can hear at this moment the trilling of that little grebe on the lake through the sounds of the traffic—"Of course, you never know with the Germans if 'Doctor' means a dentist or a lawyer." Very often you meet with some person or some event in "real" life that would sound pat in a story. It is not the coincidence in the story that bothers us so much as the coincidence of coincidences in several stories by different writers, as, for instance, the recurrent eavesdropping device in nineteenth-century Russian fiction.

_Q_. Could you tell us something about your work habits as a writer, and the way you compose your novels. Do you use an outline? Do you have a full sense of where a fiction is heading even while you are in the early stages of composition?

A.   In my twenties and early thirties, I used to write, dipping pen in ink and using a new nib every other day, in exercise books, crossing out, inserting, striking out again, crumpling the page, rewriting every page three or four times, then copying out the novel in a different ink and a neater hand, then revising the whole thing once more, re-copying it with new corrections, and finally dictating it to my wife who has typed out all my stuff. Generally speaking, I am a slow writer, a snail carrying its house at the rate of two hundred pages of final copy per year (one spectacular exception was the Russian original of _Invitation to a Beheading_, the first draft of which I wrote in one fortnight of wonderful excitement and sustained inspiration). In those days and nights I generally followed the order of chapters when writing a novel but even so, from the very first, I relied heavily on mental composition, constructing whole paragraphs in my mind as I walked in the streets or sat in my bath, or lay in bed, although often deleting or rewriting them later. In the late thirties, beginning with _The Gift_, and perhaps under the influence of the many notes needed, I switched to another, physically more practical, method— that of writing with an eraser-capped pencil on index cards. Since I always have at the very start a curiously clear preview of the entire novel before me or above me, I find cards especially convenient when not following the logical sequence of chapters but preparing instead this or that passage at any point of the novel and filling in the gaps in no special order. I am afraid to get mixed up with Plato whom I do not care for, but I do think that in my case it is true that the entire book, before it is written, seems to be ready ideally in some other, now transparent, now dimming, dimension, and my job is to take down as much of it as I can make out and as precisely as I am humanly able to. The greatest happiness I experience in composing is when I feel I cannot understand, or rather catch myself not understanding (without the presupposition of an already existing creation) how or why that image or structural move has just come to me. It is sometimes rather amusing to find my readers trying to elucidate in a matter-of-fact way these wild workings of my not very efficient mind.

Q. One often hears from writers talk of how a character takes hold of them and in a sense dictates the course of the action. Has this ever been your experience?

A. I have never experienced this. What a preposterous experience! Writers who have had it must be very minor or insane. No, the design of my novel is fixed in my imagination and every character follows the course I imagine for him. I am the perfect dictator in that private world insofar as I alone am responsible for its stability and truth. Whether I reproduce it as fully and faithfully as I would wish, is another question. Some of my old works reveal dismal blurrings and blanks.

Q. *Pale Fire* appears to some readers to be in part a gloss on Plato's myth of the cave, and the constant play of Shades and Shadows throughout your work suggests a conscious Platonism. Would you care to comment on this possibility?

A. As I have said I am not particularly fond of Plato, nor would I survive very long under his Germanic regime of militarism and music. I do not think that this cave business has anything to do with my Shade and Shadows.

Q. Since we are mentioning philosophy per se, I wonder if we might talk about the philosophy of language that seems to unfold in your works, and whether or not you have consciously seen the similarities, say, between the language of Zemblan and what Ludwig Wittgenstein had to say about a "private language." Your poet's sense of the limitations of language is startlingly similar to Wittgenstein's remarks on the referential basis of language. While you were at Cambridge, did you have much contact with the philosophy faculty?

A. No contact whatsoever. I am completely ignorant of Wittgenstein's works, and the first time I heard his name must have been in the fifties. In Cambridge I played football and wrote Russian verse.

Q. When in Canto Two John Shade describes himself, "I stand before the window and I pare/My fingernails," you are echoing Stephen Dedalus in *A Portrait of the Artist as a Young Man,* on the artist who "remains within or behind or beyond or above his handiwork, invisible, refined out of existence, indifferent, paring his fingernails." In almost all of your novels, especially in *Invitation to a Beheading, Bend Sinister, Pale Fire,* and *Pnin*—but even in *Lolita,* in the person of the seventh hunter in Quilty's play, and in several other phosphorescent glimmers which are visible to the careful reader —the creator is indeed behind or above his handiwork, but he is not invisible and surely not indifferent. To what extent are you consciously "answering" Joyce in *Pale Fire,* and what are your feelings about his esthetic stance—or alleged stance, because perhaps you may think that Stephen's remark doesn't apply to *Ulysses?*

A. Neither Kinbote nor Shade, nor their maker, is answering Joyce in *Pale Fire.* Actually, I never liked *A Portrait of the Artist as a Young Man.* I find it a feeble and garrulous book. The phrase you quote is an unpleasant coincidence.

Q. You have granted that Pierre Delalande influenced you, and I would readily admit that influence-mongering can be reductive and deeply offensive if it tries to deny a writer's originality. But in the instance of yourself and Joyce, it seems to me that you've consciously profited from Joyce's example without imitating him—that you've realized the implications in *Ulysses* without having had recourse to obviously "Joycean" devices (stream-of-consciousness, the "collage" effects created out of the vast flotsam and jetsam of everyday life). Would you comment on what Joyce has meant to you as a writer, his importance in regard to his liberation and expansion of the novel form?

A. My first real contact with *Ulysses,* after a leering glimpse in the early twenties, was in the thirties at a time when I was definitely formed as a writer and immune to any literary influence. I studied *Ulysses* seriously only much later, in the fifties, when preparing my Cornell courses. That was the best part of the education I received at Cornell. *Ulysses* towers over the rest of Joyce's writings, and in comparison to its noble originality and unique lucidity of thought and style the unfortunate *Finnegans Wake* is nothing but a formless and dull mass of phony folklore, a cold pudding of a book, a persistent snore in the next room, most aggravating to the insomniac I am. Moreover, I always detested regional literature full of quaint old-timers and imitated pronunciation. *Finnegans Wake's* façade disguises a very conventional and drab tenement house, and only the infrequent snatches of heavenly intonations redeem it from utter insipidity. I know I am going to be excommunicated for this pronouncement.

Q. Although I cannot recall your mentioning the involuted structure of *Ulysses* when you lectured on Joyce, I do remember your insisting that the hallucinations in Nighttown are the author's and not Stephen's or Bloom's, which is one step away from a discussion of the involution. This is an aspect of *Ulysses* almost totally ignored by the Joyce Industry, and an aspect of Joyce which would seem to be of great interest to you. If Joyce's somewhat inconsistent involutions tend to be obscured by the vastness of his structures, it might be said that the structuring of your novels depends on the strategy of involution. Could you comment on this, or compare your sense of Joyce's presence in and above his works with your own intention —that is, Joyce's covert appearances in *Ulysses*; the whole Shakespeare-paternity theme which ultimately spirals into the idea of the "parentage" of *Ulysses* itself; Shakespeare's direct address to Joyce in Nighttown ("How my Oldfellow chokit his Thursday-momum," that being Bloomsday); and Molly's plea to Joyce, "O Jamesy let me up out of this"—all this as against the way the authorial voice— or what you call the "anthropomorphic deity impersonated by me"— again and again appears in your novels, most strikingly at the end.

A. One of the reasons Bloom cannot be the active party in the Nighttown chapter (and if he is not, then the author is directly dreaming it up for him, and around him, with some real episodes inserted here and there) is that Bloom, a wilting male anyway, has been drained of his manhood earlier in the evening and thus would be quite unlikely to indulge in the violent sexual fancies of Nighttown. But I plan to publish my notes on *Ulysses*, and will not pursue the matter now.

Q. Ideally, how should a reader experience or react to "the end" of one of your novels, that moment when the vectors are removed and the fact of the fiction is underscored, the cast dismissed? What common assumptions about literature are you assaulting?

A.   The question is so charmingly phrased that I would love to answer it with equal elegance and eloquence, but I cannot say very much. I think that what I would welcome at the close of a book of mine is a sensation of its world receding in the distance and stopping somewhere there suspended afar like a picture in a picture: *The Artist's Studio* by Van Bock.[1]

Q.   It may well be a failure of perception, but I've always been unsure of the very last sentences of *Lolita*, perhaps because the shift in voice at the close of your other books is so clear, but is one supposed to "hear" a different voice when the masked narrator says "And do not pity C.Q. One had to choose between him and H.H., and one wanted H.H. . . ." and so forth? The return to the first person in the next sentence makes me think that the mask has not been lifted, but readers trained on *Invitation to a Beheading*, among other books, are always looking for the imprint of that "master thumb," to quote Franklin Lane in *Pale Fire*, "that made the whole involuted, boggling thing one beautiful straight line."

A.   No, I did not mean to introduce a different voice. I did want, however, to convey a constriction of the narrator's sick heart, a warning spasm causing him to abridge names and hasten to conclude his tale before it was too late. I am glad I managed to achieve this remoteness of tone at the end.

Q.   Do Franklin Lane's *Letters* exist? I don't wish to appear like Mr. Goodman in *The Real Life of Sebastian Knight*, but I understand that Franklin Lane did exist.

A.   Frank Lane, his published letters, and the passage cited by Kinbote, certainly exist. Kinbote was rather struck by Lane's handsome melancholy face. And of course "lane" is the last word of Shade's poem. The latter has no significance.

Q.   In which of your early works do you think you first begin to

---

[1] Research has failed to confirm the existence of this alleged "Dutch Master," whose name is only an alphabetical step away from being a significant anagram, a poor relation of Quilty's anagrammatic mistress, "Vivian Darkbloom."

face the possibilities that are fully developed in *Invitation to a Beheading* and reach an apotheosis in the "involute abode" of *Pale Fire?*

A. Possibly in *The Eye*, but *Invitation to a Beheading* is on the whole a spontaneous generation.

Q. Are there other writers whose involuted effects you admire? Sterne? Pirandello's plays?

A. I never cared for Pirandello. I love Sterne but had not read him in my Russian period.

Q. The Afterword to *Lolita* is significant, obviously, for many reasons. Is it included in all the translations which, I understand, number about twenty-five?

A. Yes.

Q. You once told me after a class at Cornell that you'd been unable to read more than one hundred or so pages of *Finnegans Wake*. As it happens, on p. 104 there begins a section very close in spirit to *Pale Fire*, and I wonder if you've ever read this, or seen the similarity. It is the history of all the editions and interpretations of Anna Livia Plurabelle's Letter (or "Mamafesta," text included). Among the three pages listing the various titles of ALP's letter, Joyce includes *Try our Taal on a Taub* (which we are already doing), and I wondered if you would comment on Swift's contribution to the literature about the corruption of learning and literature. Is it only a coincidence that Kinbote's "Foreword" to *Pale Fire* is dated "Oct. 19," which is the date of Swift's death?

A. I finished *Finnegans Wake* eventually. It has no inner connection with *Pale Fire*. I think it is so nice that the day on which Kinbote committed suicide (and he certainly did after putting the last touches to his edition of the poem) happens to be both the anniversary of Pushkin's *Lyceum* and that of "poor old man Swift'[s]" death, which is news to me (but see variant in note to line 231). In common with Pushkin, I am fascinated by fatidic dates. Moreover, when dating some special event in my novels I often choose a more or less familiar one as a *point de repère*, which helps to check a possible misprint in the proofs, as for instance "April 1" in the diary of Hermann in *Despair*.

Q. Mention of Swift moves me to ask about the genre of *Pale Fire*; as a "monstrous semblance of a novel," do you see it in terms of some tradition or form?

A. The form of *Pale Fire* is specifically, if not generically, new. I would like to take this pleasant opportunity to correct the following misprints in the Putnam edition 1962, second impression: On p. 137, end of note to line 143, "rustic" should be "rusty." On p. 151, "Catskin Week" should be "Catkin Week." On p. 223, the line number in the reference at the end of the first note should not be "550" but "549." On p. 237, top, "For" should be "for." On p. 241, the word "lines" after "*disent-prise*" should be "rhymes." And on p. 294, the comma after "Arnold" should be replaced by an open parenthesis. Thank you.[2]

Q. Do you make a clear distinction between satire and parody? I ask this because you have so often said you do not wish to be taken as a "moral satirist," and yet parody is so central to your vision.

A. Satire is a lesson, parody is a game.

Q. Chapter ten in *The Real Life of Sebastian Knight* contains a wonderful description of how parody functions in your own novels. But your sense of what *parody* means seems to stretch the usual definition, as when Cincinnatus in *Invitation to a Beheading* tells his mother, "You're still only a parody . . . Just like this spider, just like those bars, just like the striking of that clock." All art, then, or at least all attempts at a "realistic" art, would seem to produce a distortion, a "parody." Would you expand on what you mean by *parody* and why, as Fyodor says in *The Gift*, "The spirit of parody always goes along with genuine poetry"?

A. When the poet Cincinnatus C., in my dreamiest and most poetical novel, accuses (not quite fairly) his mother of being a

---

[2] Since Mr. Nabokov has opened an Errata Department, the following misprints from the Lancer Books paperback edition of *Pale Fire*, 1963, should be noted: on p. 17, fifth line from bottom of middle paragraph, "sad" should be "saw." On p. 60, note to lines 47–48, line 21 should be "burst an appendix," not "and." On p. 111, fourth line of note to line 172, "inscription" is misspelled. On p. 158, last sentence of note to line 493, "filfth" should be "filth." Nabokov's other books are relatively free from misprints, except for the Popular Library paperback edition of *The Gift*, 1963, whose blemishes are too numerous to mention.

parody, he uses the word in its familiar sense of "grotesque imitation." When Fyodor, in *The Gift*, alludes to that "spirit of parody"
which plays around the spray of genuine "serious" poetry, he is
referring to parody in the sense of an essentially lighthearted, delicate, mocking-bird game, such as Pushkin's parody of Derzhavin in
Exegi Monumentum.

Q.   What is your opinion of Joyce's parodies? Do you see any difference in the artistic effect of scenes such as the maternity hospital and
the beach interlude with Gerty Macdowell? Are you familiar with
the work of younger American writers who have been influenced
by both you and Joyce, such as Thomas Pynchon (a Cornellian,
Class of '59, who surely was in your course), and do you have
any opinion on the current ascendancy of the so-called parody-novel
(John Barth, for instance)?

A.   The literary parodies in the Maternal Hospital chapter are on
the whole jejunish. Joyce seems to have been hampered by the general sterilized tone he chose for that chapter, and this somehow
dulled and monotonized the inlaid skits. On the other hand, the
frilly novelette parodies in the Masturbation scene are highly successful; and the sudden bursting of its clichés into the fireworks and
tender sky of real poetry is a feat of genius. I am not familiar with
the works of the two other writers you mention.[3]

Q.   Why, in *Pale Fire*, do you call parody the "last resort of wit"?

A.   This is Kinbote speaking. There are people whom parody upsets.

Q.   Are the composition of *Lolita* and *Speak, Memory*, two very
different books about the spell exerted by the past, at all connected
in the way that the translations of *The Song of Igor's Campaign*
and *Eugene Onegin* are related to *Pale Fire*? Had you finished all
the notes to *Onegin* before you began *Pale Fire*?

A.   This is the kind of question that can be only answered by the
interrogator himself. The task of pondering such juxtapositions and
contrasts is above my capacities. Yes, I had finished all my notes
to *Onegin* before I began *Pale Fire*. Flaubert speaks in one of his
letters, in relation to a certain scene in *Madame Bovary*, about the

---

[3] Mrs. Nabokov, who graded her husband's examination papers, did remember Pynchon, but only for his "unusual" handwriting: half printing, half script.

difficulty of painting *couleur sur couleur*. This in a way is what I tried to do in retwisting my own experience when inventing Kinbote. *Speak, Memory* is strictly autobiographic. There is nothing autobiographic in *Lolita*.

Q. Although self-parody seems to be a vital part of your work, you are a writer who believes passionately in the primacy of the imagination. Yet your novels are filled with little details that seem to have been purposely pulled from your own life, as a reading of *Speak, Memory* makes clear, not to mention the overriding patterns, such as the lepidopteral motif, which extend through so many books. They seem to partake of something other than the involuted voice, to suggest some clearly held idea about the interrelationship between self-knowledge and artistic creation, self-parody and identity. Would you comment on this, and the significance of autobiographical hints in works of art that are literally *not* autobiographical?

A. I would say that imagination is a form of memory. Down, Plato, down, good dog. An image depends on the power of association, and association is supplied and prompted by memory. When we speak of a vivid individual recollection we are paying a compliment not to our capacity of retention but to Mnemosyne's mysterious foresight in having stored up this or that element which creative imagination may use when combining it with later recollections and inventions. In this sense, both memory and imagination are a negation of time.

Q. C. P. Snow has complained about the gulf between the "two cultures," the literary and scientific communities. As someone who has bridged this gulf, do you see the sciences and humanities as necessarily opposed? Have your experiences as a scientist influenced your performance as an artist? Is it fanciful to use the vocabulary of physics in describing the structures of some of your novels?

A. I would have compared myself to a Colossus of Rhodes bestriding the gulf between the thermodynamics of Snow and Laurentomania of Leavis, had that gulf not been a mere dimple of a ditch that a small frog could straddle. The terms "physics" and "egghead" as used nowadays evoke in me the dreary image of applied science, the knack of an electrician tinkering with bombs and other gadgets. One of those "Two Cultures" is really nothing but utilitarian technology; the other is B-grade novels, ideological fiction, popular art.

Who cares if there exists a gap between such "physics" and such "humanities." Those Eggheads are terrible philistines. A real good head is not oval but round.

My passion for lepidopterological research, in the field, in the laboratory, in the library, is even more pleasurable than the study and practice of literature, which is saying a good deal. Lepidopterists are obscure scientists. Not one is mentioned in Webster. But never mind. I have re-worked the classification of various groups of butterflies, have described and figured several species and sub-species. My names for the microscopic organs that I have been the first to see and portray have safely found their way into the biological dictionaries (which is poorly matched by the wretched entry under "nymphet" in Webster's latest edition). The tactile delights of precise delineation, the silent paradise of the camera lucida, and the precision of poetry in taxonomic description represent the artistic side of the thrill that accumulation of new knowledge, absolutely useless to the layman, gives its first begetter. Science means to me above all natural science. Not the ability to repair a radio set; quite stubby fingers can do that. Apart from this basic consideration, I certainly welcome the free interchange of terminology between any branch of science and any raceme of art. There is no science without fancy, and no art without facts. Aphoristicism is a symptom of arteriosclerosis.

Q. In *Pale Fire*, Kinbote complains that "The coming of summer represented a problem in optics." *The Eye* is well-titled, since you plumb these problems throughout your fiction; the apprehension of "reality" is a miracle of vision, and consciousness is virtually an optical instrument in your work. Have you studied the science of optics at all, and would you say something about your own visual sense, and how you feel it has served your fiction?

A. I am afraid you are quoting this out of context. Kinbote was simply annoyed by the spreading foliage of summer interfering with his Tom-peeping. Otherwise you are right in suggesting that I have good eyes. Doubting Tom should have worn spectacles. It is true, however, that even with the best of visions one must touch things to be quite sure of "reality."

Q. You have said that Alain Robbe-Grillet and Jorge Luis Borges are among your favorite contemporary writers. Do you find them to be at all similar? Do you think Robbe-Grillet's novels are as free of "psychology" as he claims?

A. Robbe-Grillet's claims are preposterous. Those manifestos die with the dadas. His fiction is magnificently poetical and original, and the shifts of levels, the interpenetration of successive impressions and so forth belong of course to psychology—psychology at its best. Borges is also a man of infinite talent, but his miniature labyrinths and the roomy ones of Robbe-Grillet are quite differently built, and the lighting is not the same.

Q. I recall your humorous remarks at Cornell about two writers experiencing "telepathy" (I believe you were comparing Dickens and Flaubert). You and Borges were both born in 1899 (but so was Ernest Hemingway!). Your *Bend Sinister* and Borges' story "The Circular Ruins" are conceptually similar, but you do not read Spanish and that story was first translated into English in 1949, two years after *Bend Sinister*'s birth, just as in Borges' "The Secret Miracle," Hladik has created a verse drama uncannily similar to your recently Englished play, *The Waltz Invention*, which precedes Borges' tale, but which he could not have read in Russian. When were you first aware of Borges' fictions, and have you and he had any kind of association or contact, other than telepathic?

A. I read a Borges story for the first time three or four years ago. Up till then I had not been aware of his existence, nor do I believe he knew, or indeed knows, anything about me. That is not very grand in the way of telepathy. There are affinities between *Invitation to a Beheading* and *The Castle*, but I had not yet read Kafka when I wrote my novel. As to Hemingway, I read him for the first time in the early forties, something about bells, balls and bulls, and loathed it. Later I read his admirable "The Killers" and the wonderful fish story which I was asked to translate into Russian but could not for some reason or other.

Q. As a matter of fact, Borges *does* know of your existence: he was supposed to contribute to the special issue of the French magazine *L'Arc* which was devoted to you, but, for some reason, he did not. Your first book was a translation of Lewis Carroll into Russian. Do you see any affinities between Carroll's idea of "nonsense" and your bogus or "mongrel" languages in *Bend Sinister* and *Pale Fire*?

A. In common with many other English children (I was an English child) I have been always very fond of Carroll. No, I do not think that his invented language shares any roots with mine. He has a pathetic affinity with H.H. but some odd scruple prevented me from alluding in Lolita to his wretched perversion and to those ambiguous photographs he took in dim rooms. He got away with it, as so many other Victorians got away with pederasty and nympholepsy. His were sad scrawny little nymphets, bedraggled and half-undressed, or rather semi-undraped, as if participating in some dusty and dreadful charade.

Q. I thought that you *did* allude to Carroll in Lolita through what might be called "the photography theme": Humbert cherishes his worn old photograph of Annabel, has in a sense been living with this "still," tries to make Lolita conform to it, and often laments his failure to capture her on film. Quilty's hobby is announced as "photography," and the unspeakable films he produced at the Duk Duk Ranch would seem to answer Carroll's wildest needs.

A. I did not consciously think of Carroll's hobby when I referred to the use of photography in Lolita.

Q. You have had wide experience as a translator and have made fictive use of translation. What basic problems of existence do you find implicit in the art and act of translation?

A. There is a certain small Malayan bird of the thrush family which is said to sing only when tormented in an unspeakable way by a specially trained child at the annual Feast of Flowers. There is Casanova making love to a harlot while looking from a window at the nameless tortures inflicted on Damiens. These are the visions that sicken me when I read the "poetical" translations from martyred Russian poets by some of my famous contemporaries. A tortured author and a deceived reader, this is the inevitable outcome of arty paraphrase. The only object and justification of translation is the conveying of the most exact information possible and this can be only achieved by a literal translation, with notes.

Q. Mention of translation brings me to one of the Kinbotian problems faced by critics who comment on your Russian novels in translation, but who themselves have no Russian. It has been said that translations such as The Defense and Despair must contain many stylistic revisions (certainly the puns), and moreover are in general much richer in language than Laughter in the Dark, written at about the same time but, unlike the others, translated in the thirties. Would you comment on this? If the style of *Laughter in the Dark* suggests it should have preceded *Despair*, perhaps it actually was written much earlier: in the BBC interview of four years ago,[4] you said that you wrote *Laughter in the Dark* when you were twenty-six, which would have been 1925, thus making it your first novel. Did you actually write it this early, or is the reference to age a slip in memory, no doubt caused by the distracting presence of the BBC machinery.

A. I touched up details here and there in those novels and reinstated a scene in *Despair*, as the Foreword explains. That "twenty-six" is certainly wrong. It is either a telescopation or I must have been thinking of *Mashenka*, my first novel written in 1925. The Russian original version (*Kamera Obskura*) of *Laughter in the Dark* was written in 1931, and an English translation by Winifred Roy, insufficiently revised by me, appeared in London in 1936. A year later, on the Riviera, I attempted—not quite successfully—to English the thing anew for Bobbs-Merrill, who published it in New York in 1938.

Q. There is a parenthetical remark in *Despair* about a "vulgar, mediocre Herzog." Is that a bit of added fun about a recent best-seller?

A. Herzog means "Duke" in German and I was speaking of a conventional statue of a German Duke in a city square.

Q. Since the reissued edition of *Laughter in the Dark* is not graced by one of your informative forewords, would you tell us something about the book's inception and the circumstances under which you wrote it? Commentators are quick to suggest similarities between Margot and Lolita, but I'm much more interested in the kinship between Axel Rex and Quilty. Would you comment on this, and perhaps on the other perverters of the imagination one finds throughout your work, all of whom seem to share Rex's evil qualities.

A. Yes, some affinities between Rex and Quilty exist, as they do between Margot and Lo. Actually, of course, Margot was a common young whore, not an unfortunate little Lolita. Anyway I do not think that those recurrent sexual oddities and morbidities are of much

---

[4] Peter Duval-Smith, "Vladimir Nabokov on his Life and Work," *Listener*, LXVIII (Nov. 22, 1962), 856–58. Reprinted as "What Vladimir Nabokov thinks of his Work," *Vogue*, CXLI (March 1, 1963), 152–55.

interest or importance. My Lolita has been compared to Emmie in *Invitation*, to Mariette in *Bend Sinister*, and even to Colette in *Speak, Memory*—the last is especially ludicrous. But I think it might have been simply English jollity and leg-pulling.[5]

Q. The *Doppelgänger* motif figures prominently throughout your fiction; in *Pale Fire* one is tempted to call it a Tripling (at least). Would you say that *Laughter in the Dark* is your earliest Double fiction?

A. I do not see any doubles in *Laughter in the Dark*. A lover can be viewed as the betrayed party's double but that is pointless.

Q. Would you care to comment on how the *Doppelgänger* motif has been both used and abused from Poe, Hoffman, Andersen, Dostoevsky, Gogol, Stevenson, and Melville, down to Conrad and Mann? Which *Doppelgänger* fictions would you single out for praise?

A. The *Doppelgänger* subject is a frightful bore.

Q. What are your feelings about **Dostoevsky's** celebrated *The Double*; after all, Hermann in *Despair* considers it as a possible title for his manuscript.

A. Dostoevsky's *The Double* is his best work though an obvious and shameless imitation of Gogol's "Nose." Felix in *Despair* is really a *false* double.

Q. What are the criteria of identity which have made this theme so congenial to you? And what assumptions about identity have you reacted against in fashioning your own conception of the Double?

A. There are no "real" doubles in my novels.

Q. Speaking of Doubles brings me to *Pnin*, which in my experience has proved to be one of your most popular novels and at the same time one of your most elusive to those readers who fail to see the relationship of the narrator and the characters (or who fail to even notice the narrator until it's too late). Four of its seven chapters were published in the *New Yorker* over a considerable period (1953–57),

[5] A reference to Kingsley Amis' review of *Lolita*, "She was a Child and I was a Child," *Spectator*, CCIII (Nov. 6, 1959), 636. The "leg-pulling" persists in this issue; see "*Lolita*: The Springboard of Parody," p. 220.

but the all-important last chapter, in which the narrator takes control, is only in the book. I'd be most interested to know if the design of *Pnin* was complete while the separate sections were being published, or whether your full sense of its possibilities occurred later.

A.   Yes, the design of *Pnin* was complete in my mind when I composed the first chapter which, I believe, in this case was actually the first of the seven I physically set down on paper. Alas, there was to be an additional chapter, between Four (in which, incidentally, both the boy at St. Mark's and Pnin dream of a passage from my drafts of *Pale Fire*, the revolution in Zembla and the escape of the king—that is telepathy for you!) and Five (where Pnin drives a car). In that still unlinked chapter, which was beautifully clear in my mind down to the last curve, Pnin recovering in the hospital from a sprained back teaches himself to drive a car in bed by studying a 1935 manual of automobilism found in the hospital library and by manipulating the levers of his cot. Only one of his colleagues visits him there—Professor Blorenge. The chapter ended with Pnin's taking his driver's examination and pedantically arguing with the instructor who has to admit Pnin is right. A combination of chance circumstances in 1956 prevented me from actually writing that chapter, then other events intervened, and it is only a mummy now.

Q.   In a television interview last year, you singled out Bely's *St. Petersburg*, along with works by Joyce, Kafka, and Proust, as one of the greatest achievements in twentieth-century prose (an endorsement, by the way, which has prompted Grove Press to reissue *St. Petersburg*, with your statement across the front cover). I greatly admire this novel but, unhappily enough, it is relatively unknown in America. What are its qualities which you most admire? Bely and Joyce are sometimes compared; is the comparison a just one?

A.   *Petersburg* is a splendid fantasy, but this is a question I plan to answer in my essay on Joyce. There does exist some resemblance in manner between *Petersburg* and certain passages in *Ulysses*.

Q.   Although I've never seen it discussed as such, the Ableukhov father-son relationship to me constitutes a doubling, making *Petersburg* one of the most interesting and fantastic permutations of the Doppelgänger theme. Since this kind of doubling (if you would agree it is one) is surely the kind you'd find more congenial, say,

than the use Mann makes of the motif in *Death in Venice,* would
you comment on its implications?

A.   Those murky matters have no importance to me as a writer.
Philosophically, I am an indivisible monist.

Q.   Bely lived in Berlin in 1922–23. Did you know him there? You
and Joyce lived in Paris at the same time; did you ever meet him?

A.   Once, in 1921 or 1922, at a Berlin restaurant where I was dining
with two girls. I happened to be sitting back to back with Andrey
Bely who was dining with another writer, Aleksey Tolstoy, at the
table behind me. Both writers were at the time frankly pro-Soviet
(and on the point of returning to Russia), and a White Russian,
which I still am in that particular sense, would certainly not wish
to speak to a *bolshevizan* (fellow traveller). I was acquainted with
Aleksey Tolstoy but of course ignored him. As to Joyce, I saw him
a few times in Paris in the late thirties. Paul and Lucy Léon, close
friends of his, were also old friends of mine. One night they brought
him to a French lecture I had been asked to deliver on Pushkin
under the auspices of Gabriel Marcel (it was later published in the
Nouvelle Revue Française). I had happened to replace at the very last
moment a Hungarian woman writer, very famous that winter, author
of a bestselling novel, I remember its title, *La Rue du Chat qui
Pêche,* but not the lady's name. A number of personal friends of
mine, fearing that the sudden illness of the lady and a sudden dis-
course on Pushkin might result in a suddenly empty house, had done
their best to round up the kind of audience they knew I would like
to have. The house had, however, a pied aspect since some confusion
had occurred among the lady's fans. The Hungarian consul mistook
me for her husband and, as I entered, dashed towards me with the
froth of condolence on his lips. Some people left as soon as I started
to speak. A source of unforgettable consolation was the sight of Joyce
sitting, arms folded and glasses glinting, in the midst of the Hungarian football team. Another time my wife and I had dinner with
him at the Léons followed by a long friendly evening of talk. I do
not recall one word of it but my wife remembers that Joyce asked
about the exact ingredients of *myod,* the Russian "mead," and everybody gave him a different answer. In this connection, there is a
marvelous howler in the standard English version of *The Brothers
Karamazov*: a supper table at Zosima's abode is described with the
translator hilariously misreading "Médoc" (in Russian transliteration

in the original text), a French wine greatly appreciated in Russia, as *medok*, the diminutive of *myod* (mead). It would have been fun to recall that I spoke of this to Joyce but unfortunately I came across this incarnation of *The Karamazovs* some ten years later.

Q.   You mentioned Aleksey Tolstoy a moment ago. Would you say something about him?

A.   He was a writer of some talent and has two or three science fiction stories or novels which are memorable. But I wouldn't care to categorize writers, the only category being originality and talent. After all, if we start sticking group labels, we'll have to put "The Tempest" in the SF category, and of course thousands of other valuable works.

Q.   Tolstoy was initially an anti-Bolshevik, and his early work precedes the Revolution. Are there any writers totally of the Soviet period whom you admire?

A.   There were a few writers who discovered that if they chose certain plots and certain characters they could get away with it in the political sense, in other words, they wouldn't be told what to write and how to finish the novel. Ilf and Petrov, two wonderfully gifted writers, decided that if they had a rascal adventurer as protagonist, whatever they wrote about his adventures could not be criticized from a political point of view, since a perfect rascal or a madman or a delinquent or any person who was outside Soviet society—in other words, any picaresque character—could not be accused either of being a bad Communist or not being a good Communist. Thus Ilf and Petrov, Zoshchenko, and Olesha managed to publish some absolutely first-rate fiction under that standard of complete independence, since these characters, plots, and themes could not be treated as political ones. Until the early thirties they managed to get away with it. The poets had a parallel system. They thought, and they were right at first, that if they stuck to the garden —to pure poetry, to lyrical imitations, say, of gypsy songs, such as Ilya Selvinski's—that then they were safe. Zabolotski found a third method of writing, as if the "I" of the poem were a perfect imbecile, crooning in a dream, distorting words, playing with words as a half-insane person would. All these people were enormously gifted but the regime finally caught up with them and they disappeared, one by one, in nameless camps.

Q. By my loose approximation, there remain three novels, some fifty stories, and six plays still in Russian. Are there any plans to translate these? What of *The Exploit*, written during what seems to have been your most fecund period as a "Russian writer," would you tell us something, however briefly, about this book?

A. Not all of that stuff is as good as I thought it was thirty years ago but some of it will probably be published in English bye-and-bye. My son is now working on the translation of *The Exploit*. It is the story of a Russian expatriate, a romantic young man of my set and time, a lover of adventure for adventure's sake, proud flaunter of peril, climber of unnecessary mountains, who merely for the pure thrill of it decides one day to cross illegally into Soviet Russia, and then cross back to exile. Its main theme is the overcoming of fear, the glory and rapture of that victory.

Q. I understand that *The Real Life of Sebastian Knight* was written in English in 1938. It is very dramatic to think of you bidding farewell to one language and embarking on a new life in another in this way. Why did you decide to write in English at this time, since you obviously could not have known for certain you would emigrate two years later? How much more writing in Russian did you do between *Sebastian Knight* and your emigration to America in 1940, and once there, did you ever compose in Russian again?

A. Oh, I did know I would eventually land in America. I switched to English after convincing myself on the strength of my translation of *Despair* that I could use English as a wistful standby for Russian.[6] I still feel the pangs of that substitution, they have not been allayed by the Russian poems (my best) that I wrote in New York, or the 1954 Russian version of *Speak, Memory*, or even my recent two-years long work on the Russian translation of *Lolita* which will be published some time in 1967. I wrote *Sebastian Knight* in Paris, 1938. We had that year a charming flat on rue Saigon, between the Etoile and the Bois. It consisted of a huge handsome room (which served as parlor, bedroom and nursery) with a small kitchen on one side and a large sunny bathroom on the other. This apartment had been some bachelor's delight but was not meant to accommodate

---

[6] In 1936, while living in Berlin, Nabokov translated *Despair* for the English firm, John Long, who published it in 1937. The most recent and final edition of *Despair* (New York, 1966) is, as Nabokov explains in its Foreword, a revision of both the early translation and of *Otchayanie* itself.

a family of three. Evening guests had to be entertained in the kitchen so as not to interfere with my future translator's sleep. And the bathroom doubled as my study. Here is the *Doppelgänger* theme for you.

Q.   Many people are surprised to learn that you have written seven plays, which is strange, since your novels are filled with "theatrical" effects that are patently unnovelistic. Is it just to say that your frequent allusions to Shakespeare are more than a matter of playful or respectful homage? What do you think of the drama as a form? What are the characteristics of Shakespeare's plays which you find most congenial to your own esthetic?

A.   The verbal poetical texture of Shakespeare is the greatest the world has known, and is immensely superior to the structure of his plays as plays. With Shakespeare it is the metaphor that is the thing, not the play. My most ambitious venture in the domain of drama is a huge screenplay based on *Lolita*. I wrote it for Kubrick who used only bits and shadows of it for his otherwise excellent film.

Q.   When I was your student, you never mentioned the Homeric parallels in discussing Joyce's *Ulysses*. But you did supply "special information" in introducing many of the masterpieces: a map of Dublin for *Ulysses*, the arrangement of streets and lodgings in *Dr. Jekyll and Mr. Hyde*, a diagram of the interior of a railway coach on the Moscow–St. Petersburg express in *Anna Karenina*, and a floor plan of the Samsa's apartment in *The Metamorphosis* and an entomological drawing of Gregor. Would you be able to suggest some equivalent for your own readers?

A.   Joyce himself very soon realized with dismay that the harping on those essentially easy and vulgar "Homeric parallelisms" would only distract one's attention from the real beauty of his book. He soon dropped these pretentious chapter titles which already were "explaining" the book to non-readers. In my lectures I tried to give factual data only. A map of three country estates with a winding river and a figure of the butterfly *Parnassius mnemosyne* for a cartographic cherub will be the endpaper in my revised edition of *Speak, Memory*.

Q.   Incidentally, one of my colleagues came into my office recently with the breathless news that Gregor is *not* a cockroach (he had read an article to that effect). I told him I've known that for twelve years, and took out my notes to show him my drawing from what was for one day only Entomology 312. What kind of beetle, by the way, was Gregor?

A. It was a domed beetle, a scarab beetle with wing-sheaths, and neither Gregor nor his maker realized that when the room was being made by the maid, and the window was open, he could have flown out and escaped and joined the other happy dung beetles rolling the dung balls on rural paths.

Q. How are you progressing in your novel, *The Texture of Time*? Since the *données* for some of your novels seem to be present, however fleetingly, in earlier novels, would it be fair to suggest that chapter fourteen of *Bend Sinister* contains the germ for your latest venture?

A. In a way, yes; but my *Texture of Time*, now almost half-ready, is only the central rose-web of a much ampler and richer novel, entitled *Ada*, about passionate, hopeless, rapturous sunset love, with swallows darting beyond the stained window and that radiant shiver...

Q. Speaking of *données*: At the end of *Pale Fire*, Kinbote says of Shade and his poem, "I even suggested to him a good title—the title of the book in me whose pages he was to cut: *Solus Rex*; instead of which I saw *Pale Fire*, which meant to me nothing." In 1940 *Sovremennye Zapiski* published a long section from your "unfinished" novel, *Solus Rex*, under that title. Does *Pale Fire* represent the "cutting" of its pages? What is the relationship between it, the other untranslated fragment from *Solus Rex* ("Ultima Thule," published in *Novyy Journal*, New York, 1942) and *Pale Fire*?

A. My *Solus Rex* might have disappointed Kinbote less than Shade's poem. The two countries, that of the Lone King and the Zembla land, belong to the same biological zone. Their subartic bogs have much the same butterflies and berries. A sad and distant kingdom seems to have haunted my poetry and fiction since the twenties. It is not associated with my personal past. Unlike Northern Russia, both Zembla and Ultima Thule are mountainous, and their languages are of a phony Scandinavian type. If a cruel prankster kidnapped Kinbote and placed him, blindfolded, in the Ultima Thule countryside, Kinbote would not know—at least not immediately—by the sap smells and bird calls that he was not back in Zembla, but he would be tolerably sure that he was not on the banks of the Neva.

Q. This may be like asking a father to publicly declare which of his children is most loved, but do you have one novel towards which you feel the most affection, which you esteem over all others?

A. The most affection, *Lolita;* the greatest esteem, *Priglashenie na Kazn'.*[7]

Q. And as a closing question, sir, may I return to *Pale Fire:* where, please, are the crown jewels hidden?[8]

A. In the ruins, sir, of some old barracks near Kobaltana (q.v.); but do not tell it to the Russians.

---

[7] *Invitation to a Beheading.*

[8] One hesitates to explain a joke, but readers unfamiliar with *Pale Fire* should be informed that the hiding place of the Zemblan crown jewels is never revealed in the text, and the Index entry under "crown jewels," to which the reader must now refer, is less than helpful. "Kobaltana" is also in the Index.

ISAAC BASHEVIS SINGER

I

Q. Mr. Singer, since you've been in this country you've published *The Family Moskat, The Magician of Lublin, The Slave,* a number of collections of stories, and *The Manor,* which is your latest novel to appear in English. And isn't there supposed to be a sequel to *The Manor?*

A. It's a part of two books but I don't know how to call two books: a duality? There will be a second part.

Q. Is the other book written?

A. Written, and also already translated, but I work on the translation and I work on the book itself. It happens often with me, working on the translation and working on the book itself go together, because when it's being translated I see some of the defects and I work on them—so in a way the English translation is sometimes almost a second original. I cut while I translate and I add sometimes.

Q. What kinds of things do you usually change?

Interview conducted by Cyrena N. Pondrom. The interview was edited from transcriptions of extended tape-recorded conversations with Mr. Singer on March 29, April 9, and April 12, 1968. All were held in Madison, Wisconsin, with L. S. Dembo participating on March 29. Part I is chiefly drawn from the first recorded conversation; Part II combines the second and third sessions. Mr. Singer has read the text to verify accuracy of transcription.

A. Oh, sometimes I may find a chapter that is not good enough; I think it needs some more description or dialogue, or sometimes I find the opposite: there is too much of it, it should be cut. I am not faithful to the original, because why should I be?—since the author is here, he can do whatever he pleases to correct things. So because of this, if there will ever be a student—or an amateur or whatever—who will compare things, one will be surprised to see what divergences, what differences, there are between the translation and the Yiddish original.

Q. Do you prefer that the English translation be treated as the primary text?

A. It's not a question "if I prefer," but it's treated that way anyhow, because all the translations into other languages are made from the English translation and I'm cautious. In some cases I'm pleased with it and in some cases I'm displeased, but it doesn't help me any.

Q. I remember you told me several weeks ago that when a German translation of—was it, *The Magician* . . .?

A. Yes, that they went back to the Yiddish, and they found things which I have cut—I don't know why I cut them.

Q. Were you pleased that they restored them?

A. In this case I was pleased, because I really found that by restoring the original they have improved the translation. But in other cases I would be in despair if they would restore what was in Yiddish because in Yiddish you can use a lot of overstatement, but you cannot use it in English. What seems to be quite all right in one language, looks sometimes very silly in another language.

Q. Well, Yiddish is a language of overstatement in general.

A. Yes, yes, Yiddish is a language of overstatement and English of understatement, so because of this I have had in many cases to cut. Perhaps if I could find the most wonderful translator who could make these overstatements into understatements it would be all right, but in some cases it is so difficult that I'd rather cut than leave it there.

Q. What sorts of things do you add when you translate? I noticed at one point in *Satan in Goray* what seemed to be some explanatory phrases for Gentiles. Do you ever add this kind of thing?

A. I don't think that I did this. I think that this was done by my editor, Cecil Hemley. As a rule, I don't like to explain. I say that the reader can always find a dictionary or an encyclopedia.

Q. Well, I only noticed a few such. I know you have worked with a lot of different translators. Do you always supervise the translation extremely closely?

A. Lately, yes. In the beginning when *The Family Moskat* was translated, I didn't do it, because my knowledge of English was less than today, and also it was done by a very experienced translator; he wouldn't have even allowed me to interfere with him. But since then I have to do all this; the translators I know well and they will let me do many things; they'll work together with me.

Q. Do you think you're virtually capable of being your own translator now?

A. Almost. Almost but not completely. Since I am a foreigner, sometimes when I dictate to the translator for a half an hour I will keep on and speak good English, and then I will make a mistake of a man who came yesterday from the old country, because a foreigner is never sure of himself in another language.

Q. Some of the short stories you sign along with the translator, as translator. Does this mean that you have done substantially more of the translation?

A. I can explain to you. In some cases, the translator does not know Yiddish, so I sit down with the translator and I dictate to him my translation and then he reworks the English and sees to it that it sounds better. And because of this, I sign my name. But if the translator would work from the Yiddish I wouldn't sign my name. When my name is signed it means that the rough translation was done by me, and he worked on the style.

Q. Turning to a cultural question for a minute, do you actually still consider yourself a foreigner in America?

A. Well, actually not. Certainly not from a legal point of view. If you ask me from an *emotional* point of view, I don't feel myself a foreigner because I love America and I love the American people, and I don't say this because I want to flatter anybody—I have no reason for it; it so *happens*. If you love somebody you don't feel as a stranger to him. And since my own country, Poland, where I was born, almost does not exist as far as I am concerned—it's a different world there— the U. S. is my real home now. So just as English has become to me a second original, America is to me my real country.

Q. If we can continue just a few minutes more on technical ques- tions, one of the things that I noticed about the short stories is that collections do not seem to reflect chronology.

A. Yes, yes, I mix them up always, and I don't really write down the date when they were written, so because of this there is a real mix-up. In other words, when you read a collection of short stories of mine one story might have been written twenty years ago and the other, four weeks ago.

Q. That's what I thought. Then, as a rule, you are not aiming at a central theme or development in a collection?

A. No. I just take a number of stories which I think could be pub- lished and I publish them. In my new collection, The Séance, I have some stories which are very new, and there is I believe one story called "Two Corpses Go Dancing," which I wrote twenty-five years ago. I must one day take all my stories and give the real dates when they were written, or the approximate dates because in some cases I don't know myself any more. Dates could be verified also from the Yiddish— those which appeared in Yiddish newspapers or magazines, because in Yiddish they appeared mostly as soon as they were written.

Q. To turn to questions having more to do with your basic tech- niques, one of the things that caught my attention in both The Slave and The Magician of Lublin is your use of Biblical analogues.

A. It is true, it is true. And I would say this is true almost about all my writing; you will find it even in Satan in Goray. I was brought up on the Bible. Whenever there is an opportunity I will compare something to some Biblical event, a Biblical name, or something.

Q. How does the process begin? Do such allusions present them- selves as you go along? Or do you think sometimes in terms of an over-all pattern?

A. No. I don't, because if this would be true I would know about it —as a matter of fact, you say that I use a lot of Biblical allusions: I recognize that it's true, but only after you told it to me . . . I myself do not realize it.

Q. It emerges from the text rather than your having a prior pattern in your mind.

A. Exactly.

Q. So actually it's more accidental than deliberate.

A. I wouldn't call it accidental, but it's also not deliberate. It is just in me.

Q. Do you sometimes use names themselves to suggest the allusion deliberately?

A. I think that in *The Slave*, I called my hero Jacob just because I needed a name. Why I called him Jacob, I don't know myself. But then since his name was already Jacob, the allusion to Jacob was a natural thing, and when I got the opportunity to compare him to his Biblical namesake, I did it.

Q. Yes. It seems to me that your novels differ quite a lot in structure, in plan.

A. Generally, I have two kinds of novels, the one, the so-called realistic novels or chronicles, like *The Family Moskat* and *The Manor*, which are more or less realistic novels, stories about families, the development of families, where I use very little of the supernatural. They are constructed in the way large novels should be constructed, according to my opinion. I don't tell the story straightly but I skip time and I go from one person to another; I leave one event and I go to another one and then I return to this event again, almost in the tradition of the Russian novels. And then there is the short novel, which is built around one person; it has one central hero and everything turns around him and the story goes a straight way; I keep on telling the story from the beginning to the end without interruptions.

Q. *The Magician of Lublin* would be an example of this.

A. *The Magician of Lublin*, even *The Slave* is a story like this. I tell this Jacob's story from the beginning to the end. Jacob is in every chapter.

Q.   Satan in Goray falls somewhere between the two?

A.   Yes. *Satan in Goray*, even though it's a small novel, actually tells the story not of a man but of a whole milieu. It's a small novel which should have been a large novel, but the way I wrote it demanded that it should be short, because you cannot write about hysteria and the supernatural long. . . . It's a strange thing: you can write about the supernatural a novel of 150 pages; if you will make it 800 pages there is already a contradiction, because life itself is not so full of the supernatural that you can go on for 800 pages. It would be a great disproportion.

Q.   Does the supernatural actually appear, or is it really a part of the psychology of the characters that you're developing?

A.   It is not just a method. Somehow, whenever I sit down to write a short story—not always, but in many cases—the supernatural will pop up, almost by itself, because I'm deeply interested in it.

Q.   Yes, I understand this, but take one of the stories that I felt was really electrifying, "The Black Wedding." What was happening there seemed to me a clue to what was happening with many of your other characters. It seemed to me that the girl here was really obsessed with the fact that this man was a devil, whereas whether he really was or not was not the point of the story; the point was what was happening inside of her mind. And many of your characters seem to have this obsessive quality.

A.   Yes, this is true. Obsession is really a very important theme of mine and this is the reason that I would write about dybbuks. I like a person who is obsessed by some mania or a single idea, a fixed idea, and everything turns around this idea. I think that this kind of literature is very important to me because not many writers wrote in this way. I'm glad that you mentioned "The Black Wedding" because it was not recognized by many writers as one of my best stories, but I do recognize it as such. It was also published lately in a collection of stories, psychiatric stories. In this story the woman is not only obsessed, you can call her insane.

Q.   Psychopathic.

A.   She is really psychopathic, to a high degree. But from her point of view, she's right. Assuming that all the things that happen are devilish, she's right in her behavior and everything is becoming consistent in a mad way.

Q. But isn't it extremely important that the "devilishness" of things is an *assumption*? What is the reality of the obsessions of the characters?

A. Since we don't know really what reality is, whatever we are obsessed with becomes our reality. Let's say a man who is obsessed by the idea of making money: money becomes to him of such importance that he really measures everything with money. He thinks he can buy everything with money and sell everything; and from his point of view he becomes right—everything has a price. Some men say every woman has a price, every man has a price, he can buy the Pope, he can. . . . This is the way they feel. And so with people who are obsessed by sex, or politics or many other things. In a way I would say we are all obsessed, but some more and some less.

Q. This also seems to me to be the center of *The Magician of Lublin*.

A. Yes. Here was a man who was really obsessed by women and by living in danger.

Q. He was obsessed by the idea of being Jewish, too, and what constituted a Jew.

A. Not really so much, in the beginning. I think in the beginning, the Jewish question existed for him, as much as being Jewish disturbs his obsession, because he felt guilty in a way, but at the end when he is disappointed in the worldly pleasures, he returns to Jewishness.

Q. Do you think this is a form of salvation for him or is that an unfair question?

A. If it was a salvation then how long it lasted I cannot tell you. I don't know really. First of all, I indicate in this book that, while he's already there in this little hut without a door to get out, he's still the magician of Lublin, and he still dreams about women. In one case he imagines that Emilia has a tunnel, and she comes to him right there where he repents, which shows how the mind works; he cannot really escape from anything. Any escape, wherever there is an escape, there's always a hole in it. . . .

Q. But even his playing the role of a thaumaturgic rabbi is also a form of obsession for him, wouldn't you say?

A. Yes. He's trying . . . yes, he becomes obsessed with the idea of the opposite of what he was, let's say, like a Communist may become sometimes an anti-Communist—this happens all the time.

Q. But what about his motives for building that hut and putting himself inside? Aren't the motives essentially mistaken?

A. Well, you can call them by all kinds of names—but I will tell you what his motives are. He has come to the conclusion that if there is temptation he will surrender. He cannot withstand temptation; in other words, if he would be in a house with a married woman, he would sin against God, he would break the Ten Commandments. And since he has convinced himself—or at least tried to convince himself—that this is bad, a man like him must run away from temptation. The only way the magician could run away from temptation would be to immure himself, because there was no other way.

Q. Is this then to say that the rabbi's comment is correct, that this is really an abdication of free will?

A. It is, absolutely . . . it is true, yes. In other words if you take the Ten Commandments seriously, and if you think that the Ten Commandments are the very essence of our life, and if you think that if we break the Ten Commandments we are broken too, then we have to take all the measures not to break them. And while it looks to some people like an easy thing, it's actually the most difficult thing, especially to people like Yasha of *The Magician of Lublin.* For him not to commit adultery was the most difficult thing, so he had really to use all the means. If a person has a terrible sickness, a cancer, if he would be told that by not eating certain foods and keeping away from certain spheres and certain people he would be cured, he would naturally do everything to be cured. So it is with pious men. They will do everything possible not to break the Ten Commandments or the other commandments which God has given.

Q. You don't legislate the norms of the story yourself though.

A. I don't tell the reader what I think, or what he should do. I say, assuming that we have such a hero and he had such experience, and he has such a character, he may come to such a conclusion.

Q. Yes. That's a very important *if*, that *if* it is true that you're completely immured in the Ten Commandments, *then* it is necessary for a man like Yasha to do this.

A. Exactly.

Q. But, there was an "if" on it.

A. Yes.

Q. Now, is Yasha abandoning some of the higher challenges to humanity in order to protect himself this way?

A. In a way he does, because according to Jewish religion this is not the way of salvaging your soul, because running away is not such a wonderful thing. A real man must be able to fight temptation and not to surrender to it. But in the same way, it *is* so and it's *not* so, because the Talmud has given men scores of ways to avoid temptation. That is, according to Jewish religion, if you are tempted, then you have to withstand temptation, but don't look for temptation. If you look for temptation, this means already that you want to surrender. In other words, if you happen to go on a dark street and you are attacked by somebody, naturally you will defend yourself, but if you are a cautious man you will just try not to go on dark streets to be attacked. Because how many times can a man beat the attacker; sometimes the attacker may beat the man. In life we avoid danger. And since sin is a danger to these people, they actually deal with sin the way we deal with danger: avoid it as much as possible and if you cannot avoid it, fight it.

Q. But still, when you say "these people," you're still suggesting that you are the observer, the spectator, and you are just recording. . . .

A. Yes, but I don't tell people what is good and what is bad. This I keep to myself.

Q. That's what I thought. Therefore, Yasha's sin, the depth of his sin, is a product of his own imagination. He sins deeply because he *thinks* he is sinning deeply.

A. Yes, but I may also agree with him; even if I *would* agree I would not put in my point of view there. It's enough for me if I give his story and his point of view, but naturally you can ask yourself, "Why does this writer . . . why is he interested in such a man like Yasha, why is he interested in the problem of sin?" So most probably, I myself am also interested in these things; I wouldn't just write about a thing which is strange to me and where I am not interested.

Q. Nonetheless, is there a point in your deliberately withholding an authorial judgment? In other words, are you saying something about the way you understand the world to work?

A. I would say that I was saying in this book, if I would have Yasha's courage I would do as he did—in a certain period of my life, at least in the time that I wrote this. As a matter of fact, all my life I dreamt about running away; this is always my dream, and not into a hut, although I thought about this also, but somewhere to an island. It is this idea somehow that bothers me. One day, I actually will be running away. . . .

Q. But not to Italy?

A. Italy?

Q. That's where Yasha wanted to run away to. . . .

A. Not Italy, not Italy. One day I tried to run away to Patchogue. This is one of the most ridiculous stories of my life. I had hay fever. It was a strange kind of summer: to tell you the story would last too long. And I said to myself, since it's already time for me to do something and not just to talk, let me go away to some little village and stay there. Since I have hay fever I went to my doctor and I said, "Where could I go?" So he said, "Do you know there is a town not far from here called Patchogue, somewhere out on Long Island." He said: "I have a feeling that there you will suffer less from hay fever because it's near the sea." So I said to myself, "Maybe this is my opportunity. Maybe I will go away for my hay fever, and I am going to stay there in Patchogue, running away from civilization." Well, what kind of a running away this was! I went into some noisy hotel—it was the very opposite of running away. I stayed there not more than three or four days. Really, if I will ever write this story, it will be a funny story.

Q. Patchogue. I know the village and I can think of it as the wrong place to run away to.

A. The wrong place, yes. I think that wherever a man runs away is always the wrong place—even this famous painter about whom Somerset Maugham wrote . . . Gauguin.

Q. But getting back to Yasha, judged objectively, one might say that Yasha's sin is really no great sin, except that he thinks it's so. For example, the letter that Emilia sends him at the end of the novel shows that she in her own way is culpable; she has sinned in her own way, looking at him the way she has [Singer: This is true.] and that he has not committed any serious crime against her.

A. Not against her. His real sin was that he wanted to steal—*also* stealing. And then he considered himself a murderer, that he caused the death of this woman called Magda.

Q. But did he really cause her death?

A. He really did. I mean, her suicide was caused by his behavior.

Q. But wasn't her suicide caused by her own obsession about what she thought he was?

A. Yes, this is always the case. Because, he made her believe that he really loved her—which he did—this is the eternal problem of humanity: a woman cannot really understand that a man can love many women. They just cannot, they refuse to understand it. I don't know why, maybe because women cannot love at the same time many men. Anyhow, this Magda felt that if he loves the other one, he doesn't love her, which in a way is true and in a way is false. The novel has not yet been written about a man who loves truly a few women. Why the writers wait with this novel I will never know. But why isn't there a novel written about a man who loves dearly three or four women at the same time?[1]

Q. You've continually said "she felt" that he could not have loved her, or "he felt" that the theft would be the great sin, now. . . .

A. How do *I* feel, this is what you want to ask me? I can tell you how I feel; I feel that if we break the Ten Commandments, we are

---

[1] In an unrecorded comment Singer returned to the topic: "When one tries to write such a novel, people refuse to interpret it that way. If you show a man who loves one woman 150 percent, another 110 percent, another 90 percent, people say he only loves the first one—the others he doesn't really love."

really in great trouble. If people make up their minds that in certain cases you're allowed to kill, or to steal, or to be a false witness (like these revolutionaries who would say, "for the revolution you may kill, for the revolution you may bear false witness") or also to live with another man's wife, to fool people somehow—once we allow ourselves to go on this way, we are in the open, like a man who goes out in the cold winter night in a light suit with all the winds and all the snow blowing; he must get pneumonia sooner or later. I think that the Ten Commandments contain the greatest human wisdom; the question is only how to keep them. And also the question is, is it possible to keep them?—because while Moses said, "Thou shalt not kill, thou shalt not steal, thou shalt not commit adultery," he did not tell us the details, how to avoid doing these things. And all this—our theological laws and everything which we think about today is really to find ways and means how to keep the Ten Commandments. If it's impossible, if one day we were to learn that it's impossible completely, as we say today about the Sermon on the Mount, then our despair would be limitless. If men and women are allowed to fool one another, this means that the whole institution of marriage is a joke. And if you are allowed to kill and steal, then naturally you cannot complain when somebody kills you or steals from you. Most peculiar, those people who break the Ten Commandments and say that there's nothing to it, they themselves, if somebody breaks the Ten Commandments to their damage, are in a terrible rage. In other words, the same Don Juan for whom it's nothing to live with another man's wife—God forbid if somebody will do it to him. Or the same man who will steal, if somebody steals from him he's in a rage and he calls the police and he says, "See what happened to me." As a matter of fact, I have a story which will come out in my next collection where I describe a thief who convinces himself that his wife is also a thief and he is enraged because he wanted to live with an honest woman, not with another thief. In other words, we all believe in the Ten Commandments as far as we are concerned, for our good. We stop believing in them when we think that they have hindered us from enjoying life.

Q.   But what about what you said just a moment ago—a man naturally can love, constitutionally can love, two or three women at the same time?

A.   As a reader, when I read The Magician of Lublin, although I haven't read it since it came out, my feeling was that he really loved all these women. He loved his wife and he loved Magda and he loved Emilia. The solution to his problem would have been if he could have taken them all in the same house and lived with them, and if they would let him have some other affairs in addition. If we could create such a society, it would be very convenient for Yasha, but it wouldn't have been convenient for other people. Tolstoy was the only writer who thought about these things in a very serious way, both in his creations and also in a philosophical way. He saw the problem but he certainly did not know how to solve it.

Q. So far you've been speaking ethically; let's shift now to a metaphysical standpoint. I know in *In My Father's Court* you commented upon your early scepticism, and all through the novels there are references—Asa Heshel, Yasha, Jacob even—to. . . .

A. They all doubt.

Q. Right, to the problem of doubt.

A. And so do I. I doubt. While I speak about the Ten Commandments, some voice asks, "Who made the Ten Commandments, just a man like you, and why take it so seriously?" It's my deepest conviction that it's man-made, not God-made. I don't believe that God came down on Mount Sinai. But even though they are man-made, they just express the principles of the divine, because there is nothing, nothing . . . You cannot correct it, you can only interpret it.

Q. Even if they're man-made, it really doesn't matter, does it?

A. It matters as much as if you would say $2+2=4$ is man-made. It is true they are man-made, but they are true just the same. Or if you say that the sum of a triangle is 180 degrees, naturally the 180 and the word *triangle* are man-made. But it's a truth which will remain as long as humanity. The same thing is true with the Ten Commandments.

Q. Does the very fact that you withhold authorial judgment in the novels enable you to convey your view that this may be something man-made, even if something absolutely necessary?

A. Yes, because I make Yasha say to himself, "How do I know that this particular faith is the truth? There are other faiths and other books, other sacred books." And so I express also the doubt.

Q. And you express all of this strictly through Yasha's point of view?

A. Yes, the only thing which I don't do, I don't say, "And because of this I think, dear reader, you should do this and this." This I avoid because—I *cannot* do this.

Q. But we are left unsure whether or not Yasha is doing the right thing or whether or not he's imagining, and this, in fact, corresponds very closely with your own interpretation. . . .

A. Yes, because we don't know really if he succeeded there. Maybe after a while he left—since he was such a magician, he could very well break the door or go out through the window. It's very easy to.

Q. Now, what are you saying about human responsibility? You said that Magda's suicide is his fault.

A. In a way it is, because if he would have behaved in the way that religion tells us to behave, she wouldn't have committed suicide.

Q. But can anyone really be responsible for what another person chooses to do with his life, even to take it?

A. Well, in some cases one person can be the cause of another person's death, either by just taking out a gun and shooting him, or by leading him into an abyss of such despair that nothing is left. One of the common causes is lying to a person, which we all do. At least men do. You lie to a person, and the reason that a man lies is that he cannot speak to the woman in his language. Because they really have two languages: not word languages, but emotional languages.

Q. Is it even possible to speak at all without lying?

A. Very difficult, very difficult. The very act of speaking contains already the grain of a lie. Whatever you say is a lie; if you meet a person and you say, "Pleased to meet you," it's already sometimes a lie, you may not be pleased. Or whatever—exaggerations. Language itself is full of exaggerations and little lies. But still, one can live with those little lies, but if you go on lying to a person, day after day and week after week and year after year, which many do, it can cause a great tragedy in that other person's life. But how to avoid it—again, the whole institution of marriage—is a great problem. Because the man who said, "Thou shalt not commit adultery" should have said, "Don't get married" (so there wouldn't be any adultery because, from a Jewish point of view, you don't commit adultery if you don't live with a married woman). In other words, the question is, "Can a man make a contract with a woman for life?" Can he write in this contract: "From now on until the end of my life, I will love only you and nobody else"? Isn't such a contract a lie from the very beginning? Those who said that you should not commit adultery assumed that this is possible.

Q.   So then in a sense man's condition is hopeless?

A.   It's not hopeless, but it's so entangled that we can never get out. It's becoming more so instead of less.

Q.   But he must have the Ten Commandments in order not to suffer moral and ethical collapse, and yet, if he obeys the Ten Commandments, he's going against his own nature.

A.   Yes, no question about it. At least in some cases. In my case, let's say, or in many of our cases, "Thou shalt not kill" is not a problem. We don't feel like killing. Although sometimes, when you get angry, you even think about this, but I think we have been brought up enough . . . and also, there is a punishment. Society punishes for killing, and we are afraid of doing it, while society does not punish for adultery—although in the old times it did, but it doesn't do it any more.

Q.   Are you saying then that this is really the primary ethical problem?

A.   I would say that in this book *The Magician of Lublin*, although it tells the story about the magician, it's our, it's everybody's problem. The emotions are an ocean and an abyss. There are so many and so contradictory and so strange that learning swimming in this ocean is an art which one can never learn completely. It's a real abyss.

Q.   It's an ocean in which all men drown, in other words.

A.   They drown or they choke in them. There is also a lot of enjoyment in them.

Q.   For you, then, it's paradoxical. All through your books you're affirming life and yet saying that there is really no way around the kind of suffering and injury. . . .

A.   No question about it. Everyday life shows this. Naturally, it's wonderful to be here and to see you and to sit with you quietly, but suddenly some robber or somebody could come in with two guns and try to shoot us, or rob us, or rape, or whatever he would do—life can become miserable in five minutes . . . in two minutes. It's always a stepping on a little bridge which can collapse any second. So it is with our health, so it is morally, and so it is with our abilities. And so it is with writing. You can write ten good novels and then write a very bad one, as if you would be the worst beginner, and we have seen it in many great writers who suddenly come out with the most terrible stuff. So it is with your friends, so it is with your marriage; one day it's wonderful, the next day you are going to divorce. And so on and so on.

Q.   How does this relate to what seems to me a similarly paradoxical view of free will and determinism? Let me read a very brief selection from *The Slave* to you and get you to comment on it. Jacob is speaking: "Everything was pre-ordained. True, the will was free, but heaven also made its ordinances. He had been driven, he knew, by powers stronger than himself. How else could he have found his way back from Josefov to the mountain village?"[2]

A.   Our philosophers and sages always said that this problem of free will and determinism is something which cannot be solved. It's just like the question of the squaring of the circle—you cannot solve it— you cannot find out what is the square of the circle. It *is* a contradiction, because if everything is determined there is no free will, and if there is no free will, there cannot be determinism. But experience shows us that both of them exist, and we live in this paradox all our lives. If you walk down the street and a car is coming, crossing, you will not say, "If I am determined to die, I will die, and if I am determined to live, I will live." You'll run for your dear life, knowing somehow that if you will not run, the car will hit you. At the same time we also have a feeling that things are determined, and everything just happens according to a plan and according to causes and so on and so on. We are both driven and we have the feeling of free will. There may be some answer, but the answer is not in this world, not in this little marrow which we call brain. Maybe some higher brain or a higher spirit could explain it. To us it will remain a contradiction forever.

---

[2] *The Slave*, Avon Library Edition (New York, 1967), p. 202. Further references to this edition will be contained in the text.

Q. So from the sensation of free will comes the knowledge of responsibility.

A. Yes, since we believe that we are free, we also believe that we have responsibility.

Q. And the sensation of determinism, of things being foreordained, somehow does not wipe out that responsibility?

A. It does not. It could be explained like a man who's in prison; naturally he's not a free man, he's in prison. But still he's free enough to behave badly or in a good way. Many prisoners are let out because they behaved well in prison. In a way this seems to be also our life. While we are basically in prison—we cannot do many things, we are pushed around just like a prisoner—there is still left freedom enough for us to behave badly or to behave in a good way. But this answer is not really a complete answer; it's nothing but a saying, an approximation, just like squaring the circle—while you cannot square it completely you can go on squaring it to a very high degree.

Q. What are these powers: "He had been driven he knew by powers stronger than himself." Yasha, too, feels that powers have led him "straight to Zaruski's hoard," and Asa Heshel also feels that he's being led back to Warsaw and other places as he goes. What do you mean by these powers?

A. I really mean powers. It's not for me just a phrase or a literary way of saying things. I believe that powers which we don't know take a great part in our life. After all, we have lived for thousands of years—or God knows how long humanity's old—without knowing about electricity. But still, electric power was here; the lightning and thunder was electricity, and then, when you combed your hair at night you saw sparks. . . . There are millions and millions of powers, even now, of which we have no idea, which take part in our life, push us or pull us or do all kinds of things with us. It is true I don't know what these powers are. They may be divine powers or other kinds of powers, but I will always have this feeling, and this is the reason that I write about the supernatural. The supernatural for me is not really supernatural; it's powers which we don't know. It's clear for everybody that five hundred years from now, the children who will go to school will know thousands and thousands of things which we don't know, and they will be even astonished that their great-grandparents didn't know of these things, which will look to them so simple. In a thousand years from now, they will know things which these children will not know, and so on and so on. Nature is a well without a bottom. And because of this, whatever we know is only a little, little on the surface, while below us, and above us, and on all sides, there are powers of which we have no inkling. This is what I mean by powers.

Q. But there is a difference between natural powers and, say, demonic powers.

A. I don't know. No, there may not be a difference. For example, a man who took off his wool jacket five hundred years ago at night and saw sparks might have thought that these sparks are supernatural; because there was no reason for him to think that a wool sweater should produce sparks. But we now know that they are . . . we call them natural, although we don't know what electricity is until today. We call light natural, although we don't know what light is. So most probably there is no such thing as two natures. There is one nature, but it is large and deep. The things we know we call nature and what we don't know we call supernatural.

Q. Here you may be alluding to your interest in psychic research.

A. I certainly am. I am astonished why other people are not. I think that everybody really is.

Q. Are you suggesting that it's possible to shortcut man's ignorance by mystical experience?

A. Not really, no. I wish it would—I would be very happy if this would be true, but I don't think so. With mystical experience we will never reach the moon, or we will never cross the ocean. You need an airplane, a jet plane. You need all these things. Science—I'm not against science and logic. I don't say throw away your laboratories and go into a little room and make dark and God will reveal to you things. I don't believe in this. The only thing I believe is that we should not belittle our mystical experience either. We should not say that the sparks which we don't understand are nothing just because we don't understand them. Pay attention to the things which don't fit into your sum of knowledge, because they may fit a little later.

Q. But in your novels, demons or forces always manifest themselves in psychological terms, as psychological forces, so that, say, for the reader who would not respond to supernaturalism you would still offer an insight into human nature.

A. Yes. In writing you have to find a way to say these things or hint them. I found that folklore is the best way of expressing these feelings, because folklore has already expressed them, has already given clothes to these ideas. By really calling demons names and by assigning to them certain functions, it makes it more concrete and in writing you have to be concrete; if not it becomes philosophy or brooding. But basically behind all these names and all these functions is the idea that powers exist—of which we really don't know.

Q. What about this comment of Jacob's—again going back to *The Slave*? It's just the moment very shortly before his death: "They were debating something among themselves, but without hostility. . . . Both sides were in their own way right, and . . . he was amazed. If only men could apprehend these things while they were still strong. . . . They would serve the Lord differently" (p. 251).

A. It seems that before he died, he had a feeling of revelation, that he had learned something. How do I know that it was so? I don't know. But I assume that it's possible, because people, before they are dead, have sometimes seen things. There are cases where people before they died said, "Here is father, here is mother." They even knew of people who died, although they didn't know it with real knowledge. Naturally, I use my imagination. A writer can do it—a fiction writer. If it really happens, I don't know. I always try to hint at these powers, but I am also a sceptic—in other words I don't say to you there are so many powers and here they exist and this is what they're doing. No. If I call them names, it's only because from a literary point of view, it's good. But behind all this is this feeling that maybe someday we learn the truth, like why did we die; maybe after our death or. . . .

Q. Or maybe not at all.

A. Perhaps as you say, perhaps never. I even admit this kind of thought.

Q. Would you say that Spinoza has had a strong influence on your thinking?

A. In the beginning he had an influence. I have a story called "The Spinoza of Market Street." Actually Spinoza preached the very opposite of what I think.

_Q._ It wasn't scepticism in any case, was it?

_A._ No, he considered himself a rationalist, but like all rationalists he became mystical against his will. Because, according to Spinoza, substance has an endless number of attributes and we only know two of them, thought and extension. So by giving substance an endless number of attributes he has already called millions and trillions of powers which we don't know. What are the other attributes of God? If we don't know them—and we will never know them according to him—they may be mercy, and they may be _anything_. So many of the rationalists talk so long, they talk themselves out of business.

_Q._ Would you agree with Rabbi Benish in _Satan in Goray_ that it's a sin to delve too deeply into things that were really meant to be hidden?

_A._ Well, in a way yes and a way no, because this Rabbi Benish was a leader of his community, and he knew that these people have weak little brains, and if they go into mysticism, it will only bring evil, which it really did in this particular case. If mysticism becomes a mass movement, it's always bad, because it's not for the masses, it's not for many. It should be an esoteric thing.

_Q._ Do you believe that there are absolute limits on what a man can know?

_A._ No question about it. Not only are they there, but they are very near to us. Wherever we go we touch these limits. However, I would say that men can a little bit stretch these limits, and whatever stretching he does is already a great gain. We know that man has stretched his limits in science to a great extent. We have learned in the last two hundred years things which humanity hasn't grasped in a hundred thousand. Perhaps we can also stretch the limits of our psychic knowledge, psychic powers, which are even stiffer limits and not so easy to push. But at least there is the desire in some of us to try.

_Q._ But this is still knowledge, within thought and extension, isn't it? This is not knowledge of all the myriad attributes that are possible?

_A._ No, I have a hope some way that perhaps you can find a third attribute if you try very hard. That is, it's not written in any book that these are all—although Spinoza said that these are the two, actually they are arbitrary. You could call them by different names. I'm sure that man knows more than what Spinoza said we are able to know.

Q. Can fiction help to stretch the limits?

A. Real fiction, or at least I would say the type of fiction which I like.

Q. And you write. . . .

A. . . . this kind of fiction, I hope. The kind of fiction that is written today by some writers, you know, who try to become sociologists in their writing—this is not the kind of writing which will push these particular limits. Maybe they will push other limits, social limits, I don't know.

Q. How does it push the limit? This is, I take it, visionary writing. Maybe this is not something that can be formulated.

A. No, no—it can be formulated. I would say that if a man really thinks about these things, he indulges in these problems, and also if he will live a better life, a life without guilt, without too many contradictions, he may, by this very fact, push a little bit the limits. Because we know that a man like Swedenborg really had a kind of knowledge that was to our minds supernatural. And you will be surprised that Immanuel Kant, the great philosopher, has written almost a whole book about Swedenborg—this is not known, this book; it is not well known because people just ignore it. Kant tells the miracles which Swedenborg has shown and believes that they are very possible, because according to Kant's philosophy we never see the thing-in-itself, only the phenomenon. Behind all the phenomena there is a great mystery which Kant calls the "thing-in-itself." And since we don't know anything of this mystery, we don't know the powers which may be concealed there. So Kant believed really that Swedenborg was an unusual man.

Q. Does Kant believe that Swedenborg actually penetrated into the thing-in-itself?

A. He doesn't say that he penetrated the thing-in-itself, but he tells in a very serious way the miracles which Swedenborg worked and he comments about them. So this great philosopher was able to believe that some men can have certain powers which we don't all have. As a matter of fact, we see these powers in many other ways. A talented man can do more than a man without talent—he has a certain power. It's also a power. Naturally it doesn't look supernatural to us because there are many writers and many painters. We call nature things

which we see often; things which we see seldom, we call supernatural.
But in a way nobody can really explain a man like Shakespeare or
Dostoevsky. Even though there are thousands of books about Shakespeare, none of them explains why Shakespeare was Shakespeare, what
he did or how he did it.

Q. The essence of Shakespeare, in other words, remains impenetrable.

A. Yes, the essence. So we see these prodigies, these very gifted
children—a child of five, three years, who will do calculations which
only a computer can do. These things appear from time to time to
give us a hint of the possibilities of human life in some cases.

Q. You mentioned Kant, and some of the things you say make me
think of Kierkegaard. Do you know Kierkegaard?

A. Not really. . . . I stopped my study of philosophy with Schopenhauer and Nietzsche and somehow I never went further. I convinced
myself that philosophy can never reveal anything. It can tell us what
we cannot do, but it can never tell us what we can do. I began to
read mostly books which are connected with psychic research, because
these people at least try to give us something positive, although most
of it is straw and lies and chaff.

Q. What have you read in particular? Have you gone back to the
Cabala at all?

A. Oh, yes. I studied the Cabala when I was still young, and once
in a while I will go back to it. I have even written a speech which I
call "Cabala and Modern Man." I read Hasidic books, and a lot of
books about the occult, about psychic research, like The Phantoms of
the Living, and many others. I also read a lot of magazines, and I'm
especially interested in the letters which readers write to these magazines, because these naive letters sometimes discover to me whole
worlds. Not discover, they give hints of hidden things. To me a writer
must be interested in the mystery of life. A writer who says to me
that he's a complete realist, to me he's not a writer anymore.

Q. And yet your own work often uses extremely detailed. . . .

A. Yes, realism—because the so-called real world itself is a great
secret, a great mystery. Also, I don't like writers who write about great

miracles and mysteries without even describing the background. In other words, a miracle must be invented amid realism because, if it's one miracle after the other and there's no realism, the miracle itself becomes nothing.

Q. All great literature begins in realism then?

A. I think, yes. Once a man brought me a story which began with a cut-off head which spoke. And I said to the man, "Isn't it miracle enough that a head which is not chopped off can talk?"

Q. Do you turn again to some of the things you read as a child and as a young man? I think you've mentioned Dostoevsky to me before.

A. Yes, once in a while I will open up a book and read, not from beginning to end, but a page in the middle or so. I read a lot of books in this way where I sit down sometimes near my bookcase, take out a book, and read a page inside.

Q. You know, we were talking earlier about Dostoevsky and the realistic setting and after I left you that day I began to reflect that, after all, many of the settings that you describe are actually places on a map of Poland.

A. Oh, surely. Whatever can be real, I make real. In other words, I don't believe in distortion—like Pinter who will distort the facts just to fit his purpose; I don't believe in this. Be as real as possible. But if you want to tell about a miracle, about a mystical experience, bring it into the milieu of realism. If not, it becomes nothing.

Q. Do you go to any lengths to establish this realism? I remember James Joyce used to write back to Dublin and ask for locations to be verified.

A. Well, in my case I don't need it, because I always write about a few little towns. I always come back to the same. I don't venture to go out too far, like a little child—her mother told her don't go out to the other side of the street. . . . I think that whatever I need to tell about, I can tell about the places which I know best, like Warsaw, or Bilgoray, or Frampol—because why couldn't these things have happened there? Why do I have to go into other places? But since I am already in this country over thirty years, I begin now to write about New York, about things which happen in this country.[8]

Q.   Only recently, though?

A.   Only recently, but always with people who come from the other side. I would never dare to write, almost never, about a person born here because I know that I don't know him enough.

Q.   Do you see a significant difference then between Jewish life, let's say in Poland, and Jewish life in the United States as you've lived it?

A.   Oh, there's no question. There's always a difference even between Jewish life in one little town and another; there is some difference. There is individuality in everything. There's no question that there are many differences. But at the same time, there are also many similarities . . . naturally, the life of my father as a Jew and my life is as far as heaven from earth, but still we are alike in many ways, too. This is what literature is: to describe individuality, all these differences. All the novels we read are basically love stories. Still, why do we read many novels?—because we want to see the difference between one love story and the other. And this is true about everything. History never repeats itself, and no human emotion is the same, no conditions are the same. Always, there's always a difference.

Q.   I know a number of the reviews and comments on your work, especially on The Manor, have suggested that you were interested in the problem of Jewish identity. But I noticed that you brushed the question off about Yasha. Is it fairer to say that you're most interested in human identity?

A.   Well, in Jewish identity, human identity, ethical identity, human responsibility—can man really serve God? And how should he serve God? And is there a God to serve?

Q.   I imagine you must have read some writers in what is called the modern Jewish Renaissance, the American Jewish writers such as Bellow, Malamud, and Roth.

A.   I read them a little, but I don't pay too much attention to these young modern writers. I mean, if I would find there great brilliancy

---

[8] Stories set in this country include "A Wedding in Brownsville," "Alone," "The Séance," "The Lecturer," and "The Letter-Writer."

I would be impressed; I have a feeling that modern young writers don't reveal much which is new to me. Maybe I am mistaken. Most probably I am mistaken, because all elderly people have this feeling, that whatever there is to know, they know already.

Q.   Bellow has translated a story of yours, I think.

A.   Yes, he did, he did. He translated "Gimpel the Fool" and I am grateful to him for doing this. They are talented people, but, you know, at my age, you want to read only the masters. You don't want to spend your time with reading anything which isn't first-class. So if I want to read fiction, I always go back to Tolstoy or Dostoevsky or Gogol. If I find something good in other writing I certainly am very happy, but I seldom find things which make me enthusiastic. I must confess this.

Q.   If not the contemporary American Jewish Renaissance, what about the Yiddish culture in New York when you first came?

A.   It was on the decline even then. And I'll tell you, Yiddish culture and I are two different things. Though I love Yiddish, I'm not a Yiddishist, because these people really have a kind of social ideology. They want to create a movement. They always talk about a movement—the Jewish literature, the Jewish theater, or the Yiddish theater. I'm not a man of movements at all. In other words, they considered me, in a way, selfish. They said, "You only think about your own work, about your own talent. You forget us, the movement." But I'm disappointed in movements. I know that movements and mediocrity always go together. Whatever becomes a mass movement—even if mysticism were to become a mass movement—would be bad. So, from a literary point of view, I went my own way. Also, these people were all on the socialistic side. They always thought about creating a better world. And, because of this, they were sentimental, which is not my way; I would also like to see a better world, but I don't think, really, that men can create it.

Q.   You can't be a sceptic and a socialist at the same time, in other words?

A.   Yes. They can make an effort, you know. But we cannot create a different society. We cannot do all these things which these people preach. And I have seen what happened to Russia, how they had the

Revolution; they spoke about a new man and a new way of life and actually it's the old men and the old way of life, a little changed.

Q. You go back to the masters—would you be willing to talk at all about the writers who've meant the most to you?

A. Well, I would say that Tolstoy, Dostoevsky, and Gogol meant the most to me. And also I have great respect for Flaubert, although he's not one hundred percent my kind of writer. I loved Edgar Allan Poe, although I read him in translation and I see that in this country there's a great tendency to belittle him. But I don't agree with this. It is true that I haven't read him for a long time. But my feeling is that the man was a genius, no matter what they say. And someday in the future, he will be again fashionable, they will again praise him. He is one of these writers whom I've never forgotten.

Q. What is there in Polish literature that you particularly like?

A. Oh, in Polish there is a great literary masterpiece: *Pan Tadeusz* by Adam Mickiewicz. Mickiewicz was a genius of the same kind as Byron and Pushkin and such people. The book was translated into many languages, also into English; it was translated into English only a short time ago, again. But poetry cannot be translated and he is one of those who lost a lot in translation. Another good writer among the Poles was Slenkewicz, the one who wrote *Quo Vadis*, but he is not of the size of Mickiewicz. They have a poet called Slowacki, and Bennett. But the real genius there was Mickiewicz.

Q. How about the Yiddish tradition in Poland?

A. Well, Yiddish literature in Poland is not very old. I mean the modern literature, because before this there were mostly Biblical things and religious books. But secular literature in Yiddish is not even a hundred years old. They have done quite well in a hundred years, but there is no reason for too much satisfaction.

Q. The form of your stories and some of your novels, plus the Biblical allusions, has led a number of people to talk of you as writing fable or parable.

A. Well, people always need a name for things, so whatever you will write or whatever you will do, they like to put you into a certain category. Even if you would be new, they would like to feel that a name

is already prepared for you in advance. Which is not really true. I
don't call myself a fabulist; I hope that one day somebody will find a
new name for me, not use the old names.

Q.   Have you read any Kafka? Do you like Kafka?

A.   Yes, I like him, but one Kafka in a century is enough. It's not
good to have whole armies, whole multitudes, of Kafkas. He's not the
kind of writer whom one should imitate or even emulate. There could
have been only one Kafka, like one Joyce and one Proust. While there
could have been another Tolstoy—it couldn't do any damage if you
would have a hundred Tolstoys; but a hundred Kafkas wouldn't be
good. He's a unique case.

Q.   Why wouldn't it be good?

A.   It wouldn't be good because it's description of dreams, completely
so. Kafka is not enough embedded in life—his miracles are too arbitrary to create the kind of literature that could last forever. The
reader gets very tired if life is distorted, or too much invented, completely defying the order of things. In other words, the real mystic
should describe life as it is, and then bring out the other side. But
when you begin immediately with symbolism or with distortions, you
create a kind of literature which even if it is unique, you cannot have
too much of it. Like with food, you can eat a lot of bread, a lot of
potatoes, a lot of vegetables, you cannot eat a lot of mustard. You can
only have a little bit of it. And this is true even about spiritual things.

Q.   Then you wouldn't put Kafka in the same category as you put
Tolstoy or Gogol?

A.   No, no, not at all.

Q.   What about James Joyce?

A.   Also not . . . also not.

Q.   Would you emphasize the significance of a narrative event, of
plot over symbol, from what you've just said?

A.   Well, to my mind, the symbol should be the climax of a work,
the result of a whole work. You cannot begin immediately with the
symbol and go on this way. Because if you heap one symbol upon the
other, it very often happens that one symbol neutralizes the other or
cancels the other.

Q. It's like the Biblical analogue—it's got to emerge from the work; it can't be imposed on it from without.

A. Exactly, exactly. It's peculiar—I wanted to say the same thing. When you read the Bible, you get the story and you get description, but somehow the story is also symbolic.

Q. And that's perhaps the reason why the symbol and the central figure in your novels very often coincide: the magician in *The Magician of Lublin.* . . .

A. I hope so. If you look deep into reality, reality itself is very symbolic. As I said before about a man who began his story with a cut-off head: it is true, from a symbolical point of view you can make a cut-off head talk, but you cannot write a whole play with a cut-off head because we need to step on a more familiar ground, to be able to go into what is not familiar.

Q. And Kafka writes of people with their heads cut off, who speak?

A. Exactly, quite often he does this.

Q. You said reality itself is very symbolic. At this point I'd like to come back to the question, "What is real? What is reality?"

A. We don't know; Kant and other philosophers like David Hume and John Locke or Berkeley and others have already taught us that there is no real way of defining reality. In a way we can say that reality is what is real to us. But still we assume reality is not an assumption, that there is something behind our feelings and our senses. What we call reality is the things to which we are accustomed. If you see a table every day, a table looks to you real. If you would see a table for the first time in your life, you would most probably feel that it's something not real. Or if you try to think about what a table is, you know that a table contains millions and trillions of molecules. Each molecule contains many, many atoms, and each atom contains protons and electrons; then the table stops being the table, it becomes an amalgamation of miracles. So actually what we call reality are things to which we are accustomed. The everyday things we call reality. But if you want to go into something which is not everyday, the best thing is to begin with everyday and go from there. If you begin immediately with the miracles, with the unusual, you cannot go far from a literary point of view.

Q. To go back to Berkeley then, there's a sense in which the contents of a literary work are as real as anything.

A. Surely, according to Berkeley, the whole world is ideas in God.
So since literature's full of ideas and images, it is just as real as anything.

Q. Do you think of literature as having a purpose, a function to
serve?

A. Not the kind of function which many younger people think—a
sociological function, a function to build a better society and so on. I
don't believe that literature has this power. I say that literature is a
force without direction. What I mean by this is: it moves one way
and another way; it doesn't go straight from one point to another.
Literature will never, can never, enhance the revolution, can never
enhance social reforms. And if it does, it is in a very small way, because
literature has to give many points of view: the point of view not only
of the oppressed but also of the oppressor, not only of the one who is
wronged but also of the one who is doing wrong. I say if literature
is a force, it's a vector which goes not straight but around and around
—like the waves of the oceans, they keep on going, but they go nowhere. Literature stirs the mind; it makes you think about a million
things, but it does not lead you. So the basic function of literature,
as far as I can say, is to entertain the spirit in a very big way. I mean
small literature entertains small spirits and great literature entertains
greater spirits. But it's basically an entertainment and it has only qualities of entertainment—which means, if you are not entertained while
you read a book, there is no other reward for you. While you read,
let's say, mathematics, you can say, "I'm bored now, but it will be
useful to me to build a bridge or to build a house." In literature, if
you don't enjoy it while you read, the purpose is lost. It has to be
enjoyed; like all the good things of life, it's a kind of luxury, rather
than a thing with a function.

Q. How does one enjoy literature, what does one respond to in a
piece of fiction?

A. Well, if you enjoy something, you don't really have to ask yourself why you enjoy. Naturally, professors like to analyze. But the reader
does not always need this analysis. It's only in the later years that people began to analyze every kind of enjoyment. People don't really have
to analyze the pleasure which they get out of love or sex, they enjoy

it and that's it. I would say that it doesn't do any damage if you do analyze it but neither do we bring more enjoyment by the analysis. If there wouldn't have been a single book about Shakespeare, Shakespeare would still be as good as he is. And the same thing is true about all the writers. However, it seems to me that we are reaching a point where analysis itself becomes a pleasure to some people. And if it is a pleasure, I say more power to them. Why not? If you enjoy it, and others do too, keep on analyzing.

Q. I was really driving at something a little different: the matter of aesthetic response, the way one responds to the formal elements in a work, as one might respond to the formal elements in a painting. What is your relationship to a work that you create, from this standpoint?

A. I would say that in my own small way, I'm a perfectionist. I like perfection, I like to think that I have written something which is in my way perfect—which means the construction is right, the description is right, the dialogue is right. I have not done too much or too little, everything is in its place. And this kind of enjoyment is shared by a painter or even a housewife when she thinks that she has done a good job in cleaning the house or preparing a supper. This feeling of doing a thing right is a human instinct as much as any other instinct which we have.

Q. You say that "everything is in its right place." How do you go about laying out a novel? Is it purely instinct or do you work from a plan?

A. Well, when it comes to a novel, no matter how much you plan, you can never act according to plan, because once you have written the first chapter, even the first page, you are not anymore the complete owner of the thing. The heroes themselves, the situation itself, bid for consequences and so on. In a short story, it's easier to have a complete plan and write according to it, but even in a short story you cannot do just what you please. Also there, the heroes, the characters, have their own lives and their own logic, and you have to act accordingly. But still, the very idea that you have done something right (let's say you have written an essay or a story and you read it and you think, "It is exactly what I wanted to do") is a pleasure which I cannot define, and it doesn't even have to be defined. It's as basic as any other emotion.

Q. This might sound like a cliché, but what you're saying is that the mystery in the creation of literature is as great as the mystery in the response to life.

A. No question about it. Surely, because literature is a part of life. If you go out and you see a girl and you like her, you really don't have to analyze why you like her. You don't need to measure her nose and her face and so on and so on. It's enough if you like her. By measuring, you cannot spoil it, unless your measurements are wrong, and they may hypnotize you in the wrong way. The reason we love a beautiful woman or a beautiful building or anything is that we have an instinct for proportion that we cannot explain. We will say that one nose is better looking than the other. And if you ask yourself, "What is your point of view, how do you know how a nose should be?" the only answer could be that we—Plato's explanation—that we have seen somewhere a nose above, before we came to this earth, and we know exactly what it is. But whatever the answer, there is in all human beings a feeling of how things should be and how they shouldn't be. We call a freak a freak not from any other point of view but from our point of view, from what we are accustomed to, from what we consider right.

Q. This will get back to the idea of analysis and analysis being a pleasure in itself. Could you say that in certain types of people the instinct for analysis is almost an aesthetic instinct—the instinct for seeing relationships within the work or in life?

A. Yes, yes, that may be true, because actually analysis itself is a form of creation. It is true that some people have it more and some people have it less. But there is such a thing. We like to analyze things; and in the sciences, analysis has accomplished much; the whole of science is really built on logic and analysis. In art, it hasn't done as much, but still, I'm not against literary criticism—far from it. But I'm against it when the writer himself is his own critic, while he writes. For example, sometimes in *Pale Fire*, as Nabokov writes, he says, "I could have written it so." He writes essays about his heroes. And I think this is not the right way of mixing analysis and giving images. To me this looks unaesthetic.

Q. What do you think of Nabokov in general, since you mentioned him?

A. Well, he's a good writer, but I would say he's not my writer.

Q.   Are you suggesting that the writer loses the right to define what the work is, as soon as he finishes the work?

A.   No, he doesn't lose, he has the same rights as anybody else, but not more.

Q.   And he cannot define the work while he's writing it himself either, because this would be an act of literary criticism.

A.   No, it's not really good. Let's imagine if a man would stand on his knees and declare his love to a girl. He would say, "I love you dearly, I cannot live without you," and then he would try to explain: "The reason why I love you dearly is. . . ." We feel that he would spoil his love declaration; he would become really ridiculous. It's not necessary in this case. And the same thing is true when we tell a story. Most stories are love stories also. In some way, a story is always kind of a love declaration—near to it; and explaining and using all these foreign words and saying what I *could* have done is not the right way. I don't believe the writer should interpret, just as I feel it would be a very bad thing if a rose would explain exactly what colors it used and how it is to become a rose. The beauty of the rose is its silence, its *being* a rose. And I think this is really what Gertrude Stein meant when she said, "A rose is a rose is a rose." It meant that you cannot say more.

Q.   In other words, the writer creates a coherent and self-sustaining illusion.

A.   Exactly.

Q.   And this is perhaps the reason that your work relies as heavily as it does on irony?

A.   There may be irony, but the irony should never be outspoken, not clearly. When you go into a store there's a sign which says there are shoes and so on. But literature doesn't need any signs; go into the store and see the merchandise by itself.

Q.   Perhaps the word should be paradox, not irony. Paradox certainly exists in the world.

A.   All over. Everything to me, everything is a paradox. The very existence of things is a paradox.

II

Q. Mr. Singer, if we may, I would like to discuss the short stories, since in the last interview we chiefly considered your novels. One of the things that struck me in the *Short Friday* collection is the presence of some stories in which you've assumed the point of view of a demon or a magical creature. If I remember correctly, we have spoken about demons sometimes being a manifestation of a man's inner feelings and obsessions. Is this true in a story like "The Last Demon," for example, which is written completely from the point of view of the demon?

A. Well, I think I told you that I really believe in demons. To me they are alive. If a voice from God would come out and would say, "There are no demons," there would still remain something of my way of thinking. At least to me, demons exist, just as God exists. I assume that there are intelligent powers not connected with a body, or not with a human body or with an animal body. And these powers still work, so for me they exist. About the story of "The Last Demon": I imagine that there is a demon in this little village, but since I don't know anything about demons, I always make the demon behave as if it would be a human being. In other words, he has the mind of a human being without the body of a human being.

Q. Would this make the story an allegory or fable?

A.   I wouldn't really call it an allegory. When I write about a demon, I go, so to say, into *his* point of view. I assume that he exists not only as a fable. . . . Our human existences may also be a fable or an allegory, but it's also existence: you have to eat, you have to sleep. I don't know anything about demons, so whatever existence I give them must be a kind of human existence. But still I try to find some individuality in them, taken from folklore, from stories. In other words, to me a demon is not only a fable or an allegory—he's like some separate creature which lives by its own right and by its own laws. A demon may have different laws, different ambitions, but he has to be human, not because I want to make him human to teach something about humanity, but because I have no *other* experience. I can give him, once in a while, also the powers of an animal, but anyhow, it's all taken from experience or from folklore, which is a kind of experience. And from imagination, which is also a form of experience.

Q.   Let's take up a possibly related question. In "Yentl the Yeshiva Boy" you said, "Though their bodies were different, their souls were of one kind."[4] Are you using "soul" to indicate something like human nature? What do you mean by "soul"?

A.   In this case I meant really human nature, because the soul expresses human nature. When we say the soul or the spirit, we mean actually the man, because we don't know if the soul and the body are two sides of the same coin, as Spinoza says, or if they can be separated. In this case what I meant is that they have kindred spirits: whatever it means. But I may also use the word "soul" in a different way.

Q.   That's what I was thinking. Now when you use it in the different way, do you in any sense imply the notion of *fixed* human nature?

A.   No, I don't believe in a fixed human nature, because I believe in free choice, so it cannot be completely fixed. But naturally, it has its inclinations, there's no question about it. For example, in the story you mentioned, "Yentl the Yeshiva Boy," we have to do with homosexual people. This is *their* inclination. Free choice does not really deny human nature, nor does human nature deny free choice. These two can live together. Like in a prison—although you are imprisoned, you have some freedom; some prisoners get out for good behavior,

---

   [4] *Short Friday and Other Stories* (Signet: New York, 1965), p. 145. Further references to this volume will be contained in the text.

and some prisoners stay longer because of bad behavior. In the prison itself there is a choice.

Q. Would you link the soul to the part of the person that is engaged in free choice?

A. No, I would link the soul to everything: to sin and to virtue, to passion and to insanity, to everything.

Q. So along with Spinoza you would not necessarily mean to take the soul as the opposite of body at all?

A. In some cases, I would—say, when I speak about a hereafter. Then the body has decayed and I assume that the soul remains. In literature the writer does not have to be completely consistent. He can use a term once so, in another time so. You are completely free because it's playing around. The writer plays around with words and also with ideas. Especially, when you write about demons, you are playing all the time. And since you are playing, you can change your point of view, you can change everything. Still there is a certain consistency which is connected with the writer himself. No matter how he plays, you see what is behind the play: how he reacts, how *he* plays. As a matter of fact, when we study actors, we know that they are themselves in every part. The same thing is true with writers.

Q. To go back to the story we started with, "The Last Demon": although it seems to be about a demon, there actually is in it a strong current, it seems to me, about the possibly corrupting power of literature.

A. Yes, absolutely so. In other words, this story belittles the writers.

Q. What were you doing here? The quotation that I noted was, "Satan has cooked up a new dish of kasha. The Jews have now developed writers. Yiddish ones, Hebrew ones, and they have taken over our trade. . . . They know all our tricks—mockery, piety. They have a hundred reasons why a rat must be kosher. All that they want to do is redeem the world" (p. 115).

A. Exactly. Actually I am chiding here not only the writers, but the whole Enlightenment. The Jewish Enlightenment is a kind of rationalism which came very late, a hundred years later than rationalism came to Europe. It was obsolete to begin with. And because it was obsolete, it was old-fashioned and silly. So our kind of Enlightenment, which we call the Haskalah, is something which I often chide, because Yiddish literature and Hebrew literature is always under its influence. All the writers are writers of the Enlightenment—and I would say that I am almost an exception. Maybe there is another exception, but they're very few.

In some sense I am saying that the writers actually are small assistants of Satan. They help him . . . they help the imps. In other words, what the devil did in the old time himself, now the writers have taken over.

Q.   All right, that quickly brings us to the question, if these writers are doing the wrong thing, what should a writer be doing?

A.   Well, I never say what he should be doing because I myself am in a way a split personality. If I would be a very religious man I would say that the writer should write about religion, like my father did, but this, as you know, I cannot do. I can make fun of the Enlightenment but at the same time I cannot give anything which should take the place of the Enlightenment. However, I have my kind of philosophy, which is expressed in my writings—not that I practice it one hundred percent, but at least I believe in it. What I believe is this: we don't know what God wants from us and there is no chance ever to know. Revelation is always dubious; we don't know if God has ever revealed Himself, or if He has ever told a man how we should behave, or if revelation is the nature of God—we know nothing. So our best guess is to behave in a right way towards other human beings and also towards the animals. Not that we are sure that this is going to be rewarded and that this is God's will, but this is our best bet, as gamblers will say. Since we don't know which horse will reach the aim, let's bet on the horse that looks the strongest; let's not build our fortune on other people's misfortune. And I think that this is to what all philosophers came—religious philosophers and actually all philosophers, no matter if rationalists or mystics. Somehow, if you read the history of philosophy and the history of religions, they all came to the same conclusion, because this is how far human thought, human philosophy, can reach. So let's assume that God does not want me to stab my fellow man, to gossip about him, to denounce him, and so on and so on—that God does not want us to be bad to one another. Comparing God to our father, us to the children, our father's real desire is that his children should not do damage one to the other. This is to me nothing but an assumption because, as I say, I don't know. There are many arguments which can prove that the opposite is true: God has given us power to do damage to one another, which means He does not mind. However, since we cannot go further, we have to rest here and say this is it. If we made a mistake, so still it's better to be good than to be bad.

Q.   When you use the words "good" and "bad," you're really using them on the basis of revelation, are you not?

A.   No, on the basis of human needs. I mean, you are a good man if you don't make people suffer. This is the only measure; there is no other measure. The Ten Commandments and all the commandments in the world are built on this.

Q.   On something which is fundamentally experience. . . .

A.   Fundamentally experience, and in us. Kant calls it the categorical imperative. There are all kinds of names for it, but we all know exactly what it means.

Q.   Do you see a human being as fundamentally, in part, evil?

A.   Well, I don't belong to those who say men are born good, only that civilization spoils them. This to me is completely silly. Man is born bad, with a certain goodness in him, which he can enhance and which he can completely destroy, or almost completely destroy, as we see from experience.

Q.   It seemed to me in the *Short Friday* collection that one of your concerns was a description of the nature of evil. In fact, that collection, I think, contains some of the most grotesque or horrifying of the stories you've written. I'm thinking particularly of the stories "Blood" and "Under the Knife," although there are others similar in the same collection. To begin with, in "Under the Knife" did you view Leib as a psychotic, and does this have something to do with the nature of evil?

A.   The man who murders two innocent women, because he wants to take revenge on the woman who rejected him.

Q.   Yes; he kills one woman who befriends him (the streetwalker) and the elder sister of the woman he loved. It seems to me that there are a number of possibilities here. One of them is that this is the study of a man who is totally obsessed and as a result psychotic.

A.   It is actually another story of obsession. I don't like to write about people who are indifferent, or who are only mildly interested in a thing. I think that literature can serve us best when it will write about obsessed characters, because here you can see the human being with all his qualities, good or bad. Here is a man who is obsessed by revenge, although there was no reason for him to kill this woman. (She might have loved him once and now she doesn't love him; she wants to live her own life, and she's entitled to it.) But to him, she is evil, although he's actually evil. I'm concerned with the idea that he revenges himself on people who are completely innocent. This is what happened really with Hitler; he was angry with a few Jews, a few journalists whom he considered evil. And he took revenge on people who had nothing to do with journalism, most innocent victims. This is what happens in every war; whenever people fight for something, the victim always is not the one whom they fight, but people who have nothing to do with him. For example, when we fight now in Viet Nam we are not killing the leaders of Communism, but innocent recruits. And they are not killing Rockefeller or Johnson, whom they consider evil, but again those who have nothing to do with these leaders.

Q.   In other words, the most important thing about the story is the fact that the person whom he wanted to injure escaped untouched?

A.   Yes, yes . . . and also, I make this Leib at the end sick. I show by this that nature itself takes revenge in its own way, that if you wait a little, everything is revenged anyhow, everything is in a way straightened out by nature itself. I remember that I once went in a bus and a number of people were quarreling over a seat. They began a great quarrel, and I wanted to give them my seat, but they said, "No, no, we don't want your seat." I was reading the newspaper for a few minutes, and then I lifted my eyes; they were all gone. The whole quarrel was a quarrel about sitting two minutes on a bench. It wasn't worthwhile. And I think that all human fights, or almost all of them, are of the same kind. If we just would wait a little bit, the whole thing would be over.

Q.   Are you saying something too about the randomness of suffering?

A.   I don't know myself what I'm saying; all I know is that I just got this idea of this story. And the story, in a way, is a consistent story— I mean it works itself out from the beginning to the end. And once a story is right, is done right, you can find in it many, many things. It's not the writer's ability to know everything which the story may imply.

Q.   What about "Blood" now?

A.   Here is another obsession: people who are obsessed by blood. And I also tried to show in this the nature of sadism. In a way sadism is a kind of riddle; we have a word for sadism, but we seldom really know what it is. We say that the sadist enjoys bringing suffering to people, but here I made sadism clearer than it is when you just read the dictionary. Here you see people who enjoy killing animals and you infer from this that they might have enjoyed killing people too, if they would have gone a little further. And also you see it connected with sex. The shedding of blood arouses these people.

Q.   Are you implying that there's something fundamentally associated between carnal lust and blood lust?

A.   I think, yes. For example, men's obsession for thousands of years and until today to have a virgin is only this, that the first time a man lives with a virgin he makes her suffer a little bit, and he sees blood. And men were terribly obsessed with this; to marry a woman who was not a virgin was a great misfortune and a great shame. He had to get his pound of flesh from this woman. The woman herself, even though she's the victim, was sometimes very much excited by this, as I heard women tell me, exaggerating even their suffering—which is a kind of masochism. . . . Hunting is deeply connected with sex. If you will read the Bible or Homer, you will see that sometimes the woman asks her lover to give her a few heads or limbs of the enemy. The passion of the flesh is deeply connected with the flesh itself, with the blood of the flesh.

Q.   In other words, would you suggest that all human drives, particularly sex, but all human drives, have a component which is destructive and consumptive?

A.   There is no question about it. Passion, an immense desire for the female, is kind of a strange desire to revenge himself upon a person he loves. A man may be loving a woman very much, but he's little disturbed by the fact that this woman will get pregnant and she suffers while she gives birth. He takes it for granted; in a way, it's his privilege. He feels that this is the way he can rule her. Women enjoy the fact that men go to war—not all women, but more than we dare to know.

_Q._   In other words, you're placing sexuality very much at the root of most of experience. Is that a fair statement?

_A._   There is sexuality in everything. About this I have no quarrel with Freud. The only real quarrel with him which I have—although I'm not a specialist—is about his remedies. He believes that if things become clear to us, we stop being bothered by them. The first thing is, they never become clear, so this is not going to help any . . . and even if they would be clear, it would still not help because it is not a question of being clear or not clear. If a man has a passion for somebody, you cannot talk him out of it. If a father really would like to sleep with his daughter, no matter how much he will lie on the couch and talk about it, he will still have this desire.

_Q._   When I reflect on it, actually there are very few, perhaps no, portraits in your work of passion, a clear passion, that comes to a good end.

_A._   No, passion in itself can never bring any good end. It's only when we curb our passion. . . . By the way, there isn't such a thing as a good end; what is a good end? It does not exist. The only thing we call "a good end" is if a man lives without any passion. He doesn't strive to do anything and he goes on living a monotonous life, so he may continue for eighty years or so, being bored to death and boring other people; then he dies. While "the bad end" is that of a man who goes into things in a very hard way, lives only a few years longer, dies suddenly. Both ends are actually not so good.

_Q._   Then passion is its own reward?

_A._   It speeds up human life, it gives it more content, more intensity. Passion is bad when it brings suffering to other people. But even if you damage yourself, you are sinning, from an ethical point of view. Just as a father doesn't want one child to hit another, he doesn't want that child to do damage to itself.

_Q._   Well, once again you're caught then; the alternative is boredom.

_A._   I think so.

_Q._   But any kind of passion probably. . . .

_A._   Yes, yes—it means suffering and causing people to suffer. At its best, it brings suffering to the owner, to the one who has the passion, and in most of the cases, it brings suffering to the man who has the passion and to his objects. If a man says, "I am passionately in love with a woman," it means that he suffers, and sooner or later the woman will also suffer, one way or another. If he will not marry her . . . she will suffer. If he marries her, he may be jealous, or he may cool off after a while, and get a passion for somebody else. Passion really is suffering. This, I will say, is part of my writing.

Q.   But also a basis of meaning?

A.   Surely, without it a man is a vegetable.

Q.   So we're back again to the paradox, aren't we?

A.   Yes, just as in a little village wherever you walk you come immediately into the fields, so it is in life, wherever you go you are immediately at a paradox, at a contradiction.

Q.   There was another direction suggested in the story "Blood." After the sadism and the slaughtering, as a kind of culmination of evil, Risha turned deliberately to deceiving the community about the purity of the meat she sold. You wrote, "She got so much satisfaction from deceiving the community, that this soon became as powerful a passion with her as lechery and cruelty" (pp. 40-41). Is the desire to deceive the community one of the basic or perhaps most serious expressions of evil?

A.   You cannot live in passion, really, without deceiving. Every man who has a passion must lie, especially if the passion is connected with sex. The man has to lie to the woman or the woman has to lie to the man. For Risha, deceiving the community is actually a kind of culmination of deceiving; she has deceived her husband before. She began by deceiving one man, but she deceived all men.

Q.   Is it the case then that passion always brings one into conflict with the community?

A.   I would say yes, because the community is not a passionate institution. It's an institution of curbing. People create a community only because they curb their passions, because if every member of the community would go after his passion, the community would not exist. A collective is an institution where everybody curbs himself. A really passionate man does not belong. He's either a criminal, or he's crazy, or he's an outcast. He's never really a part of the community.

Q. Unless, of course, he buys membership in the community by deception?

A. Exactly. Yes, this is true. If he deceives the community he can for a while stay within it.

Q. This returns us to the conflict between human nature and·the Ten Commandments that you discussed in the first interview, although in "Blood" it is the kosher laws that are being violated.

A. The same thing: it's always the same thing. This is also the Ten Commandments, because the Ten Commandments say you should not bear false witness; in other words, you should not deceive the community.

Q. Thus the religious laws are expressions of the community's desire to control.

A. Yes. The laws of the Torah and of all religious codes say you cannot give in to passion and still let others live. To give in to passion to the very end means that you should live, and the other one should die or should suffer the pangs of death. And the community is a kind of experiment to curb passion, and because of this to maintain life.

Q. All this discussion brings us back to the question you've treated again and again: the problem of will. To what extent are the people in the two stories we've discussed exercising free will? They are really driven people.

A. They don't. This Risha did not exercise free will at all. She has made up her mind, it seems, long ago that she has to have her way in everything. The man with whom she sins, this slaughterer, is a better person than she. He's a man who really would have been a part of the community, but she seduces him and brings out what is bad in him. At the end I make him repent. He dies in the poorhouse and confesses his sins. This woman becomes an animal at the end; she becomes a werewolf. In other words, if man completely stops curbing himself, he becomes a beast—in a negative way, because the beasts are curbed by nature, by higher powers, but when man becomes an animal, he becomes ten times worse than an animal.

Q. The situation of your characters in these two stories seems to be different from the situation of Cunegunde in the story very near the end of *Short Friday*. Now here is another woman who clearly is . . .

A.   Possessed by fear. The fear of this Cunegunde turns into a destructive power; although she does not really destroy, she wants to destroy. In other words, even though witches may not exist, potential witches there are by the millions: people who would destroy if they could.

Q.   Does it make a difference that in the "Cunegunde" story we are told of the disasters of her childhood, whereas we see Risha in "Blood" only at adulthood, making what seems to be an unmotivated choice?

A.   It is true that I did not tell about Risha's childhood. I just avoided it. But certainly there must be a good reason. One of the reasons is always heredity, in which modern people don't believe, but I do believe. I know that in our time we always believe in circumstances. We say that circumstances made the person, which I believe. But I believe that the heredity is more important. We come already to this world laden with certain powers, with certain desires and passions. So not in every case where I describe a passion do I have to describe the circumstances, because not in every case do the circumstances play such a big part. In "Cunegunde" it was necessary to give the circumstances, because to become what she was you needed also unusual circumstances, while Risha's desire for blood might have been with her from her very childhood.

Q.   Where is free will in all of this?

A.   I believe, as I said before, man is in a prison. However, in the frame of the prison, there is still a little freedom left. In the frame of our prison, we have free will and this is a great gift—because the animals and the dead things don't have even this little freedom.

Q.   Can man give away his freedom? Can he make a choice which means that from that point on he actually cannot act freely?

A.   No, I don't believe this, but I can say he can neglect the little freedom he possesses. Once it is misused and neglected, it almost stops to exist. However, a spark is always left. No matter how low a person has fallen, some voice in him will always tell him he can repent, he can change. We all feel this.

Q.   Do some people have a greater share of freedom than others?

A. I would say that people with great passion have more freedom than those who have no passion. It seems a paradox—but I believe in it. I will tell you why: the person who has very little passion lives according to a routine. And since a community means routine, he lives in peace with the community. Although he lives a moral life, it's not free will. The community itself becomes a prison to him. He's afraid of the rabbi, afraid of the priest, afraid of the elders, of his wife, of his mother-in-law. Although he behaves well, he's a prisoner. While a man with great passion—since he has learned to misbehave, since he's not a slave of the community, he can also become the opposite of evil. This is a paradox, but it makes sense just the same. Let's say that a man has decided that he's a lecher. He doesn't care about his wife, about the marriage institution; he'll just do what he wants. But since he has the courage to defy the community, he might have, in other circumstances, the courage even to defy himself and his passion and to become the very opposite. This is the reason why sinners sometimes become saints, and here we have something which is connected with Yasha the magician. Here is a man who has given in—given in to his passion, but he defied the community. So when he repents, he again defies the community, because his way of repenting is not the way the community dictated. He is again a rebel. There is a deep connection between the saint and the sinner, a fact which was known for generations.

Q. Then you would link the freedom a man possesses to courage rather than to self-knowledge. Or what is the role of self-knowledge in freedom?

A. I would say that the courage is more important than the self-knowledge because a man really does not know himself enough, and even if he knows himself, this is not always a reason for curbing himself. He may know what is right and not be able to do it. It's the kind of courage, almost a physical courage which *is* in such men—because a man of great passion is a man of great vitality. If he has great vitality, everything in him is greater, even his free will. Or it might be greater.

Q. Possibly there's another story which suggests that there are some limits upon what even the most courageous man can do in trying to control his own drives. I'm thinking of "The Fast" in *Short Friday*. To quote a line from it: "In time opposing this lusting creature becomes a habit." Then as the hero, Itche Nokhum, continues to mortify the flesh, to fast, to sleep on the bench, the specter of his former wife rises before him and he sees it as primeval substance, and it dissolves in blood spatters on the floor. The scene ends with his statement that he cannot forget her, and her lament that she is in his power. Does this suggest a qualification on what you've just said?

A.   Yes. When two persons really have a great desire for one another—which people call love, or passion, or let's call it as we want—this may become that strong. In this story I almost make the passion itself become a body. The woman whom he sees there was created by him. She's not there, but his desire for her is so great that he has given her a body, if only for a short while.

Q.   Turning to another sort of question—one of the stories in *Short Friday* fascinates me because it seems to me that the I-figure may be your own persona as well as a fictional narrator. This is the story "Alone."

A.   It's true that I went to Miami Beach; I go there sometimes in the summer because I suffer from hay fever. It is true that I was in a hotel in which suddenly for no reason—or we didn't know the reasons—they told us to leave and to go to other hotels. I have never experienced anything like it, that a hundred or two hundred guests should be told to leave. It is true that I got into another hotel, that I was there alone. The storm did not take place then, but I combined the moving with the storm. And there was a Cuban girl also, though she was not a hunchback.

Q.   The story interested me in part because it seemed to concern the nature of perception. At the first, for example, the problem was lack of understanding, as you point out; in fact the whole framework of the story . . .

A.   . . . is subjective. Yes. It is subjective because it's written in the first person, which I used not to do in the old times. Only a few years ago I decided that one may once in a while write in the first person.

Q.   Are you trying when you use first person to write as much as possible in your own voice, or are you writing in the voice of a character who views the scene?

A.   Well, I would say it's a combination of both. As much as I can give of myself I give of myself. There's no reason why not. And when I have to hide something, I let the character speak.

Q. It seemed to me also that the main character may have seen more clearly than usual. He says, "Through the heavenly channels, which, says the Cabala, control the flow of Divine Mercy, came truths impossible to grasp in a northern climate" (p. 53). And further, "At the same time the eternal questions tapped in my brain: Who is behind the world of appearance? Is it Substance with its Infinite Attributes? Is it the Monad of all Monads? Is it the Absolute, Blind Will, the Unconscious?" (p. 54) Is this sense of truth the illusion of a character in special circumstances, or is this a penetration to reality by a character who would otherwise not be able to see so clearly?

A. I gave in this story my own feelings, but the feelings in a special case, because when one is alone, one is more inclined really to philosophize than when one is in company and everything is in order. When you are alone, contact with other people is broken, and you begin to brood about something higher or lower. I mentioned here, actually, a number of philosophers, although not by name. The Substance with Infinite Attributes is Spinoza; the Monad of all Monads is Leibnitz. The Absolute can be Schelling or Fichte. Blind Will is Schopenhauer, and the Unconscious is von Hartmann. And the question, who is behind the world of appearance: this can be Plato, and Kant—and anything. Naturally I mentioned only the idealistic philosophers. I did not mention, let's say, Feuerbach, or others. I don't even have the feeling that I have to dispute with them. I don't believe in materialism.

Q. Thus in this section you simply indicate the spread of idealistic philosophy rather than suggest a position. Do you, yourself, ever adopt a position discriminating between the world as a conception of the mind and the world as a poor imitation of an absolute form?

A. I feel, like most idealistic philosophers and actually like everybody else, that what we see here is only kind of an image, a picture, which is fitted to our power of conception. To me, and I think to many others, we are living in a kind of a dream, even when we are awake. The only difference is that this dream seems to have a certain consistency. If you dream at night that you have a house, you wake up in the morning and there is no house, but your dream of a house in the day as a rule goes on day after day. So it is a consistent dream; a dream behind which there is a reality. But what reality is, we don't know and we will never know. The thing-in-itself will always be a puzzle to every human being. And when a person is alone, he's brooding, he feels these things even more than when he is with people, where the illusion of reality is a little stronger.

Q.   Interpreting the story "Alone," do you think a man gets closer to intuition of the *Ding-an-sich* when he is alone and brooding?

A.   Very much so. He has no choice, because when a person is completely alone for a time, he feels that the day is almost as dreamy as the night. Things become almost without substance. This feeling that things lose their substance is very strong when a person is alone, or in times of tragedy, in times of great confusion. And also when you come to a strange city you already feel that there is something wrong with your conception of reality, because here are people living without knowing you. You don't exist for them, and they almost don't exist for you either. The feeling of reality is actually strongest when a man sits in one place among his family or among his friends, among the things he is used to. The more you move away from your things—you don't have to be Immanuel Kant to feel that things just melt between your fingers.

Q.   The discussion of idealism leads me to an historical question. In your memoir, *In My Father's Court*, you comment that you are now "familiar with all the defects and hiatuses of Spinozaism. But at that time I was under a spell which lasted many years." [5] How long did the spell last?

A.   Really many years. I used to carry around Spinoza's *Ethics* wherever I went. But later on I began to see that Spinoza is in his own way a realist, which I did not like too much. After I read David Hume, Kant, and others, I felt that something is wrong with Spinoza's belief in reality, because to him what we see is real. And then there is his rationalism and his idea that God has no will and no purpose. I did not like that. As I became older I became more inclined to mysticism and to religion, and I felt that to say that the universe is nothing but a huge machine with no will or no purpose is minimizing creation. I will take from Spinoza his pantheism; I believe like Spinoza that everything is God. But to be sure that God has only these two attri-

---

[5] *In My Father's Court* (Signet: New York, 1967), p. 221.

butes which we know (though he says He has endless attributes) and that He has no will and has no purpose is wrong; it is to be too sure about things where men cannot be sure. I could just as well say that will and purpose are also attributes of God—and so is beauty, and so is, maybe, morality. The Cabala has both sides: it has all the good sides of Spinoza and all the good sides of Plato. This is the reason I admire so much the Cabala.

Q.   In other words, your dispute with Spinoza really turns on this question of the ideal versus the real?

A.   Exactly. And about the question of free will and purpose. Once we assume that God has will and purpose, then there is no limitation to what God can do with His creation; it may have the most wonderful purpose and the most wonderful direction. Spinoza was actually a materialist. He called matter God, because he also says that matter (extension) and thinking are two sides of the same coin, which means to him there is nothing but matter, that matter itself thinks. Since I moved away from materialism, I began also to move away from Spinoza, although he fascinates me just the same. He was a great and a deep thinker in his own terms.

Q.   Did you begin to move away from Spinoza before you came to this country or later?

A.   Before.

Q.   That means that most of what you have written was written after you became critical of some of his basic thinking.

A.   Yes, I would say so—even the story "The Spinoza of Market Street" is a Spinoza story I have written in later years. At the end the main character (who has finally married) says, "Divine Spinoza, forgive me. I have become a fool." Well, I don't believe that a man who lives with a woman is a fool. Spinoza compares people who love to the insane. He did not believe in love; at least he says so.

Q.   Thus, as it seems, the whole story is extremely ironic.

A.   It is in a way. First I describe this man who is—even though he is a Spinozaist—a deep thinker. But what I wanted to say is that if you are a human being, if you are alive, you cannot live according to Spinoza. And another thing: Spinoza belittles very much the emotions. To him the emotions are very negative. His ideal man must get rid of his emotions, at least as much as possible. Only then could he be a real thinker, and could he have what he calls the *amor dei intellectualis*—the intellectual love for God. I dispute this. I consider the human emotions a great treasure—not only a material treasure, but also a great treasure of revelation, because our emotions reveal to us things which we cannot grasp with our intellect. The only thing is that the emotions, because they are so many and because they are so intense, can also be very dangerous. They are a weapon which can be used in many ways. Man can kill himself with emotions, kill others with emotions, so he has to control them, to curb them—but not to get rid of them, not really to dismiss them, as Spinoza says.

Q. So in "The Spinoza of Market Street" the emotions really conquered the intellect and the man was better off, or wiser.

A. Yes. I think so, although he says he became a fool, I think he became wiser—that he had sense enough in his old age to get a woman, even though she was such a woman. To his heart, she was a vulgar piece, but still he had somebody.

Q. Now what about the Cabala: this was also something which you studied as a boy, wasn't it? At about the time you discovered Spinoza?

A. Almost in the same time or a little earlier—although one is not allowed to study the Cabala, from a Jewish point of view, before one is thirty years old, because it's esoteric and dangerous, according to tradition. But I stole these books from my father's bookcase and I studied them. Spinoza was not in my father's library, but I once heard my father curse Spinoza. He said he was a heretic, a disbeliever, and I became curious. My father even mentioned that what he said was also said in a different way by the famous saint, Baal Shem. Baal Shem said the world is God and God is the world. From these words I got a notion what Spinoza is. In my kind of education, in my kind of circumstances, we had to learn things very quickly and from hints. In the time when I heard the name, there wasn't anything about Spinoza in Yiddish—and also, my father forbade me to read worldly books, secular books. If my father would have caught me reading Spinoza, I don't know what would have happened in our house; there would have been a scandal. We had to steal ideas, steal emotions.

Q. About what time did you begin, then, to get rather widely acquainted with secular books?

A. Not until I left really my father's house, although I read a lot while I was in my father's house. But I had always to hide, to go up to an attic, or to the fields somewhere. Reading was an illegal business, except reading holy books. Only when I went to Warsaw to live with my brother in the early twenties could I study. But since I had then all the books which I wanted, my desire to read became smaller, you know how it is. But still, I read. Then I read Kant and Schopenhauer and Nietzsche and David Hume, whom I admire very much.

Q. During this time you must have been in your late teens and in your twenties. [Singer: Yes.] Did you stay with your brother then?

A. My brother was there, but I had a furnished room. I didn't live with my brother, but we were attached. I saw him all the time. There was a Warsaw writers' club, and at this writers' club they all came, the painters and even the actors and naturally the writers. I even met there a number of European writers, including Galsworthy.

Q. What other contact did you have with English literature at this time?

A. Not much, except that I read Dickens. I loved very much Oscar Wilde—not his plays, but *The Picture of Dorian Gray*. I read that the first time in Hebrew, and in Hebrew it was even more beautiful than in English. Hebrew is just made for this kind of writing. I also read *De Profundis*.

Q. How important was the Yiddish literary tradition to you then?

A. It was important, but not really very important. In the same time I began to read European literature in translation, and even though I was young I immediately saw that the great European writers are better than our Yiddish writers.

Q. Whom did you read?

A. Maupassant, Victor Hugo, Flaubert; and Dostoevsky, Tolstoy, Knut Hamsun, and Turgenev.

Q. So Hamsun would rate alongside the Russian realists as an important figure for you?

A. Yes. . . . Dostoevsky is not a realist. And even Tolstoy I wouldn't call a complete realist, but I loved Hamsun. There was a time when I was really drunk with Hamsun. Later on he became a realist, and when he became a realist, he became almost nothing. He lost himself; but his great works are *Pan* and *Hunger*. There he is the real Hamsun. I also translated from German *The Magic Mountain*.

Q. What is your attitude towards Mann?

A. He is, there is no question, a highly talented writer, but I like better his *Buddenbrooks* than *Der Zauberberg*. I feel that modern writers began to write essays about literature instead of telling stories. I call this modern kind of writing the epoch of the essay; they write disguised essays which they call stories. And I think that *The Magic Mountain* is such a disguised essay. I still believe in the old-fashioned storytelling; the writer should tell a story and the essays should be written by the critics.

Q. During these Warsaw years a socialist point of view was dominant among literary men, wasn't it?

A. Very dominant and very much in fashion. I never believed in it— because the first thing is, they were materialists and I was against materialism. And also I was a pessimist; I didn't believe that we can really change the human condition by changing the regime. Not that I was antagonistic, but I was sceptical about the whole thing. Today, to say that I'm sceptical about this isn't a great prowess, but in my time you had to have a lot of character, because everybody fell into this kind of faith. They all believed a new time is coming. There will be new people and a new nature . . . a new man. And it will all be brought by Karl Marx and his disciples. And even though I wasn't highly educated and I was young, I said, "I don't believe it." So I had to be for the second time a disbeliever. First I was a disbeliever in our dogma, where people screamed at me and scolded. Then I became a disbeliever for the second time, in Karl Marx.

Q. Your scepticism about Judaism began when you were very young, didn't it?

A. I always loved Judaism and I always believed in God, but as far as dogma is concerned, doubt began very early. Because I saw that these dogmas are man-made things: I did not believe that God told Moses, let's say, not to touch money on the Sabbath, or not to write on the Sabbath. They have millions and millions of little laws. They made from one law fifty, and then from the fifty a thousand, and so on. Every generation added something new.

Q.   These two kinds of scepticism then meant that from the time you were very young you were really separated from the society around you? There must have been considerable controversy with your family.

A.   With my family, with friends, with writers, with critics. I was really surrounded, so to say, with a hostile milieu.

Q.   And of course you did not go through what has become almost a cliché about writers in the century, the period of disillusionment following the German-Russian Pact.

A.   No. I never believed in them and I wasn't disillusioned; to me, Stalin and Hitler were made of the same stuff.

Q.   In a real sense then you've stood quite outside the fashions in writing.

A.   Yes, as a matter of fact, I still am outside. I'm far from being an insider even today.

JORGE LUIS BORGES

Q. In your essay, "Valéry as Symbol," you wrote that Valéry was "the symbol of a man infinitely sensitive to every phenomenon and for whom every phenomenon is a stimulus capable of provoking an infinite series of thoughts. Of a man who transcends the differential traits of self and of whom we can say . . . he is nothing in himself." What would you say of Borges as symbol?

A. Well, I don't think I can say very much, because that symbol has been invented for me by other people; I mean, I don't think about myself, but many people seem to be thinking about me. So I am, in a sense, their handiwork, not my own. When I write a story or a poem I am simply concerned about that story or that poem, but I have no general philosophy; I have no message to convey. I am not really a thinker. I am a man who is very puzzled—and generally speaking, very pleasantly puzzled—by life and by things, especially by books. My father had a fine English library, and I've always been reading and rereading those books. I was introduced to America by one of the first novels I ever read in that library: *Huckleberry Finn*. And afterwards I read *Roughing It* and other books by Twain. And then, of course, I came to Edgar Allan Poe, and also—I wonder how you'll take this—to Longfellow. Since then, of course, I discovered other writers: Emerson, Melville, Hawthorne, Thoreau, and Henry James. The very first lectures I gave when I was obliged to do so,

Interview conducted by L. S. Dembo on November 21, 1969, in Madison, Wisconsin. The interview was held in English.

113

because, well, I had to earn a living somehow, and I was hounded out of a small job I held by the dictator—the first lectures I gave were on *literatura norteamericana clásica*, and then I spoke on those authors. I had not spoken in public before and of course I was full of fear and trembling, even as I am full of fear and trembling now when I speak here. I'm always afraid the words will stick in my throat.

Q.   They somehow don't.

A.   No, but in a sense, I am quite a veteran in everything concerned with stage fright. I get more and more afraid as the years go on.

Q.   It certainly isn't obvious.

A.   Well, it's obvious to me.

Q.   Anyway, let me continue with this question: One of your chief themes seems to be the ability of the mind to influence or recreate reality. I am thinking of the consummate recreation of the world in "Tlön, Uqbar, and Orbis Tertius." The philosophy of idealism prevalent on the imaginary planet Tlön seems to be vindicated when the actual world begins to transform itself in Tlön's image. Are you in fact a philosophic idealist or do you simply delight in paradoxes made possible by idealistic reasoning, or both?

A.   Well, my father—I seem to be referring to him all the time; I greatly loved him, and I think of him as living—my father was a professor of psychology, and I remember—I was quite a small boy—when he began trying to teach me something of the puzzles that constitute the idealistic philosophy. And I remember once he explained to me, or he tried to explain to me, with a chessboard, the paradoxes of Xeno, Achilles and the Tortoise, and so on. I also remember that he held an orange in his hand and asked me, "Would you think of the taste of the orange as belonging to it?" And I said, "Well, I hardly know that. I suppose I'd have to taste the orange. I don't think the orange is tasting itself all the time." He replied, "That's quite a good answer," and then he went on to the color of the orange and asked, "Well, if you close your eyes, and if I put out the light, what color is the orange?" He didn't say a word about Berkeley or

Hume, but he was really teaching me the philosophy of idealism, although, of course, he never used those words, because he thought they might scare me away. But he was teaching me a good many things, and he taught them as if they were of no importance at all. He was teaching me philosophy and psychology—that was his province—and he used William James as his textbook. He was teaching me all those things, and yet not allowing me to suspect that he was teaching me something.

Q. But you would say that you more or less were brought up on idealism?

A. Yes, and now when people tell me that they're down-to-earth and they tell me that I should be down-to-earth and think of reality, I wonder why a dream or an idea should be less real than this table for example, or why Macbeth should be less real than today's newspaper. I cannot quite understand this. I suppose if I had to define myself, I would define myself as an idealist, philosophically speaking. But I'm not sure I have to define myself. I'd rather go on wondering and puzzling about things, for I find that very enjoyable.

Q. That reminds me of the image of the labyrinth that recurs throughout your work.

A. Yes, it keeps cropping up all the time. It's the most obvious symbol of feeling puzzled and baffled, isn't it? It came to me through an engraving when I was a boy, an engraving of the seven wonders of the world, and there was one of the labyrinth. It was a circular building, and there were some palm trees near. Anyway, I thought that if I looked into it, if I peered into it very closely, perhaps I might make out the minotaur at the center. Somehow I was rather frightened of that engraving, and so when my mother said, "Since you like the book, you can keep it in your room," I answered, "No, no, it better stay in the library," because I was afraid of the minotaur coming out. Of course, I never told her the reason. Children are very shy. You don't say those things when you are really afraid of something happening. It really was an uncanny picture.

There was also an English dictionary, with a picture of the sphinx. Then I would play with my terrors; I would say to myself, now I will look up the word "six" and see that very tiny little illustration, and then I opened the book and closed it at once.

Q.   Has the minotaur ever come out of the labyrinth?

A.   Well, I have written two sonnets; in the first, a man is supposed to be making his way through the dusty and stony corridors, and he hears a distant bellowing in the night. And then he makes out footprints in the sand and he knows that they belong to the minotaur, that the minotaur is after him, and, in a sense, he, too, is after the minotaur. The minotaur, of course, wants to devour him, and since his only aim in life is to go on wandering and wandering, he also longs for the moment. In the second sonnet, I had a still more gruesome idea—the idea that there was no minotaur—that the man would go on endlessly wandering. That may have been suggested by a phrase in one of Chesterton's Father Brown books. Chesterton said, "What a man is really afraid of is a maze without a center." I suppose he was thinking of a godless universe, but I was thinking of the labyrinth without a minotaur. I mean, if anything is terrible, it is terrible because it is meaningless.

Q.   Yes, that's what I was driving at . . . .

A.   . . . Because the minotaur justifies the labyrinth; at least one thinks of it as being the right kind of inhabitant for that weird kind of building.

Q.   If the minotaur is in the labyrinth, the labyrinth makes sense.

A.   Yes, if there's no minotaur, then the whole thing's incredible. You have a monstrous building built round a monster, and that in a sense is logical. But if there is no monster, then the whole thing is senseless, and that would be the case for the universe, for all we know.

Q.   Doesn't Thomas Hardy express a similar idea in one of his poems—I think it's called "Hap"—in which he says that if he knew that the universe were malevolent, he could resign himself, but he knows that it's haphazard, and that is the real cause of his despair?

A.   I admire Hardy's poems but I haven't come across that one. You see, I lost my sight in 1955 and, of course, I had to fall back on other readers and young minds—young eyes and young memories—and so I depend on things already read. But my consolation lies in the fact that my memory's rather poor, so when I think I'm remembering something, I'm surely distorting it and perhaps inventing something new.

Q.   Perhaps that's what it means to be an artist.

A.   Yes, well, if I could verify every one of my memories, I should be less fanciful than I am or less inventive.

Q.   Well, you're apt to turn into Funes, the Immemorious.

A.   No, in the case of Funes I think of a man being killed by his memory and of a man being unable to think, since he can possess no general ideas; that is, in order to think, you must forget the small individual differences between things. Of course, Funes couldn't do that. But that story came to me as a kind of metaphor for sleeplessness, because I suffered greatly from insomnia.

Q.   Yes, you speak about the "terrible lucidity of insomnia."

A.   The terrible lucidity of insomnia. And there is a common word in Argentine Spanish for "awaken": recordarse, to remember oneself. When you're sleeping, you can't remember yourself—in fact, you're nobody, although you may be anybody in a dream. Then suddenly you wake up and "remember yourself"; you say, "I am so-and-so; I'm staying in such-and-such a place; I'm living in such-and-such a year." But recordarse is used as a common word and I don't think anybody has worked out all its implications.

Q.   Getting back to the labyrinth, it seemed to me that this image was not only generally appropriate to your work but represented the central paradox in it; that "the rich symmetries" of the mind, and of history, and of the world, end only in confusion or mystery.

A.   But I really enjoy that mystery. I not only feel the terror of it; I not only feel now and then the anguish, but also, well, the kind of pleasure you get, let's say, from a chess puzzle or from a good detective novel.

Q. In other words, you don't feel "*angst*"?

A. No, I don't. Or if I feel it, I feel it now and then, but I don't try to cherish it nor do I feel especially proud of it. It comes on me, let's say, as a headache or toothache might come, and I do my best to discourage it.

Q. I notice that from time to time the narrator of a story will identify himself as Borges, but, as the parable "Borges and I" seems to illustrate, Borges is more than one man. Are the characters of the *ficciones* sometimes Borges' nightmares or dreams or are they in fact the works of a detached creator intellectually interested in their dilemmas?

A. Sometimes I have been influenced by dreams. But only twice have I written down actual dreams. One was in the sketch called "Episode of the Enemy"; and the other dream I had I gave the Norse name of *Ragnarök*, "The Twilight of the Gods." And those two dreams were written much as they occurred. I worked in a few details to make them more credible. In other cases I may have been influenced by dreams without being quite aware of it.

Q. I meant dreams in the broader sense of the word.

A. Well, I don't think of literature and dreams as being very different. Of course, life has been compared to a dream many times over. But I think that in the case where you're imagining a story, you are actually dreaming it; at the same time you're dreaming it in a rather self-conscious way. I mean, you're dreaming and you're trying to direct the dream, to give it an end. Now, it is quite a common experience of mine—I suppose it has happened to you also—to dream and to know that I am dreaming. And also this has happened only during the last few years of my life: to begin dreaming before I begin to go to sleep. I know, for example, that I am in bed; I know where I am, and that somebody has come into the room, that somebody belongs to a dream; and then I know that very soon I will fall fast asleep. That's a sign that sleep's coming on. I asked one of my nephews and he told me that he had the same feeling. Sometimes he had dreams not only the moment before waking up but before going to sleep.

When one dreams before going to sleep, one knows that one shouldn't worry about insomnia because in two or three minutes one will be fast asleep, and then one will be dreaming in a more intricate way, with different characters, different people speaking, and so on.

Q.   Would you say that your characters represent a part of you?

A.   Yes, they do—all of them. But I have a trick of my characters poking fun at me. I am also contemptible in my stories. Many of the characters are fools and they are always playing tricks on me and treating me badly. Actually, I often play a very poor part in my stories.

Q.   Well, as intellectually impressive as they are, all the characters seem to have some sort of weakness: Averroes, for instance. He can never determine what Aristotle meant by "tragedy" and "comedy" because he has never seen the theater, and he's limited by the concepts of Islam.

A.   Yes, in that story I write of a very intelligent man, as I imagine Averroes to have been, and yet a man who cannot possibly know what tragedy and comedy stood for, since he had never seen a tragedy or a comedy being acted. He couldn't possibly guess at that whole thing. If the story is pathetic, it is pathetic because a very intelligent man commits a very elementary blunder. That's the whole point to the story.

Q.   Would you call it a blunder or is it a necessary fallacy in his thinking? No matter what he could do, he was still limited by his environment and his experience.

A.   I also think of him as being a symbol of everybody, because after all, what any single individual must know is very little as compared to the sum of all things. But in that story you are made to feel, at least if the story's successful, that the hero is very intelligent, and yet that he could by no means understand what tragedy meant, because, as I read in Renard's book on Averroes, when he speaks of comedy, he speaks of fate as panegyric, and when he speaks of tragedy, he speaks of it as satire, because he knew about those things but not about the stage.

Q.   Well, maybe the point is that he does represent everybody. Does he represent the author, too, in the same way?

A.   Yes, of course he does.

Q. The author himself is in a labyrinth, following casuistic reasoning, but bound by the limitations of the tunnels in that labyrinth. He can never really get out and find reality.

A. But of course. When I say everybody, I include myself. I should say so. Let me tell you an anecdote now, if you don't mind anecdotes. This happened in the province of Buenos Aires. There was an actor who went all over the country, playing the story of a brave gaucho hunted down by the police. When he came to a certain town he was told to change the name of the hero to that of the local, well, the local "Billy the Kid," in order that the people might better enjoy it. Then two or three days before the play was about to be shown, an old man came to see the actor. He was a very timid man; I've seen pictures of him. He had killed many men in his day; he had a grey mustache; he was a smallish man. He didn't know quite how to speak —he had spent all his life killing or being hunted by the police. Then he said, "I heard that somebody will appear on the stage and will say that he's me. But I want to warn you beforehand that you will deceive nobody, because I have lived in this town and everybody knows who I am." The actor tried to explain to him the whole art of stage-craft, but how could this poor old gaucho understand that? Finally, he said, "Well, maybe you're right. You're a learned man, and I'm very ignorant. I spent all my life being hunted by the police and fighting them; but I want to warn you that even though I am an old man, I can still take care of myself, and if anybody appears on the stage and says he's me, then I will come on the stage and fight him." And so the play couldn't be acted.

Q. So for all his intellect, Averroes suffered from the same problem an illiterate gaucho did. But let me ask you something on a different subject. In an essay on Coleridge you examined the idea that all literary works are one work and that all writers are one impersonal writer.

A. Yes, I got that idea from Emerson, who said they were the work of one single all-knowing or all-thinking "gentleman." The word "gentleman" is beautiful there. Because if he had written "man" it would have meant very little, but the idea of a gentleman writing, well, let's say, all Shakespeare's tragedies for him . . . .

Q. Well, the word probably speaks for Emerson's own gentility.

A.   Yes, but I don't want to blame gentility. I think it should be encouraged. At least I try to be a gentleman, though I never quite succeed in that ambition.

Q.   In any case, what would you say is the contribution of *Ficciones* to this universal work? Is it part of traditional literature?

A.   Oh, I think it's made of half-forgotten memories. I wonder if there is a single original line in the book. I suppose a source can be found for every line I've written, or perhaps that's what we call inventing—mixing up memories. I don't think we're capable of creation in the way that God created the world.

SARA LIDMAN

Q. I'd like to talk a little about *The Rain Bird,* the first of your novels to be translated into English. It's evident that this is a novel about human isolation, the failure of people to communicate with one another, to understand one another, even though they inhabit a small village or are related.

A. As far as I'm concerned that novel was written during the last century.

Q. What?

A. I knew nothing about society at the time I wrote it. It all occurs within the minds of people. There's no conception of society.

Q. But certainly the novel is dealing with a universal problem. People have secrets; people have feelings; but they can never express them. Communication has become impossible. They are always posing or they're obsessed or they're decreeing laws. They can never really come together in a community.

A. Those are only symptoms. They don't touch the causes.

Q. Well, does society produce the psychological condition or does the psychological condition produce the kind of society men live in? Couldn't you say the causes you speak of are in human nature?

A. I think that human nature can change. It can change and men can become more social. We'd all be much happier if we had a society that

Interview conducted by L. S. Dembo on May 4, 1969, in Stockholm. The interview was held in English.

considered people as part of a group rather than as isolated, competing individuals.

Q. I can see why you reject *The Rain Bird* although I still can't accept your reasons. The novel is hopelessly pessimistic. There's nothing that can save these farmers you depict, for their problems lie within themselves. Take the character with which the novel opens, Egron Stahl, a religious fanatic who in spite of himself possesses tender feelings for his daughter that he cannot express without blundering. Is there any kind of society in which a man like this could be saved?

A. He would be saved in a society that was truly communal—where everyone worked together and didn't indulge in self-flagellation all the time.

Q. But can even an ideal society eliminate the individual's desire to excel or get attention or compete? Can it eliminate human egoism?

A. Not in one generation but eventually. In a truly equalitarian society people could develop their personalities in harmony with others.

Q. You seem to be saying that life is wholly rational.

A. I don't believe it is irrational.

Q. And yet you once revealed a deep insight into human perversity.

A. When I wrote *The Rain Bird* I was partly under the influence of the Swedish literary climate of the late forties. But, if I remember right, I had also been reading a good deal of Kierkegaard at the time. Really, I was so very confused then. And, of course, though my own childhood wasn't at all like Linda's [the main character in *The Rain Bird*], I was still subjected to that religion of ours, Lutheranism. I was a pious child, but I thought I had broken away from the religion; that is, I thought so until I began writing the novel and saw that I retained its negative attitude toward man.

Q. I still wonder whether the harsh religious doctrine is a cause of the psychological disturbances of the characters or a symptom of them. Or maybe the climate and the geography are responsible.

A. Anyway, Linda lived in a rigid society that gave her no means for expressing herself. She's perverse and full of faults, but she had no opportunities, either.

A.   Yes, and also his belief in superhuman or absolute forces with which man must communicate—like the Absurd. But my real complaint is that Camus is so concerned with the metaphysical question, he makes the question of colonization seem irrelevant—just a fact that's given and not worth mentioning, like the weather. The truth is that colonization is such hell, it is blasphemy to tell Meursault's story in such a setting.

Q.   Your rejection of Camus and *The Stranger* sounds like your rejection of the author of *The Rain Bird.*

A.   She, also, did not know where the real problems were to be found.

Q.   But at least she had a "style," as did Camus.

A.   At least she worked at having one.

Q.   Do you intend to do any more fiction or will you continue to write reportorial studies of various social conditions?

A.   Well, you know I've written a book about coal miners, or rather I edited their descriptions. There were moments, when I was doing this, that I felt . . . jealous, completely put aside. I felt that I wanted to add something but that I wasn't allowed to. But as to fiction, yes, I think that now and then I'll write stories if I have time, but my imagination really can't compete with today's reality. Why make up stories when life is so full of forceful and powerful events? It seems unnecessary. Anyway, I think the question is academic. The true problem, for me, is finding the means of presenting social reality—the solutions to the problems I see—in the most effective way. Whether that is done by fiction or reporting is not important.

Q.   Then actually you see no distinction between literature and journalism.

A.   An article that gives some information of the world, that's written in strong language, that's full of vitality, that, to me, is literature. We have today in Sweden a writer called Jan Myrdal, the son of the famous economist, who really does much to mold public opinion and influence other writers as well. He has written novels but they aren't so important as his articles, which come out every Sunday in the newspapers. Practically the whole population hangs on that article—it's the weekend treat. Well, these articles, as far as I'm concerned, make Myrdal a great writer. True, it's politics—but it's what I crave, what I need, what I enjoy.

There are others, of course, who write about politics but they're dull; they use flat language. And it's sad—it's really not even politics; it's nothing. It has no art.

Q.   Tell me, how do you view the literary situation in general in Sweden today? Are writers becoming more and more leftist or turning more and more to journalism?

A.   Well, the Swedish writers' union is said to have 610 members and that's quite a lot for so small a country. Their attitudes vary, of course. In fact, there is a term of abuse that is used against people like me. The English translation would be "left-screwed," twisted left. It's very abusive in Swedish.

Q.   It's not harmless in English, either. But seriously I sense the whole political climate in Sweden to be leftist. The protest against the war in Vietnam . . . it really can't be called leftist any more in the United States. . . .

A.   A lot of the leftist feeling in Sweden is superficial or limited to certain groups. There are many things wrong with this country. When I think of the condition of the workers, for example, their constant harassment in the factories, the inevitable decline in wages after forty. After fifty, you are gone, you are nothing if you're a worker in Sweden. And there's also the Swedish investments in South Africa, supporting the apartheid system. But I think the Swedes are fantastic in convincing themselves and the world that they're living in paradise. Some of them actually are, I suppose, but not the workers. I've learned some bitter truths.

Q.   I wonder what you'd think of the United States.

A.   (laughing) I'd almost be afraid to go.

PER OLOF SUNDMAN

Q. I'd like to begin by talking about your views on style. Your novels, of course, are well known for their concern with details and externals to the exclusion of character psychology or introspection. But this technique seems to be part of a general philosophy: the impossibility of discovering what lies beneath a fellow human being's exterior, as you once wrote. Would you consider yourself to be not only a realist, but a behaviorist as well? That is, do you believe at all in a psychological life that is not directly related to the material world or composed of responses to it? I have in mind the apparent inability of your characters to express emotion over anything except their immediate rational concerns and encounters with other people.

A. Well, I studied Freud when I was very young; then I came upon Watson and found he was like a breath of fresh air. I took it in whole at first, but since then I've changed my mind. But insofar as I have any psychological theory or view of the human psyche, I would be a behaviorist rather than anything else—a modern one, though.

Q. What do you mean by a modern one?

A. It means that I'm critical of certain oversimplifications that Watson was guilty of. Actually, I've also been influenced by the reflexologists, Pavlov and so on. But remember I'm not a psychologist; I'm an author and a "moralist." That is, the behaviorists scrutinize and describe human behavior, but I draw moral conclusions from it. I'm not satisfied with mere description; I judge—though with great caution.

Interview conducted by L. S. Dembo on May 8, 1969, in Stockholm. The interview was held in Swedish and English, with Lars Bäckstrom interpreting.

Q.   Yes, that is exactly what I wanted to ask. The passion of many of your characters for details, mathematical accuracy, and organization seems to make them half admirable and half absurd, admirable for their powers of reasoning, but absurd for their moral insensitivity. Could you elaborate on your moral position?

A.   I have an old program or thesis, though in a way I don't like the word "program." It says that people are generally rash at interpreting and judging other people. I have a weakness for those people who talk and judge little. But this program might be described as being one of humanist tolerance. I can give you an example from real life. I lived for fourteen years in a village in northern Sweden, in Jämtland. I had a neighbor called Jöns Andersa. I told him that he could mow the field around my house, because I had no use for it, and that he could do so free of charge. But he never did it; instead he went to a swampy part of the woods and cut down a certain grass that grows on wet ground— sedge, I think it's called. And I discussed with my neighbors why Andersa was acting so foolishly, since it would have been much easier to have taken the grass from my fields. And they said simply that Andersa doesn't "feel right" if he doesn't mow grass in the swampy part of the forest. They didn't go any farther than stating this, and they didn't try to pass moral judgment on him. They just accepted his behavior.

Q.   Does this kind of acceptance involve the idea that a man can never understand any other man? I think you wrote as much in your "Notes on a Technique." The moral is that when people do attempt to judge others in terms of their external actions, they often act badly, wrongly, or insensitively to the people with whom they're dealing, and therefore actually show a lack of true human compassion themselves. I had in mind Olle Stensson in the novel *Two Days, Two Nights*. Here is a man who seems to be the completely rational individual, describing in detail everything that happens around him, describing in detail the characteristics of Karl Olofsson. Yet Stensson reveals himself to be insensitive, essentially irrational, and wholly unable to understand the human situation in which he finds himself. He actually, it seems to me, is a cruel man too.

A.   It's sometimes stated that I write a kind of objective prose. It's really a fictional subjectivism. In this case, in *Two Days, Two Nights*, Stensson tells the story of what he has been through, and he tells it the way people usually tell about reality: he distorts, he adjusts. If you read the book carefully, you'll find that he often contradicts himself.

He hints at having had a relationship with Karl Olofsson's wife—I would guess that he is lying or at least exaggerating. And possibly it's typical of my relation to my characters that I don't really know myself whether Stensson is lying or not. We talked about the wealth of detail in my books and I think one can say that I follow the old rule that if you want to make a false or incredible story credible, you should have a lot of seemingly irrelevant detail to make it convincing.

When I lived up in Jämtland I had a sort of hotel and I remember a woman, a guest, who told a perfectly fantastic story about her bags that had got lost—wholly incredible. I have forgotten it right now, but I remember that at the time I completely believed her because she talked in such an exact manner about the changes of the weather, about time, about the way the bus driver was dressed, and how people looked whom she had met, and details made the story credible.

Q.   One of the descriptions in *Two Days, Two Nights* is very interesting. Stensson recalls "making a pass" at Maria, Olofsson's wife, and he describes her reaction in completely impersonal terms. He says that when he tried to kiss her, she raised her leg automatically: "I have read somewhere that this is a typical female reaction, and I have noticed it many times before."

A.   I was in a press conference when one of my novels had been translated into Danish and I was approached by a slightly intoxicated literary critic who told me that that description is the best piece of pornography he's ever seen.

Q.   You're not approving of Stensson, are you? But to go a step farther, while you take a moral position against the strictly behavioristic approach to experience, I think that in many ways you are also captivated by it. For example, in the short story "The Negotiators," the narrator is only partly absurd in his passion for the details. It seems to me that you are portraying him sympathetically, too, insofar as you yourself enjoy the descriptions, the manipulations, the calculations that preoccupy him.

A.   I personally love details. I am an observer. I read Sherlock Holmes when I was a young boy and the impressions were deep. But in this short story, "The Negotiators," the details play a different part from the one they play in most of my work. To a very large extent, it's a purely autobiographical story. I've been through almost everything in it exactly as it's said. There I was sitting in the small village of Strömsund, negotiating with the representative of the labor union of the municipal workers, and there we were, for hours, digging into those endless details to get a settlement for the salary of a certain charwoman. Meanwhile, the first Russian satellite was circling around the earth and there was this enormous contrast between our sort of micro-work and this huge enterprise that was also built on a wealth of details. I would say that the story brings out, finally, that this kind of negotiating micro-politics, that we were dealing with, is something much more human, much more important, than the space project. It is true that Stensson, like me, has an obsession with detail, but that's the only similarity between us. Stensson represents a kind of human being that I consider to be evil.

Q. Whereas the negotiator is essentially a humane man?

A. Yes, the negotiators are humane people. And it stands to reason that social problems should, if possible, be solved by such discussion.

Q. Is "The Negotiators" meant, in any way, to be taken as a description of the Swedish mentality in general, with its passion for organization, detail, and collective effort?

A. I did not have this intention. It's up to the reader to decide about that. I guess it's a distinct possibility that I was fascinated by the story because it is typically Swedish. But it's really a story about meaningful work.

Q. I'd like to talk a little bit about the novel *The Expedition.* I was very much surprised to see that the advertisement for the English edition speaks of the essential Western virtues of pragmatism, solidarity, and the ability to organize. The truth seems to be that the expedition operates under extremely tyrannical conditions and hardly exemplifies solidarity. Sir John, the leader, feels an abstract European solidarity with Kanyi Pasha, whom he is on his way to rescue, but no true feeling for his own staff. He attempts to make them merely extensions of his own will. The staff has no real sense of participation, but is merely instrumental, and each man is completely isolated. Therefore I was most perplexed to see that any of your critics could identify you—or themselves, for that matter—with Sir John, or even with Lieutenant Laronne, who is himself an instrument, and merely an instrument, of Sir John's power. This seems to me in many ways to be a novel with political overtones or a direct political statement about Western colonialism.

A. I think that there is something in both points of view, but the weight is rather on yours. I, myself, did not write the text on the dust jacket;

the English publishers have. That means that they probably do identify themselves with Sir John.

Q. But it seems clear that Sir John's "virtues" have led to exploitation, cruelty, and misery, not just among his European staff, but among all the men he employs. The novel, I think, comes into focus when, without any due process, Sir John has two of the native deserters executed and whimsically pardons the others. Isn't this the essence of Western injustice in the colonial world?

A. Yes, of course. And there's another scene, one that comes very near the one you pointed out: Sir John has a long speech about the time it will take to kill all the elephants that are in existence, and the amount and price of the ivory that could be recovered. This is also a clue to his character. It's been eight or nine years since I wrote the novel, but I recently talked about it at one of our folk high schools. When I reread this passage it gave me a sort of "literary experience." But, as a matter of fact, I've taken it directly from Stanley's *The Congo,* as I did the execution episode from another of his works. Still, I can't deny that these episodes are representative of British society at this time.

Q. I am very much interested in the role of Jaffar Topan, Sir John's native bookkeeper. Were you implying that he is the Eastern man, at peace with himself and his world, in contrast to the Westerners around him?

A. One might say that the character of Jaffar grew as I worked on the novel. I reread Stanley's book, *In Darkest Africa,* and I noticed that he provides detailed accounts of the Europeans that take part in the expedition, and then he says that there were, say, eight Europeans, eight hundred men from Zanzibar, six hundred from the Sudan. I noticed, then, that there was always at Stanley's side a European never mentioned by name or described, but who was essential. He was actually Stanley's valet, William Hoffman. But he was no "gentleman," so there was no need to introduce him to the reader. Most of the Europeans that took part in this expedition—and survived—wrote books about it, but Hoffman didn't. It occurred to me that I could tell the story from the point of view of this valet, but he turned out to be such a bad narrator that the novel would have been unreadable with him as spokesman. Then I created a non-European narrator, Jaffar, but even he, I discovered, couldn't bear the full weight of the story and I had to create an additional one, Lieutenant Laronne.

Q.   My question was a little more philosophic. I know that your essay "Notes on a Technique" mentions what you've just said. But one cannot help contrasting Jaffar as a man, not just as a narrator, with the Westerners among whom he lived. I couldn't quite make any definite judgment of him as I read the novel. He seemed to me to be a sympathetic character, a gentle man, who has a typically Eastern sense of tranquility; he certainly is less aggressive and less cruel than the Westerners.

A.   I agree, but since Jaffar represents the author, I would have difficulty in stating this directly—although I am an active person, while Jaffar is, at least in part, a man who's resigned himself to a certain passivity.

Q.   I thought there was a special significance in the fact that the novel ends in the middle of the jungle, the expedition being under dire threat of destruction. Am I wrong in finding a philosophical and political symbolism in this scene? A political meaning, of course, is that the scene is a warning about what will happen to Western society, and is perhaps relevant to our own times. There also seems to be the philosophic implication that destruction is the outcome of man's power to organize, which is really built upon air.

A.   I worked on this novel for three years, from 1960 to 1962, and I wrote three versions of it; in the second version I had the novel end earlier than in the first, and in the third even earlier. In the first version I had the expedition reach the savannahs—to get a certain feeling of freedom and a sense of escape from the jungle. But I found that if the end of the novel would represent what I wanted it to, it would have to finish earlier, so in the third version it ended right in the middle of the jungle. As for your philosophical interpretation of the novel, the failure of, or the futility of, the human organization in general, one might say that that is also what my book on the polar expedition of S. A. Andrée (*The Flight of the Eagle*) is about. Well, I think that Andrée was both a good and a bad planner, and one can say the novel is about the ineffectiveness of human organization. There is a really marvelous ending to the Stanley account and sometime I hope to write a sequel to *The Expedition*. When Stanley met Emin Pasha, the man he intended to rescue, he found him in a sparkling white tropical suit, surrounded by beautiful women, and at the moment very happy with his life.

Q.   Well, really, an ending like that would make the novel even more ironic.

A.   Yes. It turned out that Emin Pasha was not interested in being saved by Stanley. So Stanley had great trouble in persuading him to return to civilization. Only after a great deal of quarreling between them did they finally depart for Dar es Salaam with the Pasha's whole entourage.

Q.   The Pasha was hardly the same kind of man as Stanley. But what I was going to ask is, would it have really mattered to Sir John at all whether he saved Kanyi Pasha, no matter what Kanyi Pasha's attitude was? It seems to me to be completely irrelevant to him. All that was relevant was the expedition itself and the organization of it.

A.   That's true about Stanley, too—that the expedition somehow turned into an end in itself. But here's the end of the story. The historical Emin Pasha was originally a German Jewish doctor who had gone into Turkish employment. In time he became the governor of the Tanganyika district; it was really the southern part of the Sudan and belonged to the Turko-Egyptian sphere of influence. In any case, the return party headed for German East Africa. Messengers had been sent down and the Germans prepared an enormous feast to greet the Pasha. During the feast he got drunk, somehow fell from the second story of the house, and fractured his skull. But in my novel he's going to die.

Q.   That's quite an ending. But aside from the fact that it makes a good story, doesn't it go back to the original point, that all Stanley's labor was for nothing?

A.   Yes, it certainly does.

Q.   To change the subject, I was wondering what you feel is your position in contemporary literature in general. For example, are you in sympathy with the French *nouveau roman* writers? Or have you any special opinion of the work of Camus?

A.   That is a question I've been asked many times. Early in my career I was compared with the *nouveau roman* writers, particularly with Robbe-Grillet. That was before I read them and actually I haven't been able to read them carefully after that.

Q.   Have you read any contemporary novelists that you feel have influenced you? Or let me put the question this way, instead of talking in terms of influence: Have you read any contemporary novelists that you enjoy?

A.   I really can't mention any modern writers. I guess I'd have to go back to the Finnish classic Alexis Kivy and to the old Icelandic narrators. It's also relevant to mention the reading of my youth, Conan Doyle and Jack London.

Q.   Jack London, of course, is one of the early realists. Have you read any other American novelists, Theodore Dreiser, for example, or Stephen Crane?

A.   Yes, I have read other American novelists, and in Germany, when they translated me, they mentioned especially Hemingway, and I do admire him. But I would say that my general attitude to what I read is pretty diffuse, pretty vague. Actually, I must confess that very few literary works absorb me. And, for better or worse, as a member of Parliament I read voluminously in public documents and reports. Memory being the fragile thing it is, I often forget what I've read. This is also partly true about my own books; I may have difficulty in remembering what they really are about. The senior Swedish poet and novelist, Artur Lundkvist, said that the most important material a writer has is books by other people, but I think it's really human beings.

Q.   Do you envision your audience as being chiefly Swedish or European in general?

A.   As opposed to many other writers I'm always very conscious of an audience, and I'm very conscious of wanting to have as many readers as possible. In the beginning I was aware only of a Swedish audience, but once they began to translate me, my idea of my audience changed. I know now that I may be writing for people who have a different frame of reference, a different environment, from a Swedish audience, and this has affected my writing and my choice of subjects.

Q.   Yes, well, speaking of choice of subjects, I understand that Alfred Nobel is the subject of your current work. I wonder if you would elaborate on that a little.

A.   To me, as to all Swedes, Nobel was a remarkable man. He invented dynamite, he earned a great deal of money. When I was working on my novel about Andrée's balloon trip, I came across Nobel again. And first, it turned out that Nobel was the one who really financed, for the most part, Andrée's insane expedition. Then I discovered that he was really a Baroque character, a kind of Renaissance man, a man who was so ugly that he hardly ever permitted his photograph to be taken, full of bizarre ideas. I also learned that he really did not want to become a great capitalist, but that he wanted to be a writer. His name, incidentally, has nothing to do with the word "noble"; it comes from the village from which his forbears came, called Östra Nöbbelöv, in Scania, in southern Sweden. It's a homespun name to Swedes.

Q.   Will he be cast in the same mold as Sir John or will he be a sympathetic character?

A.   Immensely more sympathetic than Sir John and an immensely more reflective or meditative character.

Q.   When do you expect to complete the work?

A.   It's very extensive and will take many years. It's the biggest task I've undertaken. Right now I'm still reading books about Nobel, and after I've done that I'll let him rest for some time, and then I'll begin asking myself how much I remember of what I had read, and whatever I remember I will decide to treat as essential and base my book on it, perhaps while returning to some other books. Unless my work in the Parliament takes too much time, I hope to publish several other books before I'm through with the novel about Nobel. I would like to do a collection of short stories about love. After the great wave of pornography in Sweden, it's now possible to write about love.

Q.   You mean it would be a collection about women lifting their legs?

A.   Yes, indeed. But seriously, I think the Swedish public is now sated with pornography. They no longer find it remarkable to read a description of lovemaking, so they can relax and read the *whole* story.

POETS

JAMES MERRILL

_Q._ I'd like to start by asking you about your poetry course at the University of Wisconsin this semester. What did you teach in it?

A. It was described as a poetry workshop, though there was little actual writing done. The eight weeks were mostly spent reading things I liked, then towards the end we took up some student work. We spent half of the time at least on Elizabeth Bishop's last book, _Questions of Travel._ And then we read some of Berryman's _Dream Songs_ and some Lowell, and we had a glorious day on _The Rubáiyát._

_Q._ What do you think _The Rubáiyát_ offers in teaching?

A. An anonymous poem, really, where the language, the content, is drawn from a whole universe much older, say, than Greek mythology, a kind of Old Testament, as old as language itself. The wine, the bread, the wilderness, the rose—all that of course translates beautifully into just what a Victorian audience wanted to hear: those Christian words, I mean. The vocabulary of the poem works both ways, for piety and paganism alike, which perhaps explains why Fitzgerald's translation sank so quickly into everybody's consciousness. People know lines from it who have never heard of Fitzgerald or Omar—or of poetry, for that matter.

_Q._ This seems to be something of a comment about the so-called "confessional" poetry of late. Do you have any feelings about it?

A. It seems to me that confessional poetry, to all but the very naive

---

Interview conducted by Donald Sheehan on May 23, 1967, in Madison, Wisconsin.

reader or writer, is a literary convention like any other, the problem being to make it *sound* as if it were true. One can, of course, tell the truth, but I shouldn't think that would be necessary to give the illusion of a True Confession.

Q. So the division between confessional and objective poetry is, you would say, artificial in the sense that both modes are conventions.

A. Precisely. Now and then what I wrote has been true. Often, though, it's been quite made up or taken from somebody else's life and put in as if it were mine.

Q. Critics today are asserting that in poetry the period of experimentation is over and that a period of consolidation has set in, the Second World War being the Great Divide. Does this have any meaning to you, is this true?

A. I've always been suspicious of the word experimentation. It partakes too much of staircase wit. People who talk about experimentation sound as if they thought poets set out deliberately to experiment, when in fact they haven't: they've simply recognized afterwards the newness of what they've done. William Carlos Williams talks about breaking the back of the pentameter as if this had been the first step in a program. It's something I should think he'd have been likelier to recognize well after doing it—if he ever did do it. The pentameter has been a good friend to me; you'd think I'd have noticed a little thing like a broken back. As for consolidation, I'm not so sure. Anybody starting to write today has at least ten kinds of poem, each different from the other, on which to pattern his own.

Q. What kinds would you say?

A. There would be the confessional, if you will; or the personal nature lyric along the lines of Roethke; or the Chinese-sage manner, full of insects and ponies and small boats and liquor and place-names; or the kind of stammered-out neo-epigram of people like Creeley— to name only a few. And there are all sorts of schemes on the page to reproduce—the broken line, Williams' downward staircase, three paces to a step; the tight stanza; the heavy garlands of Perse; the "expressionist" calligrams of Pound or Olson. . . .

Q. Perhaps this is a false abstraction to keep pursuing, but the sort of poetry that, say, Eliot and Pound wrote, doesn't seem to be getting written today. At the same time, though, I can't imagine, without some of Pound at least, any poets writing as they do today. Do you think there exists an "influence" (if I can use that tricky word) of Eliot and Pound on poets today?

A.   Yes, if only as something to react against. Eliot and Pound, though, seem to be so terribly different in the long run. With Pound, in the *Cantos* at least, we find precious little unity except the contents of a single, very brilliant, and erratic mind. Whereas Eliot gives what may be only an illusion—I haven't read him for twenty years—of being infinitely in control of his material: so much so, that you have the sense of the whole civilization under glass. As, indeed, Eliot's poems are under glass for me. The temptation to reread them, though it's growing, is still fairly slight.

Q.   How about Wallace Stevens?

A.   Stevens seems much more of a poet, that is to say, a non-historian. There's a nice distinction in a poem of A. D. Hope's, where he says that he wanted to be a poet, the "eater of time," rather than that "anus of mind, the historian." I'm an enemy of history, by the way— absurd thing to say, I'll be condemned to repeat it if I'm not careful. Repeat history, that is. Well, my position's open to analysis; I even have a poem about Father Time. However. Back to Stevens, I think he continues to persuade us of having had a private life, despite—or thanks to—all the bizarreness of his vocabulary and idiom.

Q.   I here think of the term used constantly, "voice." As a critical term, do you think it has meaning?

A.   I think it does. "Voice" is the democratic word for "tone." "Tone" always sounds snobbish, but without a sense of it how one flounders!

Q.   Is voice a function of metrics, would you say?

A.   I notice voice a good deal more in metrical poetry. The line lends itself to shifts of emphasis. If Frost had written free verse, I don't think we'd have heard as much of the voice in it.

Q.   I'd like to ask you about your own development. I notice in your four published volumes that you seemed to have gone from a rather strict symmetrical poem to a much looser, freer poem. Do you agree with this and if you do, I wonder what led you in this direction?

A.   I always relapse into the strict poem. I'd like to think I would continue to write a strict poem when I felt like it. But what you say is true. I remember—this might modify what I said about experiment— I remember, after *First Poems* was published, having in mind the kind of poem I wanted to write. I could picture it to myself only by seeing an unbroken page of blank verse, the density of the print trailing down the page; and long before any of these poems began to turn up in the little *Short Stories*, there was this picture I had of a certain look to the poem. And with these poems came various new conversational elements—the first earmark, perhaps, of blank verse.

Q.   This is related, I think, to another point. You're probably one of the few poets who has written completely successful novels, ones that can't be termed "poetic" in the usual sense of that word. What about the prose element in poetry, in your verse particularly?

A.   I've enjoyed reading novels more often—or more profoundly— than I've enjoyed reading poems. There seems to be no poet except perhaps Dante whose work has the extraordinary richness of Tolstoy or Proust; and there are very few poets whose work gives as much fun as James. Oh, there's always a give and take. For instance, though a lot of the sound of James is prose, can't one tell that he'd read Browning? You hear a voice talking in prose, often a very delightful voice which can say all kinds of odd things. For me, to get something of that into poetry was a pleasure and even perhaps an object.

Q.   That would seem to contradict what some reviewers have said about your poems, that they have become more personal, perhaps even autobiographical. If the point is, as you were saying, to get a voice in poetry, what would you say to the critics and reviewers who claim this voice to be autobiographical?

A.   To *sound* personal is the point—which is something I don't believe, by the way, that Pound and Eliot sound very often; rather, they have impersonal, oracular voices. But so does an Elizabethan lyric sound impersonal. I'm not making judgments.

Q.   What about Auden's remark, that if the poet raises his voice, he becomes phony or dishonest. Is that what you're saying?

A.   If it's raised in all earnestness, dishonesty usually follows.

Q.   You know many European languages and speak a number of

them, including modern Greek. Are you drawn to any of the modern
foreign literatures? If so, what ones do you like especially?

A.   I began caring more about French poetry than I did about English, no doubt because there was no question of completely understanding it. But, again, my feeling for it ends with Apollinaire and
Valéry. I find very few living French poets intelligible—my French
has withered on the vine.

Q.   I noticed you recently translated Eugenio Montale.

A.   My Italian is even worse than my French, but I liked his poems
very much and felt close to the feeling behind them.

Q.   What is the feeling behind Montale's poems that struck you
especially?

A.   The emotional refinement, gloomy and strongly curbed. It's surprisingly permeable by quite ordinary objects—ladles, hens, pianos,
half-read letters. To me he's *the* twentieth-century nature poet. Any
word can lead you from the kitchen garden into really inhuman
depths—if there are any of those left nowadays. The two natures were
always one, but it takes an extraordinary poet to make us feel that,
feel it in our spines.

Q.   You mentioned Elizabeth Bishop before. A number of other
poets today have singled her out. Would you say, in terms of form,
that she has provided valuable examples for poets, especially in your
own poetry?

A.   The unpretentiousness of her form is very appealing. But I don't
know if it's simply a matter of form. Rather, I like the way her whole
oeuvre is on the scale of a human life; there is no oracular amplification, she doesn't go about on stilts to make her vision wider. She
doesn't need that. She's wise and humane enough as it is. And this is
rather what I feel about Stevens. For all the philosophy that intrudes
in and between the lines, Stevens' poetry is a body of work that is
man-sized. Whereas I wouldn't say that of Pound; he tries, I think,
to write like a god. Stevens and Miss Bishop merely write like angels.

Q.   Do you think it might have something to do with wit and
humor? Reviewers have used the term "witty" to describe your poetry;
and Stevens' is surely filled with various sorts of jokes. Reed Whitte-

more once claimed that, in recent poetry, there was an unbridgeable split between light and serious verse. Do you agree?

A.   Hardly unbridgeable. Aren't we used by now to the light poem that has dark touches and the serious poem shot through with lighter ones? The Canadian George Johnston comes to mind as an example of the first. His material is all quite shallow and amusing indeed, but leaves a sense of something unspoken, something positively sinister. . . .

Q.   Can the joke control that sort of oracular voice of Eliot and Pound, tone it down, make it more human?

A.   That is my fond illusion.

Q.   Whittemore was referring in part, I think, to the *New Yorker* sort of exclusively light verse as created by Ogden Nash. John Updike's poems come to mind.

A.   Updike's are very light indeed. Ogden Nash may be taken more seriously by another generation. The prosody—if you can call it that —is really such a delight. To me, it's a very American form—that interminable line with the funny rhyme.

Q.   In two recent poems of yours, "The Thousand and Second Night" and "From the Cupola," you've written what's called a long poem. Do you feel any distinctions between the long and short poem in terms of style, structure, and form?

A.   The length of those poems is partly accidental. I never dreamed, when "The Thousand and Second Night" began to take shape, that it would be as long as it is. I couldn't foresee the structure of the poem. I was working on what seemed rather unrelated poems, then suddenly an afternoon of patchwork saw them all stitched together. What emerged as the final section had been written quite early in the process.

Q.   This account almost seems to have a musical metaphor under it. Would you say there's any relation between music and your poetry?

A.   There's to me a tremendous relation. Certainly I cared about music long before I cared about literature. When I was eleven years old, I began being taken to the opera in New York; and the sense of a feeling that could be expressed without any particular attention to words must have excited me very much. I daren't go into the effect

Mrs. Wix would have pounced upon, of the opera on my moral sense. All those passions—illnesses, ecstasies, deceptions—induced for the pure sake of having something to sing beautifully about. Whenever I reach an impasse, working on a poem, I try to imagine an analogy with musical form; it usually helps. For instance, in "The Thousand and Second Night" the last thing I had to write was the passage at the end of section three beginning "Love. Warmth." I had no idea how to write it; I thought I would do it in free verse and made all kinds of beginnings, before the six-line stanza finally evolved. But the moment for which I'm most grateful is in the third of those five stanzas, when it came to me to make the meter trochaic rather than iambic—a stroke I associated quite arbitrarily with that moment at the end of the Rondo of the "Waldstein" Sonata, where the tempo is suddenly doubled or halved (I'm not sure which), and it goes twice as fast. "An Urban Convalescence" is in the form of an Introduction and Allegro. In between comes a trill (on the word "cold"), an organ point (following "self-knowledge"), then the rhymes, the quatrains begin, in 4/4 time, as it were. Need I say how subjective this all is?

Q.   I'm reminded of a brief essay of Valéry's, "On Speaking Verse," in which he instructs the actor to approach the line from the state of music, understanding musical form first, then letting the words and the meaning come through. Does music take us back again to voice?

A.   It does, if we're poets. The next step, for me, was listening to French art songs: especially Maggie Teyte's records of Debussy, Fauré and Duparc, where, once more, though most of the words were intelligible, they made no great demands on the intelligence. It was only the extreme beauty of the musical line that was spellbinding. At first I hadn't known any German songs, but when I began to hear Schubert and Schumann the text would often as not have some independent merit. Unlike Albert Samain and Leconte de Lisle, Heine was intense and psychological. By then, a way of uttering a line to have it make real sense, real human sense, had come into my musical education.

These were all things I could have learned from my teachers. I remember a course at Amherst that Reuben Brower gave. I now see it was chiefly a course in tone, in putting meaning and the sound of meaning back into words. He made very clear connections; so that by the time we read some Frost poems, we could see certain relationships to E. M. Forster and Jane Austen, whom we'd read earlier.

Q. If, as you say, rhythm often has its own sense and meaning and energy, could it sometimes so shape the line or stanza (or even whole poem) that it dictates what words will work? Has this ever been your experience?

A. Oh absolutely. Words just aren't that meaningful in themselves. De la musique avant toute chose. The best writers can usually be recognized by their rhythms. An act of Chekhov has a movement unlike anything in the world.

Q. I think here of Frost's idea of "sentence sounds." Is this more or less relevant to what you're saying?

A. I think so. The point about music and song is that theirs is the sound of sheer feeling—as opposed to that of sense, of verbal sense. To combine the two is always worth dreaming about.

Q. I'd like to ask you about "From the Cupola." The poem uses Greek myth, but (perhaps to distinguish it from an Eliot poem) one couldn't say it was at all "propped up" by the Eros-Psyche story. What shifts and transformation were involved in making the myth relevant to the poem?

A. Again, this is all afterthought. In the poem there are, let's see, three stories going. There's the story of Eros and Psyche which is, if not known, at least knowable to any reader. Then there is the contemporary situation of a New England village Psyche and her two nasty sisters and of somebody writing love letters to her. And finally there is what I begin by describing as an unknowable situation, something I'm going to keep quiet about. But, in a way, the New England village situation is transparent enough to let us see the story of Eros and Psyche on one side of the glass and, perhaps, to guess at, to triangulate the third story, the untold one.

Q. Then it's the contemporary situation that unified the mythic and the unknowable situations?

A. If anything does. I suppose the two twentieth-century writers who have used myth most brilliantly are Joyce and Cocteau. Joyce teaches us to immerse the mythical elements in a well known setting; Cocteau teaches us to immerse them in a contemporary spoken idiom. Although I can't pretend I planned on doing this, what pleases me in the poem are precisely those two effects: a great deal of setting and a great deal of contemporary idiom.

Q. The (Diblos) Notebook also uses myth. Is the same thing involved?

A. Not really, because there's no myth underneath; that is, there's no structural use of myth in *The (Diblos) Notebook*. Rather, it is used as ornament; the central character's attitude towards myth is the issue, not myth itself.

Q. Does this apply to "From the Cupola"? The poem is perhaps the most difficult of yours to understand in that its experience (which may well be the speaker's attitude towards it) seems to be so elusive.

A. It is elusive. As I said, the poem begins with the statement that it's not going to be a confessional poem. To be honest, I don't understand the poem very well myself—at least not the first third. I've been helped, though, by the times I've read it aloud. I trust the way it *sounds* at any rate; though I find that I have to read sections of it very rapidly indeed, like that long speech of Alice's: there's next to no meaning in the speech, except for a few nuggets for a clever reader to unearth. She does ramble and that may be part of her terror. In this sense, her speech is a device out of theatre: a ranting scene that goes on for its own sake, in which every word doesn't count.

Q. I seem to hear vague echoes somewhere of Plato: the poet composing without understanding his poem, in a kind of inspired frenzy.

A. In a way, yes. I'm not sure about frenzy, though: "From the Cupola" was not composed in a frenzy. Yet certainly there wouldn't be as much pleasure in writing poems if one understood exactly what one had in one's heart and head. The process of writing discovers this—if we're lucky.

Q. Would you say that "From the Cupola" represents anything new in your career? Is a new idea involved in this poem, a new technique?

A. The newness would have to do with the narrative elements, I suspect. Without these to carry it forward, "From the Cupola" mightn't seem drastically different from those two sets of "variations" in *First Poems*.

Q. The speakers in a number of your recent poems seem to be concerned with the difficulties or joys of being a poet. Is this a new subject for you?

A.   It's one I've tried to resist. In principle, I'm quite against the persona of the poem talking about the splendors and miseries of writing; it seems to me far too many poets today make the act of writing one of their primary subjects. Obviously I'm following the crowd myself, but I've hoped as much as possible to sugar the pill by being a bit rueful and amusing about having to do so.

Q.   The fourth section of "The Thousand and Second Night"—the academic parody—is surely quite amusing about it.

A.   A friend of mine urged me to take that section out, saying it was hard enough to create an illusion, and that to shatter one would be disastrously perverse. I left it in, though, because, well, I wanted something to delay the final section. Also, the parody of the classroom was a structural equivalent, it occurred to me later, of the use of quotation, interspersed throughout the poem—the little snippets from Eliot, Yeats, Hofmannsthal, and so forth. It did in terms of structure what those did ornamentally. Once I thought of that, I had a sounder reason to leave it in.

Q.   You've used the words "ornament" and "decoration" a number of times. Would they possibly relate to what a number of readers have felt in your work: that the novels, plays, and poems project in toto a particular sort of social milieu? I'd define the term along the lines, say, of taste, intelligence, and manners rather than class or family. Am I right in saying that there is a more or less unified social world in your work?

A.   We all have our limits. I draw the line at politics or hippies. I'd rather present the world through, say, a character's intelligence or lack of it than through any sort of sociological prism. It's perhaps why I side with Stevens over Eliot. I don't care much about generalizing; it's unavoidable, to begin with. The point about manners is that—as we all know, whether we're writers or not—they keep the ball rolling. One could paraphrase Marianne Moore: using them with a perfect contempt for them, one discovers in them after all a place for the genuine. In writing a novel or poem of manners you provide a framework all the nicer for being more fallible, more hospitable to irony, self-expression, self-contradiction, than many a philosophical or sociological system. Manners for me are the touch of nature, an artifice in the very bloodstream. Someone who does not take them seriously is making a serious mistake. They are as vital as all appearances, and if

they deceive us they do so by mutual consent. It's hard to imagine a
work of literature that doesn't depend on manners, at least negatively.
One of the points of a poem like Ginsberg's "Howl" is that it uses
an impatience with manners very brilliantly; but if there had been
no touchstone to strike that flint upon, where would Ginsberg be?

And manners—whether good or bad—are entirely allied with
tone or voice in poetry. If the manners are inferior, the poem will
seem unreal or allegorical as in some of Stephen Crane's little poems.
Take the one in which the man is eating his heart and the stranger
comes up and asks if it's good. Those are bad manners for a stranger.
Consequently the poem ends shortly after it begins because they have
nothing more to say to each other. On the other hand, a poem like
George Herbert's "Love" goes on for three stanzas; in a situation fully
as "unreal" as Crane's, two characters are being ravishingly .polite
to one another. Manners aren't merely descriptions of social behavior. The real triumph of manners in Proust is the extreme courtesy
towards the reader, the voice explaining at once formally and inti-
mately. Though it can be heard, of course, as megalomania, there is
something wonderful in the reasonableness, the long-windedness of
that voice, in its desire to be understood, in its treatment of every
phenomenon (whether the way someone pronounces a word, or the
article of clothing worn, or the color of a flower) as having ultimate
importance. Proust says to us in effect, "I will not patronize you by
treating these delicate matters with less than total, patient, sparkling
seriousness."

Q. Reviewers have sometimes used the word "elegant" to describe
your poetry. How would you react to this term?

A. With a shrug.

Q. I'd like to ask you about *The Seraglio*. I'm tempted at times to
read Francis Tanning as something of a paradigm. That is, I see a
young man who struggles to see the world singly, but somehow seems
doomed to see it doubly; mirror and dreams figure prominently. Is
this young man a sort of Ur-character? And are his struggles some sort
of Ur-plot in your work?

A. He seems to me, with a few superficial differences, the kind
of young man one finds in nearly any first novel. As far as an Ur-
character goes: well, four or five years after I'd written the novel, I
came upon some books from my childhood. I reread one of them,

having no particular memory of ever reading it before, yet I must have, since I found—to my horror and amusement—that, by and large, its plot was that of *The Seraglio*. Both novels involved the effort to re-introduce an exiled mother into an atmosphere of ease and comfort; both scenes were dominated by an irascible grandfather-figure. Of course, the children's book was *Little Lord Fauntleroy*.

Q.   Again, one hesitates to use the word influence. To return to *The (Diblos) Notebook*, the novel has raised what is perhaps a side issue: how it actually was composed. Did it really grow out of a notebook?

A.   Yes. I had the story in mind several years before I found myself writing the book. During that time I had no idea how to write it, although I made a few conventional beginnings. Then, one summer, when I'd been traveling in Greece, unable to do any real work, I kept a journal. But whenever I tried to inject any of those impressions into my conventional narrative, they went dead on me. The notebook itself, though, still seemed comparatively full of life. It took a while to realize that this was a possible technique, and use it. It's a technique I might have discovered much earlier from, say, that edition of Keats' letters where the deletions are legible; and, of course, from letters one receives oneself: the eye instantly flies to the crossed-out word. It seems to promise so much more than the words left exposed.

Q.   You've written for the theatre as well, one of your plays—*The Immortal Husband*—receiving highest critical praise. Have you an opinion on the "verse drama" so many modern poets have attempted —Eliot, Yeats, Pound, even Wallace Stevens, as well as Ted Hughes and Robert Lowell more recently? What aesthetic problems does a poet face in writing plays?

A.   I loved the first act of *The Cocktail Party*—that unmistakable sound of Eliot, his line, hired out in the service of smalltalk. You couldn't imagine a suaver bartender. The poet writing plays faces the same problem that the playwright does. Borges has a piece on Aeschylus as the man who introduced a second actor onto the stage, thus allowing for an infinite dialogue. The problem from then on has been to decide on the dimensions of that dialogue for one's particular purpose. We spoke of structural rhythm a while back. One responds to that in plays more immediately than in poems. It's virtually one's entire first impression of any play by Beckett.

Q.   Have you found any older—that is, pre-twentieth-century—poetry
relevant to your work?

A.   Actually, I'd read little twentieth-century poetry until I'd been
writing for several years. My first efforts, sonnets of course, were written at fourteen when I knew only bits and pieces of Shakespeare,
Mrs. Browning, some pre-Raphaelite verse. My first twentieth-century
passion, two years later, was Elinor Wylie. I was a retarded child. No
reflection on her—I still think she's marvelous, far and away the most
magical rhyming we've ever had. There's a glaze of perfection to con-
tend with but I ate it up, it never put me off—not at least until I
went on to Yeats. Older poets, though. Pope, Keats, "Lycidas." I was
out of college by the time I read Herbert. Much later, though I'd
never looked at more than a page of *Don Juan* and knew about Byron
only through Auden's "Letter" to him, I knew that he had been an
influence on "The Thousand and Second Night." When I checked,
I found very much the tone I'd been trying for: that air of irrelevance,
of running on at the risk of never becoming terribly significant. I see
no point, often, in the kind of poem that makes every single touch,
every syllable, count. It can be a joy to write, but not always to read.
You can't forego the whole level of entertainment in art. Think of
Stevens' phrase: "The essential gaudiness of poetry." The inessential
suddenly felt as essence.

Q.   This attitude is fairly directly counter, isn't it, to the one underlying so much earlier twentieth-century poetry: the desire for concen-
tration and concision in poems.

A.   Yes, it may well involve a fatigue with all that. How can you
appreciate the delights of concision unless you abuse them?

Q.   One of the perennial questions asked any artist is whether he
has any particular method of composition. Would you care to reply?

A.   Usually I begin a poem with an image or phrase; if you follow
trustfully, it's surprising how far an image can lead. Once in a great
while I've seen the shape of the whole poem (never a very long one,
though) and tried simply to follow the stages of plot, or argument.
The danger in this method is that one knows so well where the poem
is going that one hasn't much impetus to write it. In either case, even
before the poem is fully drafted, my endless revisions begin—the one
dependable pleasure in the whole process. Some poets actually say

they don't revise, don't believe in revising. They say their originality suffers. I don't see that at all. The words that come first are anybody's, a froth of phrases, like the first words from a medium's mouth. You have to make them your own. Even if the impersonal is what you're after, you first have to make them your own, and only then begin to efface yourself.

Q. Novelists sometimes speak of characters "taking over" and the work "writing itself." Has this been your experience, either as a novelist or a poet?

A. As a novelist, no, I'm not good enough. That kind of submission must be one of the darkest secrets of technique. With poems I don't know who or what takes over, unless it's I who do, and that's not what you mean. Sooner or later one touches upon matters that are all the realer for not being easily talked about.

KENNETH REXROTH

_Q._ Last night before reading your poetry, you told students you wondered whether to give them sex, revolution, or mysticism. You decided
to give them chiefly sex and revolution. What would you have read
if you had given them mysticism as well?

A. Well, actually, many of my poems deal with mysticism, including, for example, a number of those in _The Signature of All Things_
(1949). And _The Heart's Garden, The Garden's Heart_, which came
out in 1967, particularly treats the subject. After all, some of my
poems were written in monasteries, like Holy Cross Monastery in up-
state New York and Santa Barbara, or the Cowley Fathers in Cambridge, or the Daitokoji Monastery in Japan, where _The Heart's
Garden_ was written.

_Q._ What about poems from _In Defense of the Earth_ (1956), like
"Time Is the Mercy of Eternity"? There you write: "Far away the
writhing city / Burns in a fire of transcendence / And commodities. The
bowels / Of men are wrung between the poles / Of meaningless anti-
thesis. / The holiness of the real / Is always there, accessible / In total
immanence." Don't these lines suggest that the empirical and trans-

---

Interview conducted by Cyrena N. Pondrom on March 23, 1968, in Madison, Wisconsin, where Mr. Rexroth read his poetry to a university audience,
and in Milwaukee on March 24. Also incorporated are tape-recorded answers
to written questions. Mr. Rexroth graciously consented to read the final text.

All short poems quoted may be found in _Collected Shorter Poems_, New
Directions, 1966, and require no page citation. For lines from long poems page
numbers in _Collected Longer Poems_, New Directions, 1968, have been given,
with the abbreviation _CLP_.

cendental are not really antithetical, that real objects possess transcendent meaning? To make the question more general, doesn't your
view of mysticism contain a certain view of reality, and if so, what is
that view?

A.   Yes, it is true that poems like that one imply a view of reality. My
point in those lines—and in poems that follow—is that if reality can
be apprehended without grasping, the epistemological problem disappears.[1] The beginning of the experience of reality is the same as the
end of it. The source or spring of experience is an experience like that
of final illumination. That is to say, rather than being built on perception, on receiving and sorting sense data, our experience of reality
begins and ends in illumination. Jacques Maritain talks again and
again about the idea, although this is not really Thomism. It is an
idea that goes back to medieval mystical philosophy, to the thought
of Richard of Saint Victor. Experience begins with illumination;
since this is true, there ceases to be a problem of transcendence of the
mundane world. This idea occurs over and over again in my poetry. I
think one of the clearest expressions of it is in *The Heart's Garden:*
"He who lives without grasping/Lives always in experience/Of the
immediate as the/Ultimate. The solution/Of the problem of know-
ing/And being is ethical./Epistemology is moral" (*CLP*, 294-295). In
both *The Heart's Garden* and "Time Is the Mercy of Eternity" there
is a philosophy; in fact, there is a complete *Weltanschauung.* And in
The Heart's Garden, as in all my longer poems written earlier, there is a
dramatic form: there is a conversation between two or more persons,
a dialogue concerning the nature of reality.[2]

Q.   You suggest that these poems illustrate the apprehension of
reality without grasping. The question is, how are the epistemological
steps bypassed? A little further in "Time Is the Mercy of Eternity" the
mystical experience seems to be presented in terms of the erotic experi-

---

[1] This comment may be seen as a further reflection on the thought expressed
in *An Autobiographical Novel:* "I looked at maps of India and South America
and strove to convince myself they represented immense countries full of people
living and dying. I suppose it is at this time that a child first faces the solipsistic
dilemma to which we can never know the answer. Are the other people there or
is the world just something going on in my own head?" (p. 47)

[2] One should remember in this context that the *Upanishads*, too, are
dialogues on the nature of reality.

ence ("The thighs of the goddess/Close me in"). Is there a close
relationship between erotic experience and mystical?

A.   The epistemological steps are bypassed by direct experience; and
erotic experience is one type of direct experience—though only one
type. It is the experience of otherness, presumably at its most intense.
Apprehending reality without grasping is rather like Sam Johnson
kicking the rock and saying, "This is the ineluctable modality of the
visible." Direct experience is like the *cogito*—the analytic process lies
ahead of it and there is no getting beyond it. The epistemological
process of, for example, Locke and Hume in English philosophy is not
anterior to direct experience. The process doesn't come first, it comes
afterwards, and the direct experience is the main thing.

Q.   Is this like the existentialist emphasis on experience?

A.   It's something like existentialism, but not quite the same. The
existentialists are obsessed with the primacy of self. It is hard to talk
at once about both French and German existentialism, but French
existentialism starts from Cartesianism; it is completely dominated by
the consciousness of self-identity. It really does begin with the *cogito*
and remains dominated by it. We are not aware of "I think" but of
reality as such.

Q.   Is it correct to say then that you are emphasizing the experience
of otherness, in contrast to the existentialist emphasis on the self?

A.   Actually, the experience of otherness is the first polarizing; it's the
polarizing that comes immediately after the direct experience. That's
the first thing one experiences after one ceases to possess the direct
experience itself. It's very easy to talk about these ideas in Buddhist
terminology. In the Western tradition we could turn to Richard of
Saint Victor who says that the direct experience of reality precedes, I
suppose you would call it, the Aristotelian sensing process—since that
is really the foundation of Locke and Hume.

Q.   This is actually like the nominalist position?

A.   What do you mean by "nominalist"? It means so many different
things to different people.

Q.   By nominalism I mean a sensual response to a tangible reality,
in which the reality is prior to thought about it. Hence generalization

and classification of the object is a kind of illusion, rather than a reference to a transcendent Idea.

A.   Well, perhaps it's something like that. Actually, the whole nominalist controversy is meaningless in the face of direct experience, the simultaneous apprehending of the object and its meaning.

Q.   Does that mean—and I notice that in your work you do make reference to him—that you are very close to Buber and to *I and Thou* in your philosophy?

A.   Yes, you could say that. Yes, I'm very close to Buber. Among those who are called existentialists, I'm closest to Buber and to Gabriel Marcel. Of course, a number of people are called existentialists, whether they really are or not. Marcel doesn't really belong in the tradition of French existentialism, if by that you mean the tradition that goes from Scheler through Sartre and Merleau-Ponty. Marcel, Berdeyaev, and Buber interest me most of that generation.

Q.   Let's go back to the nature of the direct experience; the last lines of "Time Is the Mercy of Eternity" seem to convey such an experience. You write: "At last there is nothing left / But knowledge, itself a vast / Crystal encompassing the / Limitless crystal of air / And rock and water. And the / Two crystals are perfectly / Silent. There is nothing to / Say about them. Nothing at all."
    The image "crystal" seems one key to understanding the experience, for you use it or its derivative five times in the last twenty lines, culminating in the lines just quoted. I appreciate that you are emphasizing the clarity of crystal and the emptying of the mind that yields a crystalline (in the sense of translucent) "knowledge." Do you also mean to draw on the structural connotations of the word "crystal"?

A.   Yes. Besides or even more than the clarity of crystal and the emptying of the mind that results in a sense of translucent knowledge (a kind of merging of the Buddhist doctrines of mind only and the doctrine of the void, you might say), "crystal" really, besides the actual physical thing, means to me the structure, lattice or otherwise, of solid state physics.

Q.   Do you mean through this image to present knowledge as a perception of pure forms, as well as a kind of emptying?

A.   Well, this has so many hangers on it. In Plato's or Whitehead's sense, I suppose no. Of course, what you're trying to do in a poem is to create or recreate the poetic situation, to put the reader in a situation which is analogous to that of yourself, or into one which would produce the poem, or simply into one which you want deliberately to manipulate and produce. The images, whether they exist in the form of symbols and metaphors and similes or in straight description or whatever, are ultimately designed to create a kind of ecology of the momentary sensibility. And the reiteration of "crystal" of course is designed to produce this. There is quite a bit of this stuff that goes on in poems of mine, quite consciously—things concerning light and rays of light, images from projective geometry, terms like harmonic pencil, things like this: ice, crystals, rays. These have a certain relationship to the idioretinal phenomena that accompany a rather low order of visionary experience, the type that is thought of as illumination by, you know, the people who think you can buy it in pills. And of course, it's also produced by certain disorders—there's a long analysis of the visions of Saint Hildegard of Bingen described in a book on migraine and certain epileptiform disorders. They reproduced the color, and the visions are very similar to the things described by the LSD people. But I think you notice that there's a difference in the things that I talk about, because they are much less spectacular—they're not like fireworks, and the reference is not to idioretinal sources. (Whatever the drugged person may think, I mean, idioretinal phenomena are actually what he's talking about—you know, the visions like fireworks whirling around a dark cone, or the illusion of being in a tunnel, or bursts of light and blue crystal and stuff floating around. Everybody knows the literature of the subject. It's enormous now.) Well, the things that I am talking about are quite different, and they are ultimately designed to produce an entirely different kind of rapture. "The / Two crystals are perfectly / Silent. There is nothing to / Say about them. Nothing at all." And the void and mind only have merged.

Q.   In the context which we've been using, how does the form of your poem contribute to its meaning?

A.   I suppose that this sense of the form of a poem—because this is the form of the poem, the poetic situation that it creates—and the meaning, are the same thing. And of course, the structure of this poem, "Time Is the Mercy of Eternity," the aural structure, is a great deal more complicated than you would assume from the lineations, and if it's read carefully aloud, this is obvious. At least it is to me when I read it.

_Q._   How does the form take concrete shape in your poetry?

A.   When I write poetry, what I really get first is one or two phrases with a very insistent rhythm. The phrases keep insisting and the poem builds up by a process of accretion. This process of accretion sometimes is conscious and sometimes is unconscious, and of course it varies from poet to poet.

_Q._   Could you elaborate on how structure and conception in a mystical poem can lead toward the knowledge that is really a kind of emptying?

A.   Actually, mystical poetry communicates a kind of trance state, an emptiness which is a state of not grasping. The creation of such poetry is like the slow development of a state of bliss in which grasping disappears. This is what Buddhism is talking about, in, for example, _The Diamond Sutra._ It's a state of not-being and not not-being. It is an idea like those of the school of Buddhism taken up by neo-Confucianism; really it's a general Oriental philosophical idea, not one specific to Buddhism or neo-Confucianism, and it can even be stated in English philosophical terms. It is what Wittgenstein was talking about in his study—not of course in his philosophical works—but in his study.

_Q._   What in neo-Confucianism do you find most Buddhistic?

A.   Tu Fu, perhaps? I suppose his work is very close to a philosophy of the Void. One could also point to the philosophy of Chu-Hsi, who really is the major philosopher of neo-Confucianism. I have discussed him before in my essay on neo-Taoistic philosophy.[3] When ideas like those of Lao-Tze are restated in popular terms, they become simply

---

[3] "Sung Culture" in _Assays._ A comment in that essay bears on the foregoing discussion of form in poetry: ". . . Chu [Hsi] and Lu [Hsiang-shan] both developed reality from Not-Being, the unconditioned, through the interaction of form (_li_) and potentiality (_ch'i_). For Chu, these two metaphysical principles always interacted, although the world of form was, eventually, one—pure, empty—the Void of the Buddhists. For Lu, form was always primary, its substantiation an illusion. . . . For Chu, man's mind was a combination of _li_ and _ch'i_. For Lu, man's mind had strayed from the world of _li_, pure form, to which it had originally belonged, and the aim of the wise and good man was to find his lost mind or true nature again by quiet meditation and begin to understand its relation to the whole. At the end would come, without words or ideas, the sudden illumination, the knowledge that the individual was in fact the totality" (p. 7).

another kind of occult religion; eventually, of course, all these tendencies converge in the eighth century A.D. Jung's description of the golden flower cult, for example, is really the description of a little slum sect of Toynbee's cultural Proletariat, one which grew and fell apart; certainly it didn't last long. Jung's whole relation to that description is in many ways very amusing. He includes in his book plates important to the cult, but he doesn't even reproduce the significant plates having to do with spiritual alchemy. The final plate in the group is one of a little man with limbs coming out all over him, with alchemical apparatus inside. Jung deliberately suppresses this. What's more, I once bet someone twenty-five dollars that he couldn't find Thomas Vaughan (the brother of Henry) listed in the index to Jung's book, because Thomas Vaughan—though his account is rather difficult to understand, rather occultist—was the greatest of the English spiritual alchemists. He explains all the golden flower symbolism and therefore anticipated Jung. And Jung wanted to believe that he was the discoverer of it himself. A. E. Waite was one of the few people who appreciated all of this. In fact, I've long planned to do a new edition of A. E. Waite's Vaughan, though I haven't yet found the time. Of course, one has to remember that when any of these mystical and occult theories become popular culture—and Taoism, for example, has been very popular culture—they eventually become hocus-pocus.

Q. Your reference to A. E. Waite reminds me of a comment you made in an essay of yours—I believe in your introduction to the new edition of Waite's *The Holy Kabbalah*. In that essay you said you saw mystic or occult theology as "seeking the basic pattern of the human mind in symbolic garb." Do you see poetry as acting in much the same way?

A. Well . . . yes. But there is really a difference. I suppose when you deal with these great logical systems—such as Gnosticism, the Cabala, or others like that—you find that all such systems are manipulative. Poetry, of course, is not manipulative. Poetry deals with much more concrete things. It possesses an intense specificity—the intense specificity of *direct* contact and direct communication; rather than dealing intellectually and discursively with permanent archetypes it does so directly, via Whitehead's "presentational immediacy."

Gnostical cosmology, for example, represents the fundamental way in which the human mind is organized. It asserts or posits a physiological substratum that conditions mental activity. That is to say, it presents generalities which are the opposite of poetry. It contains no specificity, although it deals with the same problems poetry deals with. We could think, for example, of Anubis and Thoth weighing the soul, the Book of the Dead, and the account of the stations of the soul, which haunt Gnosticism. You know the picture from all the Books of the Dead, the stations where the soul is tested, where it is eaten by the crocodile if it doesn't know the right answer in the testing. This is a fundamental human experiential archetype. It is a repetition of how the human mind operates. These patterns abide, but they are great generalities, and such generalities are almost the opposite of poetry. Both occult theology and poetry deal with the same thing, however, in the sense that they both reorganize experience in terms of permanent symbolic structures. Such structures, whether presented in generalities or specifics, are actually based on the physiological: the fact that a man has a liver and two kidneys. This is the kind of thing that is built into the organism.

Q.   I see. What you're saying is that a poem, with its specificity, acts on us like experience. It should be approached with illumination first.

A.   Yes, that's right. A poem is an efficient vehicle for focusing attention, for giving direct experience. A work of art is, in a sense, a function of the perceiver's attention. If you're a paralytic, the spots on the ceiling are or can be a work of art. If you want an illustration of this, you can turn to some of the final forms of Brancusi's fish. These forms provide an extremely frictionless experience of a work of art. This is attention focused at its most intense. But of course it's true that the mind can be so refined that any old fish or any old rock, for that matter, will do—it doesn't have to be Brancusi's fish. But let me be very clear: art is not a substitute for the mystical experience. In its most highly refined forms, art may communicate the mystical experience. Poetry may be an expression of the direct apprehension of reality—but it may do a great number of other things as well. There's erotic poetry, nonsense poetry, satiric poetry; poetry does a lot of things besides communicate the mystical experience.

Q.   The poem that does communicate the mystical experience is actually the poem that communicates the idea of harmony, isn't it? This reminds me of the last poem of In Defense of the Earth, "They Say This Isn't a Poem." Isn't the idea of harmony that we see there characteristic of the poem that communicates mystical experience? I mean particularly the lines "The harmony of all that is / Without man can unite with / The harmony of all that is / Within man as a knowable / Good, an inner moral good."

A. That's right. But that poem says two things. It says the other thing too. There are two parts to the poem, and the two parts represent two different views. The poem bifurcates the two views of reality and juxtaposes them. In the first section there is the idea of harmony, and in the second, the idea that man's view of the universe imposes moral order on reality.

Q. But in the first section of the poem, the last three lines ("How beautiful and specious/And how stinking with the blood/Of wars and crucifixions") comment ironically on all that goes before. Now it struck me that what you had to say about harmony in the first part of that poem was really what you were saying about harmony in a large number of your other mystical poems. Is that not the case?

A. Yes, it's exactly what I was saying in others of the poems.

Q. Well then, how is it that the last lines comment ironically on the first? Is it this way: that the harmony that you mentioned in the first part of the poem is the knowledge that is achieved without grasping, is the knowledge of direct experience. . . .

A. That's right, that's what it is.

Q. Then is it true that what has led to wars and crucifixion is the other kind of knowledge, the kind of knowledge of the bourgeois world, the kind of knowledge that is achieved by grasping—and that this knowledge has led the world into chaos?

A. Yes. Man kills himself by defining the indefinable, grasping the inapprehensible. We do not apprehend reality, since this implies an outreaching effort; rather it apprehends us. We are simply in reality. We are in being like fish in water, who do not know water exists.

In the second section of the poem we come to understand that the forces that operate about us in the universe do not in fact possess the moral order that we can postulate as possible, or create among men. The order we perceive in the universe is one imposed upon it, not simply the order of direct experience. All the myths are constructed things. After all, Aphrodite and Artemis, when thought of literally as persons, are vicious or silly.

The thing that baffles writers on ethics is the difference between moral and physical evil. A. E. Taylor, for example, confuses the waste of value in the world of nature with relations among men. That difference, really, is quantitative, not one of "value"—a qualitative one.

There is nothing privative in the relations among men as there is in nature. There are no explosions of stars, for example, or the destruction of millions of salmon to produce one salmon. What I mean is that there is a difference between the order of nature and the moral order of men. There's a difference, in other words, between physical and moral evil. To confuse the two is a vast confusion. Actually, what happens is that you not only take the physical realm to be evil, you also assimilate the relations between men to the physical. That is, you take the relations between men to be privative when they are not, and to be somehow excused by the analogy with the physical realm. This is the subject of my *Phaedra*. Coleridge's "Rime of the Ancient Mariner" is also concerned with this, although as a myth it's almost too contrived: "Christabel" has more insight into the problem. Actually, tragedy makes clear the distinction between the natural order and the moral order of man. Thus it comes back to a question of will. Basic to all great tragic literature is the Socratic dilemma, the fact that an ethic is not a way of life. It is really not true that if men are presented with rationally defined alternatives—the greater good and the lesser good—they will infallibly choose the greater good. In this, Socrates is simply wrong. An ethics tries to set up a system of guarantees by which men can choose the greater good. This is really what Sir Thomas More's *Utopia* is all about: his society produces a whole system of checks and balances that is supposed to work automatically in the individual, and thus tries to guarantee that men will choose the greater rather than the lesser good. But it's not even true that men will merely choose the lesser good; there are men who will choose positive evil.

Q.   You said the subject of your *Phaedra* is that "men take the relations between men to be privative when they are not. . . ." In your play Hippolytus rejects Theseus' proposal that Hippolytus take Phaedra to Crete to restore the kingdom; do you see this as Hippolytus' assumption that human relations are privative?

A.   The problem is that Hippolytus and Phaedra come unprepared to vision. All these things have been made disgustingly popular by the wrong people since, but it is as though a tantric couple—or an alchemical couple—had achieved ultimate illumination in the yoga of the sexual act, but because they had brought acquisitive and privative demands to vision, the vision destroys them.

Just recently I did an introduction to the alchemical works of Thomas Vaughan for University Books. Apparently what happened to Thomas Vaughan was that he and his *soror mystica*, his actual wife, at

an inn called The Pinter of Wakefield essentially destroyed themselves in the erotic, yogic practices that are symbolized by the language
of alchemy.

Q. Your play, with consummated love between Hippolytus and
Phaedra, is very different from the myth as Euripides and Seneca used
it, with their suggestions that Hippolytus' unnatural rejection of love
contributes to disaster.

A. Seneca I've never been able to take seriously. I've always thought
that he really belonged in the old-time Hurst Sunday supplement, or
in one of the lower order of fantasy and science-fiction magazines, and
I abominated his Latin, which is spuriously, you know, "pure." Euripides is another matter, but I would say that superficially my play is the
opposite of Euripides'.

Q. Do you reverse the theme, then, to suggest that human intentions—however natural—are never freed from disaster, or that vision is
temporary, even when it derives from love rather than from Artemis,
and that horror is certain to overtake anyone?

A. It just overtakes them. Nothing is said one way or another about
other men. I think my other plays go on from there. *Iphigenia in Aulis*
is a long conversation between Saint Augustine and Saint Mechtilda of
Magdeburg—I mean that's where a great deal of what Iphigenia and
Achilles say to one another comes from. And the final play, which is
a two-part play, *Beyond the Mountains*, is of course a redoing of the
Oresteia. At the very end of Greek civilization as such, these people
far away in a mountain valley above the Kabul River go through like
sleepwalkers all the motions of Agamemnon, Clytemnestra, Aegisthus,
Orestes, Electra.

Q. Earlier you said that tragedy makes clear the distinction between
the natural order and man's moral order. Do Hippolytus and Phaedra,
for example, suffer because they are part of the natural order and do
not create a moral order—because, as Hippolytus says, their coming
together was accidental rather than an act of will?

A. The question of moral order is a question of the stability and the
availability of the mystic experience. Moral order, in the individual or
in society as a whole, depends upon precisely that, society as a whole;
and when the light of contemplation goes out, the civilization collapses,
and there is a kind of ecological point of no-return. (When you kill

off enough California sardines, the enemies of the sardine take over, and although they seem to be very abundant still, lo, in three years they have vanished. Of course, the people who ground them up for fertilizer in great factories in the sea say that's not the reason—it was an atom bomb, or some mysterious disease that's not been diagnosed, or something else like that.) The interrelatedness of contemplatives is a skeleton or web which holds the social body. There is a critical point when there isn't enough of this web. We have long since reached that and passed it in America, and the society goes completely to pieces, however healthy it may seem. And of course the participants in the society violently deny that this is happening. In the darkest moment of American history, just before Christmas 1967, the infamous and evil Lyndon Johnson said that Utopia was just around the corner, that he had brought the dreams of mankind to fulfillment. Appalling. Even Stilicho or Galla Placidia had more insight into the situations in which they were than he. And the reason for this is the loss of vision.

It doesn't do any good when the vision secedes from the society— I mean the hippies, even those who don't take drugs, who sit in contemplation and are true visionaries. They're not going to say they're in society because they have already left it. (The relationship of the church to contemplation in the days of Galla Placidia is another question altogether and a very complicated one.) But that's what the plays are all about. The plays are really about contemporary society, which is now past the position of *Beyond the Mountains*, of the Bactrian Greeks being overwhelmed by the Kushans or whomever. And of course, this is the inability of a people, not of individuals, to achieve and to hold the experience of unity and certainly of spiritual integrity.

Q. Let's go back to the poetry that even in this society does communicate a mystical experience, poetry you said is at its most refined. Could one say that what such poetry does is to communicate a sense of the absolute?

A. Well, in a sense one of the things poetry has been doing from the early teens or twenties, from the time of cubism on, is to drift toward absolutes, and I do mean exactly "drift toward." Poets and critics have been involved in endless discussion of aesthetic theory, and aesthetic discussions tend to define poetry in terms of absolutes. Aestheticians have even been talking about poetry itself in terms of being absolute, though there is no such thing as an absolute definition of poetry. But this is to limit attention to certain kinds of poetry.

From another standpoint, the notion of the Absolute with a capital "A" is meaningless in terms of the unqualified experience, the mystical experience. I take it your question really was the following: does a poem about a mystical experience put the reader in touch with the Absolute? As for that, I'd have to say, "No." A poem is only an adjustment of instruments.

Q.   In other words, you are saying that the Absolute is just another limited concept, that it is not to be understood as the same kind of thing as the generalized mystical experience. Is that correct?

A.   Yes, that's it. The Absolute is just another definition—a limitation, a grasping. A certain type of experience deals with absolutes. But experience has to disqualify itself before it permits mystical experience. When this is placed in the context of poetry you have to realize that there's a difference between an aesthetic and a mystical experience—and this is an argument I've carried on with other poets, from André Breton on, for many years. The aesthetic experience is an experience of maximum specificity, whereas the mystical experience is unqualified, even in terms of things like absolutes. What this means is that the aesthetic experience is not the same as the religious experience or the mystical experience. The poetic experience is something completely different.

Q.   Is this the foundation for the poem in The Art of Worldly Wisdom, "Fundamental Disagreement with Two Contemporaries"? You dedicated that to Tristan Tzara and André Breton, I believe.

A.   Yes, one of my basic arguments with Tzara and Breton and others of this same period is the confusion of poetic with religious experience. Of course, that poem in the first part is a parody of Tzara and in the second, a parody of Breton. But the fundamental disagreement here is the confusion in the role of poetry.

Q.   I believe about that time you were also involved in putting out a dadaistic magazine. Does your disagreement with your contemporaries have anything to do with differing attitudes toward dadaism?

A.   Someone else asked me about that recently. Actually, we never put out the magazine; the point of it all was a parody of dadaism in which a lot of noise deliberately came to nothing. We had a number of parades, we beat a lot of drums, but we never did do anything. The dada movement did have a real political content, but our own efforts never resulted in a magazine. We called it "Escalator." I think you can find Escalator poems in the *Milwaukee Arts Monthly* by Sam Putnam.

When you look at it, the whole Chicago Renaissance, of which surrealism and the dada movement was a part, was really very much more closely connected with Munich and Düsseldorf, Amsterdam and Rotterdam, than it was with Paris. For example, Ben Hecht brought back the first pictures of George Grosz, Paul Klee, and John Hartfield long before we heard of anything from postwar Paris. It was through this route, from Germany, that the cubist movement got started in Chicago.

Q. That leads to a question concerning cubism. You do accept the word "cubism" as the description of one period of your poetry, don't you?

A. Yes.

Q. One of the most difficult questions in the discussion of cubistic poetry, it seems to me, is the application of the term "cubism." For example, painting is a "simultaneous" art form, whereas poetry is apprehended sequentially . . . .

A. That's true, and one of the things that happens in cubism is that the multiple aspects you get in cubist painting introduce into art the temporal sequence of poetic form or music.

Q. But how do the principles of cubist painting apply to a description of poetic technique?

A. In both painting and poetry there is simply a radical dissociation and a reasoned recombination of elements.

Q. What exactly are the principles of recombination?

A. Well . . . it's a matter of mathematics, for one thing. Most cubist paintings of the synthetic period are based on the golden section. For instance, in the work of Juan Gris, Albert Gleizes, and Metzinger—who incidentally remained golden section painters—you find mathematical principles at work. And in the earlier stage of cubism, analytical cubism, you actually had people taking a Cézanne watercolor and turning it upside-down or on one of its edges and copying it in their painting. Now when they did that they were after two things. They were after first of all the purity of geometric construction; but they were also after a kind of dynamic *einfühlung*, the stress and strain of form against form. Thus that which you saw in Cézanne was carried to its fullest extent in analytical cubism. This is actually a classical, an architectural, notion. The many works of Jay Hambidge on "Dynamic Symmetry" represent the largest body of golden section theory.

Q.   Yes, but the architectural notion is one particularly applicable to painting. How do you make the transition between painting and poetry?

A.   Well, just as Gris was the perfect cubist painter, Reverdy and to a lesser extent Apollinaire were the perfect cubist poets. They were doing the same thing that Gertrude Stein was doing in *Tender Buttons* —paragraph upon paragraph of simple scenes, juxtaposed like still lifes. I write like Reverdy. I started out writing that way, and I still do, although often now I paint it over to look like something actual like babies or flowers. It's the kind of writing that captures the sense of everything happening at once. The real influence here is not Reverdy, but the *Un Coup de dés* of Mallarmé. Mallarmé is usually described as a symbolist poet, but in *Un Coup de dés* the poetry is very simply presented. It is really an objectivist poem, not a symbolist poem at all. In fact, Mallarmé pushed symbolism to the point that it became anti-symbolist.

Q.   Both your comments on cubism and the imagery of your own poetry place frequent emphasis on the geometrical. In fact, you've given your last two collections of poetry titles from mathematics or mathematical logic—like *Gödel's Proof*. What is the relationship between these systems of mathematics and your poetry?

A.   Well really, that's what *Gödel's Proof* is all about: that there is a relationship, that no system is self-contained. And this, of course, is related to the generalized experience that we've been talking about in connection with mystical poetry.

Q.   Is there possibly, in this very abstract system, mathematics, a core of form which is also applicable to poetry?

A.   Yes, mathematics is very abstract, abstract like music. And I suppose it is true there is also a core of form in the world's poetry, likewise very abstract and applicable to a large number of poems. But getting to mathematics itself—Whitehead's textbook on projective geometry is pretty. I enjoy mathematics; it's the same thing as poetic form, but non-specific rather than specific. And it seems to me that mathematics is at its best as a pure art, that is, when it is not going anywhere. That's why mathematics is a study for the young. Incidentally, it was the Buddhists who invented the zero—between the negative and double negative.

Q. Your references to Buddhism are very frequent. In *The Dragon and the Unicorn*, for example, you speak of Shiva ("You are Shiva, but you dream"; *CLP*, 279) and often use images of fire and cycle ("All things are made new by fire"; *CLP*, 95; "the concept/Of time arose from the weaving / Together of the great organic / Cycles of the universe"; *CLP*, 96). Would you elaborate on your relationship to Zen, Gary Snyder, and more generally, to Eastern meditation?

A. Specifically, the statement "All things are made new by fire" is from alchemy; that's an alchemical slogan. And the reference to cycles of the universe—well, of course, that's obvious; I mean, time arises from the weaving together and the turning of the earth and the movement of the earth around the sun, movements of planets through the sky and so forth. But I suppose of all of American intellectuals—and this was sort of contemporaneously with Huxley's change of mind—I was probably the first to have any great interest in Eastern religion. I've had this all my life, as it says in my autobiography. Long before anybody else was talking about it, I was reading people like Suzuki, and eventually, I suppose, I came to read everything in English on Buddhism, particularly, but on Oriental religion in general; and I've read an enormous amount. Although I am quite familiar with hatha yoga and the practices of sexual yoga and so forth, and I think I understand their relationship to the occult tradition in the West (this *is* what is occult in the occult), it is more than this. Nevertheless, my interests have always been more or less occultist. I would say that just reading in Buddhism and knowing Buddhist people—I knew Suzuki and I've known various Shinshu people in San Francisco in years gone by—has all had a very considerable influence on me; and of course there's the influence of Oriental poetry, at least Far Eastern poetry.

Q. And what about your relationship with Gary Snyder—especially since your references in *The Dragon and the Unicorn* to "Buddha / Mirror" in the hearts of all creatures, Kew Gardens, cedars of Lebanon, California sequoias, and smoke (*CLP*, 118) all appear a few years later in Snyder's *Myths and Texts*?

A. Gary Snyder has been called a disciple of mine. I think in his young days it is to a certain extent true that he did pick up a lot of stuff from me. I hadn't even noticed in Snyder the allusions to Kew Gardens, cedars of Lebanon, California sequoias, and smoke, which echo this poem of mine. You see, all scattered around amongst younger poets are people who have read my longer poems with a great deal of attention. And the poems have meant a great deal to them, so to speak, philosophically, although they have been dismissed with contempt by the Trotskyite Ku Klux Klan literary establishment that ran the quarterlies in the thirties and forties. But this was all sort of underground in the years after the war; we were not-people. I still am a not-person; to the best of my knowledge, for instance, I have never been mentioned in *The New York Review of Books*. I hope not.

Q.   Could we explore a representative of those longer poems a little more fully then? In *The Dragon and the Unicorn* two apparently important comments are: "This necessitous character / Of consequence is what / Has given rise in the West / To the conception of sin, / In the East to that of Karma" (*CLP*, 129) and "being is / Responsibility ... Ontology is ethical" (*CLP*, 130). Do you mean that it is impossible to "be" at all without subsequent states or acts being consequent, and thus that ethics is built in to metaphysics?

A.   Well, yes. But that particular aspect of it is treated at greater length in the sort of pendant poems to *The Heart's Garden*, that are in the *Collected Longer Poems*. The question is really epistemological, and for me, in fact, the epistemological problem does not exist, because, as I said, knowledge, which is an act of love, precedes its materials, its "Lockeian data."

Q.   That reminds me of the statement you attributed to the "Philosopher" in *The Dragon and the Unicorn*: "The noblest way to possess / A thing is to possess it / In an immaterial / Manner. . . . / This is the definition / Of knowledge" (*CLP*, 104).

A.   Yes, well of course, possession ultimately is the possession of love, is the possession of vision. There is no other possession. The knowledge that is grasping is not knowledge.

Q.   How are you using the word "love" here? And you say "Ultimately the fulfillment / Of reality demands that / Each person in the universe / Realize every one of the / Others in the fullness of love" (*CLP*, 140). What. . . .

A.   Well, this isn't really any longer such a very complicated idea or such a very outrageous idea, because it has been widely popularized by Teilhard de Chardin. The personalization of reality, I think, is its terms, that is, its poles. Reality flows between the two poles of person-alization, and the fulfillment of reality is its, so to speak, saturation with this charge. That's all it is.

Q. What do you mean here by love? Certainly your use seems more complex than either a reference to purely sexual emotion or to the abstraction of the Platonic idea. Do you mean in part "the tran-scendence/Of the self, what I have called/Extrapersonalization" (*CLP,* 141)?

A. Well, the answer to that question is the subject of, you know, my whole work. What is love? Of course, what love is ultimately is responsibility. That's only an aspect of it, but in the section we're dis-cussing that is brought up again and again. Sexual love, of course, is one sacramental, one outward, vesture of an inward spiritual reality, and I suppose this is extrapersonalization. That is not a term that I would use anymore, but what I meant by extrapersonalization was that the person is realized in his reflection in other persons, and there is no end to this process. You see, back of this lies a kind of vision, a universe made up of an infinite number of contemplatives, a picture which opens the Avatamsaka Sutra of Kegon Kyo. Of course, the dynamics of this process is endless; realization of the one in the other constitutes the flow of reality.

Q. Are the narrative descriptions—like the accounts of bicycling (e.g., *CLP,* 144-145)—"real" because the "we" of the poem see with the eyes of love?

A. Yes. Experiences that do not have a "love perspective" (*CLP,* 145) are unreal, or pallid approximations of the real. An experience exists only to the degree that it is a love perspective.

Q. Does the physical act of love have a privileged place in the ful-fillment of reality? (See *CLP,* 149.)

A. Here of course the answer is yes.

Q. You speak of three ways of loving, one physical and two others. What do you mean when you call "touch[ing] each other through . . . the earth/Center . . . or by means/Of ultimate inclusive/Action" (*CLP,* 150) two other ways of loving?

A. Again here we're talking about the poles of reality, the undeter-mined substratum, *Ungrund,* and the ultimate realization in the final illumination. You see, the influences go back to our previous discussion of Eastern religion.

Q. I see. Well, later you explicitly connect love and being: "Love, like all the sacraments, is a/Miniature of being itself./All things have an apparent / Meaning and an opposite / Hidden meaning brought forth by fire" (CLP, 154).

A. Yes; there you have two notions from two different sources— medieval Catholic mystic and a mystical alchemical text.

Q. Are you saying by the combination that just as being looks real, but is not until raised to its fulfillment in love, so love looks purely physical or emotional until the dissolution of knowledge has taken place, and love is revealed as a direct intuition of the meaning of the universe?

A. The answer to that, of course, is yes. Except that the word intuition is so loaded that I never use it.

Q. A final question, then, about the role of poetry in achieving the vision you describe. You cite Zoroaster's statement that "poetry presents us / With apparent pictures of / Unapparent realities" (CLP, 154). Does poetry, under the guise of concrete images, reveal the "opposite hidden meaning" of both love and being?

A. Well, some poetry does. I mean, some poetry doesn't. The poetry of the aestheticians, the sort of ideal of what poetry should be, does. Incidentally, one of the reasons for my great interest in Buddhism is that no matter how far it moves from the historic Buddha, Sakyamuni, the inner core is always the judgment of the religious experience as such; that is, it is radical religious empiricism. Generally speaking, my attitude towards life is one that avoids imperatives; where they're used in my poems they are kind of like quotations, so they're used ironically. I simply don't believe that art should do anything. Art can be used to flatter Louis XV or it can be used to lick the boots of a Stalin, or it can be used to overthrow the Polish government, or it can be used to glorify God, or it can be used for anything; it can be used to seduce your mistress or excite your wife, or it can just be used to idle away the time. I think it's a great mistake to approach philosophy or religion or aesthetics with anything except a simple, naive attitude: "What happens?" What happens in life? What happens in philosophy? What happens in art? And avoid the imperative . . . .

Q. I'd like to begin with some facts about your life, Mr. Oppen. You've lived many years in New York City, haven't you?

A. Yes, although I spent my boyhood in San Francisco. I was born in New Rochelle. My father, having married a second time, moved to California when I was about ten. I guess I was about nineteen when I left college, the University of Oregon, with Mary Colby, my future wife, and eventually hitchhiked to New York. A young instructor by the name of Jack Lyons had given me Conrad Aiken's anthology of modern poetry. It was my discovery that there was such a thing as modern poetry other than what I had been writing. I could say there was nobody at college with whom I could discuss modern poetry — but now I'm not so sure. I think I was afraid that somebody *would* tell me something about it and I didn't want to be told.

Anyway, we got to New York and started looking for people like Sherwood Anderson and even Vachel Lindsay and Carl Sandburg, who still have a kind of importance to me. Mary and I happened to be walking past the Gotham Book Mart one day before going to a party and we dropped in to waste some time. I saw *Exiles, 3*, edited by Ezra Pound, and he was one of the names I knew I was looking for. And I stood there and read the first poem which was called "Poem Beginning 'The'" by Louis Zukofsky, and went on to the party where someone said, "Oh, you're a poet. We have a friend who's a poet; you should meet him; his name's Louis Zukofsky." I said, "He wrote 'Poem Beginning "The,"'" and they said, "That's true, but you're the only person in the world who knows it."

Interview conducted by L. S. Dembo on April 25, 1968, in Madison, Wisconsin. Quotation from "Of Being Numerous," © 1967, 1968 by George Oppen (in the volume of the same title, New Directions/*San Francisco Review*, New York, 1968) is by permission of the publisher. Oppen's other volumes include *Discrete Series* (To Publishers, New York, 1934), *The Materials* (New Directions/*San Francisco Review*, New York, 1962), and *This In Which* (New Directions/*San Francisco Review*, New York, 1966).

Q. Unfortunately, you're still in the minority.

A. That's possible, that's possible. Let's see, then. When I was twenty-one, Mary and I went to France to begin what was called To Publishers for reasons which I forget; it became The Objectivist Press. We printed *An "Objectivists" Anthology,* Pound's *ABC of Reading,* and so forth, but financially the undertaking became impossible. The books were paperbacks and the New York bookstores refused them. The customs officers made trouble, too. Louis did the editing and we did the printing. All that The Objectivist Press meant was that people paid for their own books.

Q. Why was it called "Objectivist"? Was there any sense of a movement?

A. That was Louis' term, as far as I know. When we sat down to write a statement on the book covers, Charles Reznikoff, who had legal training, produced at the right moment his statement: "The Objectivist Press is an organization of poets who are printing their own work and that of others they think ought to be printed." It was a little beyond the fact because there were differences of opinion on what should be included.

Q. Were there any criteria for what got published?

A. Well, Louis put into *An "Objectivists" Anthology* people whom he liked or admired. He was, however, operating on a principle; there was some agreement among the poets. I think that all of us had considerable area of agreement, very considerable, but nobody signed a manifesto, and, as I said, certainly not everybody was of the same opinion. But there is no question that there was a relationship among these poets. The poets Louis liked all held a certain attitude toward poetry.

Q. Just what was that attitude?

A. Let me see what we thought and whether I can generalize about it. I'll just put it in personal terms. What I felt I was doing was beginning from imagism as a position of honesty. The first question at that time in poetry was simply the question of honesty, of sincerity. But I learned from Louis, as against the romanticism or even the quaintness of the imagist position, the necessity for forming a poem properly, for achieving form. That's what "objectivist" really means. There's been tremendous misunderstanding about that. People assume it means the psychologically objective in attitude. It actually means the objectification of the poem, the making an object of the poem.

Q. Williams, in fact, speaks of the poem as object.

A. Right. And this existed in the context of the sloppy American imagism descending out of Amy Lowell and a thousand others. The other point for me, and I think for Louis, too, was the attempt to construct meaning, to construct a method of thought from the imagist technique of poetry—from the imagist intensity of vision. If no one were going to challenge me, I would say, "a test of truth." If I had to back it up I'd say anyway, "a test of sincerity"—that there is a moment, an actual time, when you believe something to be true, and you construct a meaning from these moments of conviction.

My book, of course, was called *Discrete Series.* That's a phrase in mathematics. A pure mathematical series would be one in which each term is derived from the preceding term by a rule. A discrete series is a series of terms each of which is empirically derived, each one of which is empirically true. And this is the reason for the fragmentary character of those poems. I was attempting to construct a meaning by empirical statements, by imagist statements.

Q. Each imagist statement being essentially discrete from the statement that followed or preceded it?

A. Yes, that meaning is also implicit in the word "discrete." The poems are a series, yet each is separate, and it's true that they are discrete in that sense; but I had in mind specifically the meaning to the mathematician—a series of empirically true terms.

Q. In any case, the "discrete" aspect seems to be reminiscent of the cubist approach, if I'm not being farfetched—hard, sharp fragments of theme or experience joined mosaically rather than integrated organically.

A. I'm really not sure what troubles the cubists had, but I had trouble with syntax in this undertaking and, as a matter of fact, I still have trouble with verbs. It's not exactly trouble; I just didn't want to put it too pretentiously. I'm really concerned with the substantive, with the subject of the sentence, with what we are talking about, and not rushing over the subject-matter in order to make a comment about it. It is still a principle with me, of more than poetry, to notice, to state, to lay down the substantive for its own sake. I don't know whether that's clear.

Q. Please go on.

A.   A statement can be made in which the subject plays a very little part, except for argumentation; one hangs a predicate on it that is one's comment about it. This is an approximate quotation from Hegel, who added (I like the quote very much): "Disagreement marks where the subject-matter ends. It is what the subject-matter is not." The important thing is that if we are talking about the nature of reality, then we are not really talking about our *comment about it*; we are talking about the apprehension of some *thing*, whether it *is* or not, whether one can make a thing of it or not. *Of Being Numerous* asks the question whether or not we can deal with humanity as something which actually does exist.

I realize the possibility of attacking many of the things I'm saying and I say them as a sort of act of faith. The little words that I like so much, like "tree," "hill," and so on, are I suppose just as much a taxonomy as the more elaborate words; they're categories, classes, concepts, things we invent for ourselves. Nevertheless, there are certain ones without which we really are unable to exist, including the concept of humanity.

I'm trying to describe how the test of images can be a test of whether one's thought is valid, whether one can establish in a series of images, of experiences . . . whether or not one will consider the concept of humanity to be valid, something that is, or else have to regard it as being simply a word.

Q.   What you're saying now seems to be a part of the view of reality that's presented in your poems: the belief that conceptual knowledge or generalization is inadequate or misleading in man's relation to reality. Your poetry seems to suggest that physical reality or the environment is mysterious and has to be, in a way, sensuously rather than rationally apprehended; the poet's response is the pure awareness of being, so to speak. In "Psalm" [*This in Which*], for example, you write, "In the small beauty of the forest/The wild deer bedding down—/That they are there!" And this seemed to be characteristic; the poet does not respond intellectually or discursively, but as a "nominalist," only to the physical tangibility or reality of the object he views.

A.   Yes, if one knows what "physical" means or what it contrasts with. But responds by faith, as I admitted somewhere, and to his own experience. All the little nouns are the ones that I like the most: the deer, the sun, and so on. You say these perfectly little words and you're asserting that the sun is ninety-three million miles away, and that there is shade because of shadows, and more, who knows? It's a tremendous structure to have built out of a few small nouns. I do think they exist and it doesn't particularly embarrass me; it's certainly an act of faith. I do believe that consciousness exists and that it is consciousness of something, and that is a fairly complete but not very detailed theology, as a matter of fact. In "Psalm" I was constructing what I felt to be a pretty emotional poem out of those few little words isolating the deer. And I just said, in this poem, these little nouns are crying out a faith in "this in which" the wild deer stare out. ["The small nouns/Crying faith/In this in which the wild deer/Startle, and stare out."]

Q.   What exactly is the faith? Is it in the world as world or is it in man's ability to know the world?

A.   Well, that the nouns do refer to something; that it's there, that it's true, the whole implication of these nouns; that appearances represent reality, whether or not they misrepresent it: that this in which the thing takes place, this thing is here, and that these things do take place. On the other hand, one is left with the deer, staring out of the thing, at the thing, not knowing what will come next.

Q.   Yet you do say in "A Language of New York" [This in Which] that the world "if it is matter/Is impenetrable."

A.   Ultimately, it's impenetrable. At any given time the explanation of something will be the name of something unknown. We have a kind of feeling—I described doubts about it—but we have a kind of feeling that the absolutely unitary is somehow absolute, that, at any rate, it really exists. It's been the feeling always that that which is absolutely single really does exist—the atom, for example. That particle of matter, when you get to it, is absolutely impenetrable, absolutely inexplicable. If it's not, we'll find something else which is inexplicable.

Q.   Is that what you meant when you said in "A Narrative" [This in Which], "Things explain each other,/not themselves"?

A.   That's it.

Q.   There's a passage in "Of Being Numerous" that seems to sum up your attitude. Let me quote it:

The power of the mind, the

Power and weight
Of the mind which
Is not enough, it is nothing
And does nothing

Against the natural world,
Behemoth, white whale, beast
They will say and less than beast,
The fatal rock

Which is the world—[#26]

A. That's right. Then, having said that, I went on to something I
called "the lyric valuables" somewhere else ["From Disaster" in *The
Materials*]. I suppose what I'm saying really is that there is no life for
humanity except the life of the mind. I don't know whether it's useful
to say that to anyone. Either people will have discovered it for themselves or else it won't be true for them.

Q. Well, exactly what do you mean by "the life of the mind" in
this sense?

A. I mean the awareness . . . I suppose it's nearly a sense of awe,
simply to feel that the thing is there and that it's quite something
to see. It's an awareness of the world, a lyric reaction to the world.
"Of Being Numerous" ends with the word "curious" partly as a joke
on Whitman, but also because men are curious, and at the end of a
very long poem, I couldn't find anything more positive to say than
that.

Q. Then by "life of the mind" you mean something intuitive, not
something analytical.

A. Yes, or just my word "faith." I said life of the mind and perhaps
I spoke a little carelessly. I was anticipating, as its opposite, all the
struggles for happiness, all the search for a morality of altruism, all
the dependence on the poor to confer value—and eventually the poor
might one way or another disappear. I was anticipating the whole
discussion of "the good," of an ethic, and leaping ahead. I don't
mean that there isn't anything to do right now, but I was thinking
about a justification of human life, eventually, in what I call the life
of the mind.

Q. I don't quite follow you. Are you suggesting that "the life of the
mind" replace social values?

A. Not "replace," no. There have been certain bases for a purely humanist or secular ethic which have worked—in the first place, the presence of the poor makes possible an ethic of altruism. That is, to want a good job and whitewall tires and a radio and so on is the very symbol of bestiality, isn't it? But if one can go and find that there are people in the South who don't have these things, then a good job and whitewall tires and a radio become positively spiritual values. I don't mean to mock the kids who went to Mississippi; they were heroic and they were doing what needed to be done. But the ethic isn't permanent and it isn't going to answer the problems. However one names that problem—the outcome of the process of humanity—it won't solve it.

One's afraid of the loss of an ethic because, of course, one does have ethical feelings. One does object to the war in Vietnam, for instance. One has trouble coming to terms with these things. We don't actually know if human life is operable without an ethic. There's the wonderful business of Socrates' defense of himself, with the beautifully worked out, entirely rational principle that one behaves ethically because one has to live in society after all and if one injures society, he will be acting against his own interest. For the sake of this doctrine he was about to drink the hemlock—which is a kind of contradiction that my poems often raise. Why do we do it? My last book tries to say that there is a concept of humanity, there is something we want humanity to be or to become, and this would establish the basis of an ethic. But that's pure metaphysical sentiment. It can't be done the way Socrates was doing it.

Q. I'm beginning to see what you mean by sincerity. Your obligation is to your feelings alone. If it so happens that they are ethical, so much the better.

A. So much the better, or at least so much the more ethical. But of literature surely we both know that a student having once experienced the meaning of sincerity is hooked; he will know what literature is though he may have only that one quotation to prove it all his life long. And out of the same emotion, the same compulsion, one says what he thinks is true, not because he would like it to be true, still less because he thinks it would be good for the reader. I'm just reporting my experiences in life, including the one that when they drop enough jellied gasoline on children, you can't stand it anymore. I'm just stating a fact about what you can and cannot stand. If it didn't bother one to burn children, why say it does? I don't understand inventing an ethic;

I'm just trying to understand what the ethic is, how long it can last. An ethic is a funny thing: when it's gone, it's gone and you can't mourn it. You can only talk about what you actually feel.

Q.   There is a difference between an ethic that is gone and one that is merely unfulfilled, though. Napalm may represent the failure of an ethic, the failure of a people to meet an ideal, but does it represent the actual passing of a value? We feel guilt in violating it.

A.   Right. Again, I think I did work it out some in *Of Being Numerous* on the basis of pure metaphysics. We care about the idea of what's going to happen to humanity, including after one's death. I think in some other poem I argued it out; it's a little difficult to go through it tactfully in prose. Young people, even people of thirty, have an uninterrupted memory of twenty years of life and their life expectancy is much more than that, an infinity, more or less. They can reasonably expect to live longer than they can imagine. At a certain time of life, that ceases to be true. People know the most distant date on which they will die, and it does not seem far off. If they knew the world was going to end within that length of time, I argue, they would not bother to live their time out. There are other situations any of us could imagine in which people would not be willing to live, would find it impossible to live, without some concept of sharing in history or humanity—something which is happening after their death. Socrates obviously did because he drank the hemlock. I'm still not inventing or trying to be good for anyone. I'm trying to say how or why it is that one does live.

Q.   But you feel that you yourself have a commitment to an ethic. You are not just an observer.

A.   Since I have a commitment to it, then I do something about it. If I didn't have the commitment, I wouldn't—the commitment being a sentiment, a something, a "gene." We simply have an ethical motivation and we must deal with that fact; if we didn't have it, it wouldn't be a problem.

Q.   Then you're an observer of your own feelings, which are inherently ethical. The idea of sincerity really seems to be the crucial one here. Well, perhaps we can go on to a different kind of subject. I was wondering whether you had any special ideas on prosody. I know that in an early essay Zukofsky talked about "objectification" in prosodic terms.

A.   Yes. Well, I do believe in a form in which there is a sense of the whole line, not just its ending. Then there's the sense of the relation between lines, the relation in their length; there is a sense of the relation of the speed, of the alterations and momentum of the poem, the feeling when it's done that this has been rounded. I think that probably a lot of the worst of modern poetry, and it would be true of some quite good poetry, such as Creeley's, uses the line-ending simply as the ending of a line, a kind of syncopation or punctuation. It's a kind of formlessness that lacks any sense of line measure.

The meaning of a poem is in the cadences and the shape of the lines and the pulse of the thought which is given by those lines. The meaning of many lines will be changed—one's understanding of the lines will be altered—if one changes the line-ending. It's not just the line-ending as punctuation but as separating the connections of the progression of thought in such a way that understanding of the line would be changed if one altered the line division.

Q.   Do you agree at all with Williams' notion about "breaking the back of the iambic pentameter"?

A.   I don't subscribe to any of the theories that poetry should simply reproduce common speech, and so on. My reason for using a colloquial vocabulary is really a different one. It may be touched by populism as Williams' is, but in general I don't agree with his ideas on the subject.

Q.   What do you mean by populism in this sense?

A.   Williams likes to name those objects: wheelbarrow, white chickens, etc. I, too, have a sense—I hesitate to say it because I have no way of defending it—of the greater reality of certain kinds of objects than of others. It's a sentiment. I have a very early poem about a car closed in glass. I felt that somehow it was unreal and I said so—the light inside that car. Shall I read it? It's very short.

Q.   By all means.

A.   In fact a lot of the poems talk about that sort of thing.

> Closed car—closed in glass—
> At the curb,
> Unapplied and empty:

A thing among others
Over which clouds pass and the
          alteration of lighting,

An overstatement
Hardly an exterior.
Moving in traffic
This thing is less strange—
Tho the face, still within it,
Between glasses—place, over which
          time passes—a false light. [*Discrete Series*]

There is a feeling of something false in overprotection and over-luxury—my idea of categories of realness.

Q. That's very interesting. It reminds me of another poem in which the light is illusory but does not seem to be false, the poem called "Forms of Love" in *This in Which.*

A. I suppose I would have to say to you at this point the terrible word "love," which seems to me to have a category of reality too. The car in the poem I just quoted is detached from emotion, from use, from necessity—from everything except the most unconscionable of the emotions. And that lake which appears in the night of love seemed to me to be quite real even though it was actually fog.

Q. But only two lovers—because of their heightened state of mind or heightened sensitivity—would have thought that the fog was a lake.

A. Yes, I think that's true. Certainly I was assuming that in the title.

Q. So the vision was actually a form of love.

A. That's right.

Q. I notice you quote Kierkegaard in "Of Being Numerous" 16, and I wonder if his view of life has in any way influenced you.

A. I liked the passage I used very much, although out of context it's a little different. I was very moved by the passage, but I don't think Kierkegaard in general has been very important to me.

Q. You also cite Heidegger and Maritain elsewhere.

A.   They have been very important to me. Maritain's *Creative Intuition in Art and Poetry*, not any other work though. Ideas like Heidegger's have been important to me for a long time, as early as the first poem in *Discrete Series*. It says, "The knowledge not of sorrow, you were saying, but of boredom/ Is . . . Of the world, weather-swept, with which one shares the century." The word "boredom" is a little surprising there. It means, in effect, that the knowledge of the mood of boredom is the knowledge of what *is*, "of the world, weather-swept." But these phrases I use here to paraphrase the poem are phrases from Heidegger's Acceptance Speech [of the Chair of Philosophy at Freiburg] made in 1929, the year I was writing the poem. And the words "boredom" and "knowledge" are, in their German equivalents, the words he used. So I feel I have a natural sympathy with Heidegger— that he should use as a philosophic concept a mood of boredom. And the word is rather strange in the poem, too. The statements are identical.

Q.   Just what do you mean, he used as a philosophic concept a mood of boredom?

A.   I was referring to one of the major concepts in the Acceptance Speech: the mood of boredom and the recognition of what is.

Q.   You also mentioned Maritain.

A.   Yes, well, what I quoted in the first book is the sort of thing I value most in him: "We wake in the same moment to ourselves and to things." That's pretty central to my own thinking. I don't like his religious apologetics, though.

Q.   We've been talking about philosophers that interest you; what about poets? I was wondering what your attitude is toward, say, Pound or Williams.

A.   It's true, of course, that Pound and Williams were both extremely important to me. But some people think I resemble Williams and it seems to me that the opposite is true. Pound unfortunately defended me against the possible charge of resembling him in the original preface to *Discrete Series*. The fact has always haunted me. At any rate, my attitudes are opposite those of Williams. Certainly one would have needed a great deal more courage, without his example, to begin to find a way to write. He was invaluable and many of his poems are beautiful, though I've always had reservations about *Paterson*. I think "The Asphodel" is a most beautiful and profound poem.

Q. I was under the impression that one of the basic themes in *Paterson*, "no ideas but in things," would appeal to you.

A. I have always wondered whether that expression didn't apply to the construction of meaning in a poem—not necessarily that there are out there no ideas but in things, but rather that there would be in the poem no ideas but those which could be expressed through the description of things. I took it that he meant the latter until I found that the expression was frequently understood in a different way. As for Pound, of course, a lot of his things stay in one's mind forever. Again, I have a great many reservations about Pound.

Q. Anyway, if your interpretation of the Williams line is correct, it seems to me you would in fact partly resemble him.

A. Perhaps.

Q. What about the *Cantos*? They seem to be arranged according to a "discrete series," by the "ideogrammic method."

A. Pound's ego system, Pound's organization of the world around a character, a kind of masculine energy, is extremely foreign to me. And Pound's root in Browning, which is so much more tremendous than any other root he has, is also foreign to me. What I really read in Pound are passages and lines. Just about the time I'm beginning to consider Pound an idiot, I come to something like the little wasp in the *Pisan Cantos*, and I know that I'm reading a very great poet.

Q. At least a poet capable of great lyricism.

A. Yes.

Q. Toward what recent writers do you feel the most sympathetic? I know you mention William Bronk in your poems.

A. I admire Bronk, but I'd prefer not to run down a list of others. I have no system for judging them. I can name the poets who really have been of decisive importance to me—Charles Reznikoff and Zukofsky as a person, his conversation, not his poetry—although, again as with Pound, while I can make an awful lot of objections to parts of A, the opening words, "A/Round of fiddles playing Bach," have rung in my ears for a very long time and always will, I imagine. Reznikoff has been the most important to me, consciously at least. And otherwise—this is what I have to explain—really Blake is more important to me than Williams, and several philosophers may be more important than Pound. The contemporary poets aren't the most important thing in my life, with the exception of those few things that really matter to me. Wyatt's poems, and several Middle English poems, among other antiquities, mean more to me than any except one or two of the contemporary. It must be some habit of life that makes it seem to young poets that all the other young poets are the major factors in his life. At any rate it's not true.

Q. It would seem to be at least partly true of writers like Olson, Duncan, and Creeley. Have you read much of them?

A. I've read a lot of Olson. I think "In Cold Hell, In Thicket" is a very fine poem. I don't really like the *Maximus Poems* nor accept them at all. I admire Duncan insofar as I can understand him, which is very rarely.

Q. I notice that in the poem called "Route" in *Of Being Numerous* you devote a whole section in prose to a story about Alsatian men who tried to avoid being conscripted into the German army during the Second World War by hiding in holes. Evidently that story meant a lot to you.

A. Yes, and I had to undertell it all the way because it's terribly dramatic and it got hold of me. I really had to tell it as quietly as I could, and, besides, it's a public story, the account of a terrible experience. But that's what these men did: they spent two or three years in a hole in the ground. They could get out of them only once in a while when it was snowing and their tracks would be covered.

Q. Were these holes actually caves or what?

A. Foxholes or trenches, with logs laid down and covered over with sod after the man had gotten in. Pierre Adam, who told me the story, would help the men and bring them food when he could. It's a painful story to tell. I wrote it down as simply as I could and the language partly reflects the fact that Pierre told me in French and my French is limited. We spoke a very simple language to each other. It's the kind of story any existentialist—Sartre specifically—might tell except that it did happen to me and it was as important to me as the poem indicates. And Pierre knew what he was telling me; he knew the point he was making. He knew that I was very positive about politics, about a social and political morality—very positive about judgments concerning the war.

Q.   And this story is related to the rest of the poem?

A.   The poem is about some of the things that have happened to me; the story is part of the meaning of that poem and all of the experiences told in it to record what I learned. "Route" is very closely connected to "Of Being Numerous," the learning that one is, after all, just oneself and in the end is rooted in the singular, whatever one's absolutely necessary connections with human history are. The section plays that part in the poem.

Q.   Then even though "Route" and "Of Being Numerous" seem to be speaking about the general human condition, they are actually very personal poems, aren't they?

A.   That's right, but I'm also writing about the human condition. All I actually know is what happened to me and I'm telling it. There wasn't any time in my life when I suddenly decided that now I'd write some philosophy. I'm just telling about what I encountered, what life was to me. In places I think I insisted upon this—"the things which one cannot not see," I wrote, and "not the symbol but the scene." I've written about what happened and the place it happened in, and that, I suppose, is the only philosophy I could possibly understand anyway, except for some kind of mathematical philosophy.

    I wouldn't, for instance, talk about death with any great intensity unless I thought I was going to die. As close as I come to a philosophic statement is in that poem in which I wrote, "we want to be here"—just to set the fact down because the poems do have a kind of pessimism; and I'm reminding myself that I do want to be here, that I would not lack the courage to cut my throat if I wanted to do so. I don't do so. In fact I enjoy life very, very much. I wrote that poem in case there was any misinterpretation of that. And I set myself again and again, not in the spirit of any medical pragmatism, any philosophy offering to cure everything, nor in any effort to improve anybody, but just to record the fact, to saying that I enjoy life very much and defining my feeling by the word "curious" or, as at the end of "A Narrative," "joy," joy in the fact that one confronts a thing so large, that one is part of it. The sense of awe, I suppose, is all I manage to talk about. I had written that "virtue of the mind is that emotion which causes to see," and I think that perhaps that is the best statement of it.

Q. This is "the life of the mind" again.

A. Yes, and that's what I really mean by mind. If the virtue of the mind is missing, if somebody is "wicked" in my sense, I have nothing to say to him and it is this fact that causes me to mourn, now and then, for large sections of humanity. I don't know whether I can tell a whole city or a whole college or a whole class full of people that their minds should possess that virtue. If they do not possess it, I really feel despair when I face them, and I do not know what to tell them.

Q. And this virtue is the primary feeling of the poet, a kind of sensitivity?

A. Yes, it is an emotion. The mind is capable not only of thinking but has an emotional root that forces it to look, to think, to see. The most tremendous and compelling emotion we possess is the one that forces us to look, to know, if we can, to see. The difference between just the neuro-sensitivity of the eye and the act of seeing is one over which we have no control. It is a tremendous emotional response, which fills us with the experience that we describe as seeing, not with the experience of some twitching nerves in the eyeball. It can only be interpreted emotionally, and those who lack it I despair of. And that's when the poems sort of stagger now and then, when I talk about despair.

Q. But in a sense it's this very sensitivity that isolates the poet or makes him a lonely man, isn't it?

A. Yes, I quoted from a letter I received from a very young student at Columbia, Rachel Blau: "whether as the intensity of seeing increases, one's distance from them, the people, does not also increase." It was a profound and painful question that I had asked myself in her words. And that's what you are asking me again, for all that I've written a whole poem to establish, if I could, the concept of humanity, a concept without which we can't live. And yet I don't know that poetry is not actually destructive for people, because what you are implying is true. It does lead to the growing isolation of the poet; there's no question in my mind about it. I can only say that for all one's fears and hesitations and doubts, and for my rejection of poetry for twenty or twenty-five years, I think that what we really want is not to establish a definition of the good and then work toward it, but rather to see what happens happen, to go wherever we are going. I think a poet comes to feel that this is all he does—moves us in the direction we are going.

Q. I think it's interesting that for all your desire merely to report your feelings and to repudiate an ethical aim for your poetry, you do have strong ethical convictions to express. But, as you've said, the important thing is that the ethic be felt and not merely constructed. I notice that your poetry does refer to the Depression on occasion, and I imagine that your feelings during this period were particularly intense.

A. That's true. I think it was fifteen million families that were faced with the threat of immediate starvation. It wasn't a business one simply read about in the newspaper. You stepped out your door and found men who had nothing to eat. I'm not moralizing now—and I've been through this before—but for some people it was simply impossible not to do something. I've written an essay that appeared in *Kulchur* 10 in which I explained that I didn't believe in political poetry or poetry as being politically efficacious. I don't even believe in the honesty of a man saying, "Well, I'm a poet and I will make my contribution to the cause by writing poems about it." I don't believe that's any more honest than to make wooden nutmegs because you happen to be a woodworker. If you decide to do something politically, you do something that has political efficacy. And if you decide to write poetry, then you write poetry, not something that you hope, or deceive yourself into believing, can save people who are suffering. That was the dilemma of the thirties. In a way I gave up poetry because of the pressures of what for the moment I'll call conscience. But there were some things I had to live through, some things I had to think my way through, some things I had to try out—and it was more than politics, really; it was the whole experience of working in factories, of having a child, and so on. Absurd to ask myself whether what I undertook was right or wrong or right for the artist and the rest of that. Hugh Kenner interrupted my explanation to him of these years by saying, "In brief, it took twenty-five years to write the next poem." Which is the way to say it.

I probably won't stop writing poetry this time, not because I've changed my evaluation of things but partly because I feel I have only so much time left and that's what I want to do. During those years I was perfectly aware of a lot of time before me and I at no time thought I wasn't a poet. I don't remember saying it clearly to myself, but I never felt that I would never write a poem again.

Q.   What did you actually do during the thirties?

A.   Oh, well, we were Communists, all right. I don't know whether to say we had philosophic doubts, but we knew that some forms of activity were of very questionable usefulness. We made sure that what we were doing was not politicalizing but something we really intended to do. We were in a way isolated; all our friends were poets and most of them were poets of the right wing. We joined the movement to help organize the unemployed. There're little accounts of it in the poems, which I think I muffed. The story has to be told very forthrightly and somehow I couldn't do it. It was a matter of going from house to house, apartment to apartment; I think we knew every house in Bedford-Stuyvesant and North Brooklyn and all the people in them. We wanted to gather crowds of people on the simple principle that the law would have to be changed where it interfered with relief and that settlement laws would have to be unenforceable when they involved somebody's starvation. And we were interested in rioting, as a matter of fact—rioting under political discipline. Disorder, disorder—to make it impossible to allow people to starve. It also involved the hunger march on Washington as well as local undertakings.

Q.   For how long were you active?

A.   Not so many years. Then there's the well-known story of the difficulty of escaping from the Communist philosophy and attitudes and one's Communist friends. And then there came about a situation that made it impossible for us to participate anymore, even after the difficulty with our own thinking. We were under threat by the McCarthy committee and had to flee the United States. I don't think I have to tell the whole story about that. You get questioned as to who you knew and you refuse to answer and you get jailed. We did not want to get jailed; that would have been only a matter of a year—we weren't terribly important—but we had a child and it would have been a bad thing. Mexico wasn't an absolute refuge, but it made it a little more difficult to get us and we knew we needed only to make it a little difficult. Nobody was very excited about us. But we did have to flee. It was actually more dangerous to drop out than not because the McCarthy committee would figure you were ripe for becoming an informer and we needed our friends badly—and there was the fact of the child too. But this is a little difficult for me to say. There is a difference in one's attitude, in what one wants to say and doesn't want to say, doesn't want to put down on paper, when one is speaking to a child—well, I can't say I was speaking to our baby daughter. I'll simply say I was being a father, and fathers don't confess to fears even to themselves. That is in its way political, too. It's part of the whole pragmatism of social and political attitudes, the test of goodness, which extends awhile when one is thinking of a child. But it's much more complex. It was actually sort of a different time of life that I sat down again and set myself, for the first time really, to complete a poem, to really finish a poem and be sure I felt I had completed it. It was as a matter of fact in 1958.

Q.   Was this while you were still in Mexico?

A.   Still in Mexico. The first poem I wrote was one of the long ones in *The Materials*. I think it was "Blood from a Stone." It was a fairly rough poem which I knew I just had to write. It took three years to write the whole collection. I don't know what proportion of the poems were written in Mexico and what in New York.

Q.   Just how long were you in Mexico?

A.   From 1950 to 1958.

Q.   That's a long time.

A.   A long time.

Q.   Did you get involved with Mexican culture?

A.   Yes, some, unsuccessfully. I think every American's experience is unsuccessful in this regard. I could tell very nice stories about Mexico, but I also have a lot of negative feelings I don't even want to state. The fact is that it's not a very good place for Americans to be.

Q.   What bothered you in particular?

A.   I really will be attacking Mexico if I get into that, and there's no particular reason. But it had to do with my sense of being a craftsman, for whatever it's worth, and my sense of not being an executive. In Mexico foreigners are not permitted to produce objects, and the law is rigorously enforced. I set up a small business, which was not easy.

One becomes accustomed to paying bribes everywhere and with the greatest possible tact and skill—a situation of infinite corruption, to begin to tell it, a society, a culture really trapped and not the fault of the people. They are trapped by their culture, by the relation of men and women, by the absolute corruption of government, by the habits of bureaucracy, the habits of people. One is forced to change class very sharply in Mexico; if one is a foreigner, one has to be an upper-bourgeois citizen, as a matter of law or necessity. None of these things was easy for us; they were by no means easy.

Q.   What kind of a business did you manage to set up?

A.   I made—"made" in the upper-bourgeois sense—furniture. I never touched a tool. I set up with a Mexican partner, a very wonderful man and a very fine craftsman.

Q.   Was there any specific reason for your coming back in 1958?

A.   Just that we could; the McCarthy thing was over. We only went to Mexico in the first place because we couldn't get passports. We weren't illegally in Mexico but we were helplessly there, and we paid an infinite series of bribes.

Q.   What did you do when you got back to New York?

A.   Sat down and wrote poetry. We just found a place in Brooklyn which was easy enough to pay for, and I started writing again. I knew James Laughlin of New Directions Press would give me some consideration and that Rago of Poetry knew my earlier work or at least recognized my name, so I wasn't entirely without connections. I felt that people knew me a little.

Q.   Mr. Oppen, I am deeply grateful for your willingness to discuss your poetry and your life.

A.   I have a liking for openness and a willingness to talk and question, and if one says something that is wrong, so one says something that is wrong. One tries not to write anything that is wrong, but conversations are another matter. Sometimes it turns out that people can find common ground or that they have that virtue of the mind I was talking about when they read your poetry—which is just another way of saying that they give a damn.

CARL RAKOSI

Q. I wonder whether we could begin, Mr. Rakosi, with biography. You consider yourself a Midwesterner, don't you?

A. Actually, I was born in Berlin, Germany. My parents were Hungarian Jews who happened to be living there at the time. When I was a year old, the family moved back to Hungary and I lived in Baja, a small town in the south, until I was six. And then my father, my brother, and I came to this country—that was in 1910. We came first to Chicago, then moved to Gary, Indiana, and finally wound up in Kenosha, Wisconsin. So Kenosha was really my hometown. That's where I was brought up and went to school. Then I went to the University of Wisconsin and got a degree in English and a master's in educational psychology.

Q. How did you end up in social work?

A. It was sheer accident. This was a period of severe economic distress and it was extremely difficult to get a job anywhere. I happened to be talking to somebody who was also looking for a job and he said, "Why don't you go into social work?" I didn't even know what it was. He didn't either, but he told me there was an office in Chicago where they were hiring people, so I went down there. This was the American Association of Social Workers office, and if you were alive and had a degree, they hired you, there was such a shortage of personnel. And if you were a man, they spread out the red carpet for you. I started out with an agency in Cleveland. I had not by any means given up the idea of writing; I thought I could do both. But I fell in love with social work and that was my undoing as a poet, in a sense. I didn't actually give up the idea of trying to write poetry until the

---

Interview conducted by L. S. Dembo on April 4, 1968, in Madison, Wisconsin. All poems referred to are contained in the volume *Amulet* (New Directions, New York, 1967).

late thirties when I was fooling around with different things. I left social work for a while and came back to the University. . . . I thought maybe if I went into psychiatry, this would give me something I could do and still write. Anyhow, social work just drew me very strongly. But it wasn't until the late thirties that it seemed impossible for me to be a social worker and to write at the same time.

Q. That's very interesting because the dust jacket on *Amulet* states that you stopped writing because you were disillusioned with a world in which poetry no longer had a place.

A. That is another element, too. During the thirties I was working in New York—this was during the very depth of the Depression—and any young person with any integrity or intelligence had to become associated with some left-wing organization. You just couldn't live with yourself if you didn't. So I got caught up very strongly in the whole Marxian business. I took very literally the basic Marxian ideas about literature having to be an instrument for social change, for expressing the needs and desires of large masses of people. And believing that, I couldn't write poetry, because the poetry that I could write could not achieve these ends.

Q. Perhaps we can talk for a while about the kind of poetry you had been writing. I know that your work appeared in Louis Zukofsky's "Objectivists" Anthology and that you are presently considered to be one of the objectivists *per se*. Williams mentions in his *Autobiography* that he got together with Zukofsky, Charles Reznikoff, George Oppen, and Basil Bunting to launch the movement around 1928 or so. I was wondering whether you participated in any of the discussions.

A. That is not correct. Williams did not get together with those men to found the objectivist movement. And I doubt whether it is a movement in the sense in which that word is generally used. The term really originated with Zukofsky, and he pulled it out of a hat. It was not an altogether accurate way of designating the few people assembled in the anthology and also in the "Objectivist" issue of *Poetry*. But he wanted some kind of name, and he checked out the term with me and, I assume, with some of the other people. The name was all right, but I told him I didn't think some of the poems in the anthology were "objectivist" or very objective in meaning. He said, "Well, that's true," but I've forgotten the reasons he gave for sticking to the name. It didn't matter. But Williams had very little to do with it. He was included, but it didn't come from his initiative.

Q.   I see. Well, in any case, would you say that you could write poetry that was "objectivist"—whatever it meant—whereas you couldn't write poetry that was Marxist? And that finally because objectivist poetry had no social implications, it became meaningless to you, and that was perhaps one of the reasons you simply gave up poetry?

A.   No, no. I never took my association with Zukofsky and the others that seriously. After all, I was living in the Middle West, except for a brief period in New York when I was seeing Zukofsky, and I didn't even know any of the other people.

Q.   Did Zukofsky himself make an impression on you?

A.   He came along at a time when it was very important for me to have someone like him around. I'd send him something to look at and it would come back with just a few comments, but they were always right on the nose. He seemed to know better than I what was true Rakosi and what was not. I really have a very warm feeling for Louis for this critical feedback. We had a most interesting correspondence. I still have his letters, incidentally, although I don't think Louis would want them revealed. They're very short, like some of his poems. If Louis could get something on a postage stamp, he'd do it.

Q.   What about Zukofsky's poetry?

A.   I believe it has a strong sense of form—it is very firmly structured; the interstitching, you might say, is extremely fine and stands up remarkably well. I also feel, however, that there are some self-defeating things in his work; his personal self, his humanity, seldom comes through the way it really is. I find this regrettable because fundamentally I think he is a warm person. The many ellipses in his work bother me because they represent, perhaps, his subconscious way of preventing this human part from coming out. On the other hand, there is a real dignity there and a compact solidity. I wish, however, that Zukofsky had never met Pound. I think that maybe his direction would have been different.

Q.   How so?

A.   First, I had better admit that I believe that Pound's critical writing—particularly the famous "Don'ts" essay—is an absolute foundation stone of contemporary American writing. But in his own work I think he's been disastrous as a model, totally disastrous to younger writers. I'm thinking particularly of the *Cantos*, of its epic tone. What was this based on, after all? On man's experiences? Certainly not. The experiences of men in the *Cantos* have only a highly specialized, idiosyncratic interest. On his view of the nature of man? Ridiculous! In Pound's view he is a boob or a crook or something equally bad. On his theoretical systems? His choices here are not even interesting. Why then an epic tone? Because of Pound's own personal need for supremacy, grandiosity. One has the feeling that everything was fed into his exciting lyrical machine to serve this purpose. It's not honest. He pretends that his material is epic when it is only a device to achieve grandiosity at the expense of the reader. All that pretense and double-dealing are nauseating to me. And irrelevant. People today are not heroic, and modern human nature is not epic. It's just human, and anything else is just playing games.

Q.   And you believe that Zukofsky is grandiose?

A.   No. Actually the long form of *A* is better suited to Louis than the shorter forms, since more of him comes through in it. But Pound has provided him with a large-scale model of unconnected fragments and has led him to believe that it's all right to make the most recondite, specialized references, as if it could be taken for granted that a literate reader would be familiar with them and have Pound's attitude towards them. If I'm reading a poem by Pound, why should I care what he read somewhere? It's of absolutely no interest to me.

Q.   Don't you think he's able to make it interesting to you by putting it into a poem?

A.   No, he's not. He pretends to know what he does not know and is contemptuous of all the boobs who don't understand his references and have not realized what is obvious to him; for example, that Confucius had all the answers. The final image that comes through in the *Cantos* is of a master of language and cadence, but the man who is speaking, the person, is preposterously grandiose. And a terrible example to others, who have a hard enough time keeping their own streak of grandiosity under control so as to be able to have an authentic encounter with a subject, without having a Lorelei chanting to them what they yearn to hear but know cannot be, that the road to greatness lies in grandiosity. But that's Pound's song, and once a person has been exposed to Pound's aura, it is difficult not to succumb. After all, who doesn't want to be great?

But there's a lot of this stuff around. Poetry gets judged, for example, as great; greater than; not so great as; good but not great, etc. Also, from Pound's grandiosity it is only a short step to the bewitching notion—which, incidentally, Zukofsky is far too selective to fall for—that everything that comes into the mind is precious. The long poem thus becomes a necessity for some writers. Before they have learned how to write an authentic short poem, it is announced that they are at work on a long one—meaning they're on something really big. Which leads to an irrational, philistine system in which one had to feel apologetic about "Brightness falls from the air, / Queens have died young and fair" because it is only two lines long.

Q. Getting back to my original question, what kind of poetry did you hope to write?

A. Well, at first I was very much seduced by the elegance of language, the imaginative associations of words; I was involved in a language world—a little like the world of Wallace Stevens, who was an idol of mine during a certain period. But at the same time, another part of me did not get away from social reality. You'll find in the Youthful Mockeries section of Amulet a lot of scorn for what was going on in the social world. In my recent work I'm doing something different and for me very difficult, and that is to take something quite personal and turn it into poetry. After all, nobody is interested in Rakosi as a person; why should they be? It's a tremendous challenge, therefore, to see whether the person Rakosi and what is happening to him can be turned into poetry. Now Americana is different. In these poems I was fascinated by folklore and I was searching there for basic American types that have really influenced our thinking—and these types are in all of us in a way. I'm sorry I petered out on Americana; I was hoping to go on.

Q. I'd like to get back to the problem of an "imagined language world" in a moment, but in the meantime could you elaborate on what you were just saying about the Americana poems? Perhaps you could comment on "Americana 1" [Amulet, p. 38], that short piece about a pioneer who is asked why he's taking his gun into Indian country, since "If your time has come, you'll die anyway," and replies, "I know that, but it may be the Indian's time."

A. Well, who was the American settler, what was he really like? It seemed to me the truth about the pioneer was not that he was romantic, but that he was practical. His reply is very primitive and shrewd.

This is my own personal concept of what the pioneer must have been like, not in the way he appears in American folklore, of course, where he's made heroic.

Q. I had the idea that the poem was simply based on a punch line. But you are actually saying that one should reflect on the speaker who has made the utterance, rather than on the utterance itself.

A. Well, I think so. Although it's true I tried to pack a lot into that last line.

Q. But to get back to the main body of your poetry, in "Shore Line" you wrote, "This is the raw data. / A mystery translates it / into feeling and perception; / then imagination; / finally the hard / inevitable quartz / figure of will / and language." It seems to me that this is an indication of how you view the poetic process in general. Wouldn't this passage be in accord with what you were saying about an imagined language world?

A. I think that's true, though it's not the whole thing. The first draft of what I want to write will be pretty much raw data that's been changed around. Then I keep changing it around some more, but it's still raw data. It hasn't been converted yet to a . . . I would say a mystery changes it. I really mean a mystery because I don't know what it is that makes the conversion possible. I only know when I haven't done it. What is it in a person that doesn't let him be until he has transformed an experience, certain feelings and observations that are related to each other and suddenly strike him as important subject-matter? I don't know the answer.

Q. Well, actually I had in mind the state of some of the perceptions and images in the finished poem. "The Lobster," for instance, seems to be presenting raw data, although if you look at it carefully, it's not raw data by any means: "Eastern Sea, 100 fathoms, / green sand, pebbles, / broken shells. / Off Suno Saki 60 fathoms, / gray sand, pebbles, / bubbles rising. / . . . The fishery vessel *Ion* / drops anchor here / collecting / plankton smears and fauna."

A. Well, there are a lot of details here, but they're certainly not just raw data; they add up to the sea, the mystery and coldness of the sea. By the way, this poem has been reprinted more than any other; for some reason people have liked it. I really don't know why; in a way, it's less Rakosi than almost any other of my poems because it doesn't have people in it. What I was trying to project here is a depersonalized something which is the sea.

Q. What about the person of the speaker as he sees each of these items brought up from the bottom? Isn't the reader viewing this "raw material" through the eyes of a man located on the fishery vessel?

A. That's so, but what I was trying to do was to write a poem without the poet.

Q. Do you believe that's possible?

A. It's possible (perhaps only relatively), though I really don't enjoy doing it that way.

Q. The poem called "Time to Kill" seems to raise the same questions. It seems to be giving raw data, objective description—though, when you consider it, the observations are clearly those of a man with time to kill, someone who is bored, perhaps.

A. That's right, up to a point. This was a hot summer afternoon and you know how everything thickens and slows up when it's hot, so that one's perceptions of what's going on become slower and denser. Then along comes an old man into the scene, and I felt and tried to convey a bit of pathos there.

Q. But you would say then that there is a human subject, a perceiver?

A. Oh yes, it's very different from "The Lobster" in that respect. And "Time to Kill" was written recently, whereas "The Lobster" was written thirty years ago. I couldn't have written "Time to Kill" as a young man.

Q. Why not?

A. I wasn't related to reality in that way then.

Q. What do you mean?

A. A lifetime of involvement with people in social work came between these two periods. This might make me a poorer poet in some ways because I'm not so completely subsumed by language as I was then. I'm equally interested in subject-matter.

Q. You mentioned Stevens before. By my calculations your poem

"Homage to Stevens" must be an early one since it seems to be chiefly a linguistic exercise.

A. Yes, very early. If I had had more poems to put into *Amulet* I would have left that one out.

Q. Why so?

A. It doesn't really say anything. I was just enjoying the pleasures of the images and the language. I don't know what kind of experience Stevens started with, but if you take one of his poems and try to understand it as a man saying something, you're lost. Its beauties are something utterly different. He's killed all subject-matter.

Q. Would you say that Williams has done the same thing?

A. Oh no, Williams had a great respect for subject-matter.

Q. Well, *Paterson* is concerned with a human subject and a human world, but I had in mind some of the earlier poems that were simply formal presentations, matters of perception again.

A. Perhaps, but with Williams you always have the feeling that there's a man there talking. With Stevens, you don't get that feeling. He's transformed himself into something wonderful and beautiful, but he's not a man talking.

Q. But you must admit that some of your own subjects are not always immediately apparent. That poem called "The Gnat," for example, or "The City, 1925."

A. I had a little trouble with the gnat poem, too, when I reread it. The subject-matter really is winter—if you will imagine the rigors and the enormity of winter (the winter is especially enormous in Minnesota). And what is one person? He's really a gnat. That's me, a gnat in winter.

Q. Well, what are the "six rivers / and six wenches / the twelve / victories" in the lines that end the poem?

A. I can't answer that. I may have left the subject of winter in the middle of the poem and gone on to something else, in which case the two halves may not go together, I'm ashamed to say. Or the six rivers and six wenches, which I would consider twelve victories anytime, anywhere, may have flashed through my mind *because of the winter*, to triumph over it, as it were, and so on. In any case, I am not comfortable with the poem's ellipses.

Q. Don't you have another poem called "January of a Gnat," which repeats some of the images?

A. That is one of my first poems. It's all imagery, really. The subject is really my own imagination playing around with what winter felt like.

Q. What winter felt like from a highly imaginative point of view, not what it felt like literally.

A. Right, right.

Q. Does "The City, 1925" also have a subject, even though the images don't seem to have any logical connection between them?

A. Well, let me say this about it. I'm a young man of twenty-two, timid and lonely, and I come to New York from a small town and it's overwhelming—the immensity, the profusion, the infinite variety, the people. The poem is an effort to come to terms with this overwhelming impression. Since this is my first exposure, there are all kinds of objects to be described—objects which have no connection with each other. The connection is through my perception, through my receiving of them in their tremendous multiplicity.

Q. So once again the perceiver becomes the important element in the poem.

A. That's true. But intuitively I intended to keep these objects as intact as possible, to keep their integrity intact. So there is this element of an adherence to the integrity of the object that makes it different from mere description. At the same time, you are right. The real subject of the poem is not the objects themselves, interesting though they are, but what this young man is experiencing in their presence. What is important is that the integrity of both the subject and the object be kept. That is, I respect the external world—there is much in it that is beautiful if you look at it hard. I don't want to contaminate that; it has its own being; its own beauty and interest that should not be corrupted or distorted. But so does the poet have his own being.

Q. What would you say are some of the forces corrupting perception of the actual world in its intrinsic beauty?

A. Well, here let me speak as a psychologist. There's the strongest kind of pull in a poet against subject-matter—in fact, against writing a poem at all. No psychologist understood this as well as Otto Rank. He called this force the counter-will. This force is always around when the urge to write is felt, and is a match for it, and often more than a match. The fine hand of this counter-devil is evident, of course, in a writer's procrastination, but also operates behind the scenes in other more subtle and devious ways whenever one is evading subject-matter, by being rhetorical or elliptical, for example. On the surface this looks innocent, as if it were just a literary matter, but if the writer himself thinks so, it just means that its protective purpose has been achieved and he has been conned by his counter-devil. In the process, he may make something as good, or even better, but the fact remains that he did not retain the integrity of his original impulse, he had to appease or deceive his counter-will with a substitute. You can see this counter-devil is a very live fellow to me.

Q. What about the matter of abstraction? This brings us back to Pound's "A Few Don'ts."

A. Abstraction, of course, is the most common deadly offender. When you write about something as though it were a principle or a concept or a generalization, you have in that moment evaded it, its specificity, its earthly life. You are talking about something else. Really a different order of reality.

Q. Let me see if I understand you. You seem to be saying here that there are two kinds of corruption that are at the extreme of one another. One is a complete evasion of the subject by the use of formal devices in the poem, and the other is an excessively rational apprehension of the subject, so that the subject is transformed into the poet's conceptions about it rather than presented in its so-called inherent being.

A. If you change the word "conceptions" to "generalizations," you're right. It's extremely difficult to present the subject, the object that has been the cause of your experience, in its integrity—and you, the portrayer of it, in your full integrity.

Q. Actually, it is precisely this kind of approach that might be called "objectivist." Does this correspond to your idea of what the term really means?

A. I think so. It was the reason I thought the term was pretty good originally, when Zukofsky thought it up. One way to see what it is is to see what it is not—how objectivism differs from imagism or symbolism, for example. You might think for a moment that, after all, objectivism is a form of imagism or naturalism. But imagism as I recall—and I haven't read any imagist poems in thirty years—was a reaction to the period immediately preceding, against literary affectations. So the imagists set out to do what the French impressionists in painting did: go out into the open and look, see what you see, and put it down without affectation of the then dominant literary influences. And that's as much as they did, but it wasn't complete. It was only the first step in a poetic process. That's why imagism is not altogether satisfying; the person of the poet is not sufficiently present.

Now symbolism, of course, is more in contrast with objectivism. It seems to me that the subject of symbolism is a poetic state of feeling and its aim is to reproduce it. It really didn't matter much what you started with—whether it was a flower or the moon. All the poet was concerned with was his own feeling. And for that subject, symbolism is suitable, but it's a very narrow subject.

Q.   A state of feeling that was far removed from the object itself?

A.   Simply his own state of feeling. He didn't care about the moon really, or about a flower, the real character of the flower.

Q.   The radical difference then is between a state of feeling per se and one resulting from a direct perception of the object.

A.   Let me put it this way. This was a generalized state of feeling that the poet carried around with him. An object was simply an occasion for him to project this feeling.

Q.   This feeling that the symbolist possessed—his approach to reality —was in a sense a priori . . .

A.   Absolutely.

Q.   . . . whereas the objectivist has an a posteriori approach. He let his feelings depend upon the object and was faithful to the object.

A.   Right. Now take my poem "To a Young Girl." The girl is not an abstraction; she remains real all the way through the poem. She's not the epitome of a young girl, she is not a beautiful ideal of a young girl, she is a real young girl. Now she becomes subjective in the sense that I, or the speaker, carry on a certain inner dialogue about her, but that's my business, that's my reality which I project into the poem. But the girl is a real person. I respect her reality.

Q. This gets us back to "Shore Line," doesn't it? You begin with the raw data and then, being faithful to it, you transform it into perception and feeling and then into something imaginative.

A. I think so. I didn't realize when I wrote those lines that they were such a true expression of what goes on in me and of my view of poetry, objectivist poetry. But that's true.

Q. "To a Young Girl," then, while being based on an external object, really describes something that is going on in the mind of the poet; he's imagining what the girl herself might be thinking and he carries on an imaginary dialogue with her. It seemed to me that the point of the poem was the liveliness, to say the least, of the old man's thoughts and feelings.

A. Yes.

Q. In fact I was reminded of Humbert Humbert and Lolita. The nymphet turns out to be partly a creature of an old man's imagination.

A. I agree, I agree. You know, speaking of fidelity to the object, something else just occurred to me. *Amulet* was reviewed in a new British journal called the *Grosseteste Review* by a young poet who found a similarity between me and a young Czech poet named Holub. Holub is a physician and he's reported to have said that he was influenced by Williams, whom he read in translation. I have Holub's book at home and it's true that there are similarities. It seemed to me that maybe one reason Williams, Holub, and I have something in common is that none of us has been a professional poet or an academic person; we've all had similar professions and perhaps our experience in them has led to a similarity in our poetry. Williams always had a feeling of respect for the object. Actually, as a pediatrician, his work was as much psychological—establishing a rapport with mothers and children, being reassuring and understanding—as it was medical. And this is true for the social worker. I don't know which medical specialty Holub was in, but he may also have had this kind of experience. Williams, of course, never stopped writing, as I did; I suspect his first response to experience may have been like mine, but that he was more in the habit of transforming it into literary material.

Q. An interesting idea. So you feel that your poetry is closest to that of Williams?

A. Well, no. I would say the one who is closest to me is Charles Reznikoff.

Q. From what you've been saying, I can see what you mean.

A. I think that Reznikoff comes through in his earlier poems as a thoroughly compassionate man. He comes through as a person. When he's observing something, you're inside him.

Q. Your *Americana* poems seem reminiscent of some of the things he was doing in *Testimony*.

A. I was fascinated with that book. But what he was saying there is that the raw data can speak for itself. It was what happened, what was in the law books and court records, and it's poetry.

Q. So he's looking at reality from his own professional viewpoint, as a lawyer.

A. Not exactly. He's simply recording it with the homely specificity and phraseology of legal language in the way it would be done in a good court record. That book did not get good reviews, as I recall. I think the critics said he hadn't done enough with the material. But my first reaction when I read it was that maybe Reznikoff is right. Maybe the material can speak for itself. But my assumptions in the *Americana* poems are different. I don't assume there that the raw data is the poetry. One thing that is similar though is that Reznikoff seems to have been fascinated with legal language and let it stand that way. In *Americana* I was fascinated with the unique flow of colloquial language, and I kept it that way.

Q. Would you call Reznikoff an objectivist?

A. Yes. I would think he goes about writing a poem pretty much as I do. Not so much in *Testimony* as in the earlier poems. Years ago Zukofsky told me that I must get together with Reznikoff because we had a lot in common. We've never met, though.

Q. Did you ever meet George Oppen?

A. No. But I respect his poetry. It can come through with brilliant perceptions of reality, in which the self is interesting, as well as the object. But I can't warm up to it. It's stripped down too much.

Q. I wonder whether I might change the subject completely now and ask you a personal question. What made you decide to start writing poetry again after a lapse of over two decades?

A. Well, that's a very good story. I got a letter one day that had gone the rounds of a number of different cities, before it finally reached me, from a young Englishman named Andrew Crozier. He said that he had run across my name in an article by Rexroth, had looked up my work in magazines, and copied every single poem I had written. He had made a bibliography and wanted to know whether I had written any more. Well, the thought that somebody his age could care that much for my work really touched me; after all, there were two generations between us. And that's what started me.

There's an amusing bit to that letter. You know my legal name is Callman Rawley, not Carl Rakosi, and Crozier had a great deal of trouble tracking me down. Fortunately he was not discouraged by a letter from my publisher saying that he doubted if I was alive and that he had heard that I may have been a secret agent for the Comintern and died behind the Iron Curtain. However, this was only a rumor and Crozier must not breathe a word of this to anyone! I can guess where this rumor might have come from. My publisher must have gotten to someone who knew my old friend, Kenneth Fearing. Fearing and I had been roommates at the University. This is just the kind of prank he would play. I can hear him laughing like hell over it.

Q. At least the letter reached you and that was fortunate. One final question. Did you revise any of the earlier poems that were included in Amulet?

A. Actually I made a lot of changes in the magazine versions I incorporated into my first book, Selected Poems, in 1941. Zukofsky said I had ruined some of them. He was right. I cut out too much. In Amulet I changed some of them back closer to the original, and others forward, as it were, to the 1960's. But I'm never satisfied. I could keep rewriting them all my life. It's a good way to get nowhere, because a person is constantly changing, and what satisfies him one day is bound to dissatisfy him the next. Unless one's critical judgment has improved, therefore—and there is no reason for that to happen after a certain age—the third version is apt to be as good as the fourth, or even better, because it's closer to the original stimulus. But it's no use telling myself that. I can't keep hands off. There's a dunderhead in me somewhere that persists in believing that a fresh perception of a poem is more right than the old. The oaf refuses to face up to the fact that every new occasion is a new situation and has to have a new poem. What a battle I'd have with my counter-will if I ever adhered to that!

CHARLES REZNIKOFF

_Q_. Mr. Reznikoff, could you start with a few comments about your participation in the so-called objectivist group and perhaps draw some conclusions about what "objectivism" was?

A. Yes, let me start by reading something I ran into only a few days ago, from a book of late T'ang poetry. Right in the beginning there's a quotation or translation from something written a thousand years ago. I suppose I oughtn't go back that far, but, like a lot of people, I like to find ancient authority. The introduction is by a man named A. C. Graham and he begins by quoting the remarks of a Chinese poet of the eleventh century. This is his translation: "Poetry presents the thing in order to convey the feeling. It should be precise about the thing and reticent about the feeling." And further on, commenting on another poet, Mr. Graham says, "A rigor in seeking the objective correlative of emotion is a strong point of most Chinese poetry of all periods." I thought that these comments, particularly the first, are a very accurate expression of what the objectivists were trying to do. Of course, the feeling is there in the selection of the material; you pick certain things that are significant—that's your feeling. You don't go into the feeling; you portray it as well as you can, hoping that somebody else reading the poem will get your feeling. Now, as part of that, I should perhaps say that I try to be as clear and precise as possible. I think that's the very word that was used in the translation of the Chinese poet: "precise." It's perhaps a far cry from what the symbolists meant when they said, "To name is to destroy; to suggest is to

Interview conducted by L. S. Dembo on May 2, 1968, in Madison, Wisconsin. Reznikoff's poetry has been collected in _By the Waters of Manhattan_ (New Directions/San Francisco Review, New York, 1962). _Testimony: The United States, 1885–1890_ was brought out by the same publisher in 1965. Reznikoff's verse plays appear in _Nine Plays_ (privately published, New York, 1927).

create." I was very much moved by that when I first read it, but my own belief is to name and to name and to name—and to name in such a way that you have rhythm, since music (and I think George Oppen would agree with me) is also part of the meaning. If you try, for example, as I have done, to express what you see from the roof of a building—chimneys and so on—the rhythm should convey your sense of depression without your saying, "What a horrible sight!"

I suppose you could ask me why one writes this way in the first place. Why do you write in the rhythms you do? How do you get to the feeling? I'd like to read from something I've written down; is that all right?

Q. Certainly. Go right ahead.

A. I have written here that first there is the need, the desire, the necessity of doing it; then the way, which you find out for yourself after, perhaps, a lot of experimenting; then you give it a name, the name, and then you come to, let's say, a formula. When I was twenty-one, I was particularly impressed by the new kind of poetry being written by Ezra Pound, H. D., and others, with sources in French free verse. It seemed to me just right, not cut to patterns, however cleverly, nor poured into ready molds—that sounds like an echo of Pound—but words and phrases flowing as the thought; to be read just like common speech—that sounds like Whitman—but for stopping at the end of each line: and this like a rest in music or a turn in the dance. I found it no criticism that to read such verse as prose was to have a kind of prose, for that was not to read it as it was written.

Q. Could we go back for a few moments to the object itself? Wouldn't you say that the objectivist poet has a certain subjective response to a thing and tries to portray his feeling, or else he simply tries to depict an object as it is? In any case, he's not a symbolist.

A. I see something and it moves me and I put it down as I see it. In the treatment of it, I abstain from comment. Now, if I've done something that moves me—if I've portrayed the object well—somebody will come along and also be moved, and somebody else will come along and say, "What the devil is this?" And maybe they're both right. But what I've written here will perhaps answer your question more directly. "By the term 'objectivist' I suppose a writer may be meant who does not write directly about his feelings but about what he sees and hears; who is restricted almost to the testimony of a witness in a court of law; and who expresses his feelings indirectly by the selection of his subject-matter and, if he writes in verse, by its music." Now suppose in a court of law, you are testifying in a negligence case. You cannot get up on the stand and say, "The man was negligent." That's a conclusion of fact. What you'd be compelled to say is how the man acted. Did he stop before he crossed the street? Did he look? The judges of whether he is negligent or not are the jury in that case and the judges of what you say as a poet are the readers. That is, there is an analogy between testimony in the courts and the testimony of a poet.

Q. Exactly what are you testifying to as a poet—the world or your own feelings or both?

A. The world is very large, I think, and I certainly can't testify to the whole of it. I can only testify to my own feelings; I can only say what I saw and heard, and I try to say it as well as I can. And if your conclusion is that what I saw and heard makes you feel the way I did, then the poem is successful.

Q. Well, I was thinking of a particular example, a very moving poem. It's number thirteen in "Autobiography: Hollywood" [By the Waters of Manhattan, p. 71]. The poet observes a swarm of flies around him as though he were a shepherd watching his sheep. When only one fly is left, he still counts his blessings, and the poem concludes with the lines, "I, too, am learning how to be silent,/and have learnt long ago how to be alone." The whole poem crystallizes here as the vision of a lonely man—only a lonely man could look at flies the way he did.

A. All right, perhaps I can tell you the origin of this poem and that will explain how I felt when I wrote it. I had a job in Hollywood at the time—a nice office, although I wasn't doing anything nor getting anywhere. I just sat there waiting for something to do and the only thing I could notice in the office were these flies and I came to the conclusion that you see. What I was describing was exactly what "C.R.," if I may use my initials, was experiencing, with no future that he could see and his only companions these flies. I had behind me, of course, the Bible, maybe the Psalms. I suppose I was thinking of "The Lord is my shepherd"; I felt myself to be something of a shepherd and it seemed to me to be amusing.

I don't know whether it's fair to get off on the subject of flies right now, but I found something particularly impressive in Shakespeare. In one of his early plays, Titus Andronicus, a man hits something and his companion asks, "What did you do?" The reply is, "Nothing, I just killed a fly," and his companion answers, "You killed a fly!," and has a few lines to show what a horrible thing has been done. And you feel instantly what a sensitive creature Shakespeare was. If he had written a play about Guildenstern and Rosencrantz, he would have done, of course, a much better job than what they did in New York. What a terrible thing: two young people caught up in a machine over which they have no control and crushed, as it were, as some of us would be if we were drafted for a war in which we had no interest and had to go along. Had Marlowe been handling the situation, he would have stopped with one line. It would have been a magnificent line. But Marlowe starts to write about the Jew of Malta, as you know, and his character becomes more and more comically evil. Shakespeare, on the other hand, creates a Shylock for whom we can have some sympathy.

Q.   Let me get back to the flies for a moment. They seem to be concrete and symbolic at once: the destruction of a fly can be made into a symbol of one's own condition, not just in an abstract, allegorical way, but the very feelings of killing a fly can be extended to the general feelings of being a victimizer or victim.

A.   I think poetry deals essentially with feelings, the feelings of the man who writes it and the feelings of the reader, though it may fail in either direction. That perhaps is one of the distinctions between poetry and prose. The latter can be written admirably without evoking any feeling, but poetry is inherently an expression of feeling. I was impressed by Stanislavsky's statement that art is love with technique. Once you say there's love, you're in the realm of feeling. Technique, of course, isn't, but is an adjunct to express it.

Q.   To go on to the historical side of my first question, I wonder whether you might speak for a while about your conversations, if any, with George Oppen and Louis Zukofsky on objectivist technique. I'd also be interested in hearing what you think about their work.

A.   Well, I hate to take any aura from our talks as I remember them, if they have any to begin with, but we talked about something quite practical. We couldn't get our poetry accepted by regular publishers, so we thought it would be nice if we organized our own publishing firm, with each of us paying for the printing of his own book. We picked the name "Objectivist" because we had all read Poetry of Chicago and we agreed completely with all that Pound was saying. We didn't really discuss the term itself; it seemed all right—pregnant. It could have meant any number of things. But the mere fact that we didn't discuss its meaning doesn't deprive it of its validity.

Q. Where did Williams fit in?

A. He was a friend of Zukofsky, and Zukofsky said he was the first we ought to publish. I had seen some of Williams' verse in *Poetry* and Harriet Monroe's anthology, but I hardly knew him. Anyway, we published his first book, I believe. Zukofsky was right, not only from a critical or poetic point of view but from a practical one: the book, to my surprise, was reviewed on the second page of *The New York Times Book Review* and the edition of five hundred copies almost sold out.

Q. Was there anything similar in the approaches that you, Oppen, and Zukofsky were taking?

A. I think we all agreed that the term "objectivism," as we understood Pound's use of it, corresponded to the way we felt poetry should be written. And that included Williams, too. What we were reacting from was Tennyson. We were anti-Tennysonian. His kind of poetry didn't represent the world we knew—the streets of New York or of East Rutherford or Paterson. It might have represented the idyllic countryside where Tennyson lived, I don't doubt, or the world in which Swinburne lived—that semi-classical world. We recognized its validity; I'm sure we all felt how good were things like "the hounds of spring are on winter's traces" or the beginning of "The Lotos-Eaters." Some of it was magnificent, but it wasn't us. And certainly what was not us was the kind of poetry Austin Dobson was writing.

Q. What did you think of Zukofsky's essay on objectivism in the February 1931 issue of *Poetry*? Didn't he talk about "sincerity" and "objectification," and didn't he devote a good part of the piece to your poetry?

A. I was not displeased, of course, but I confess that I could not follow all that Zukofsky had to say about "objectification" or, for that matter, "sincerity." That may have been my fault, certainly, and I might have kept on trying. I remember that Pound praised him.

Q. Zukofsky can be very difficult to understand, both in poetry and prose.

A. To me the use of language means communication. If you write, you write to be understood, and if you're not understood, you've failed. I'm a great believer in clarity and I try to practice it; that's why I'm interested in precision in the use of words, which is a part of clarity. I think the only importance in writing is to convey meaning or emotion.

Incidentally, speaking of technique, I came across an interesting statement in The New York Review of Books some time ago. The reviewer, commenting on translations of Sappho, said this: "At her most intense, she writes the kind of poetry that Stevens dreamed of, a poetry that 'without evasion by a single metaphor' sees 'the very thing itself and nothing else.' English poetry is in this special sense incurably evasive and requires a richer medium to achieve equally powerful effects." I'm not so sure that English poetry needs the use of metaphor, as this reviewer suggests, despite all the magnificent examples we have of it. But the difficulty in talking about Greek poets like Sappho or Archilochus is that we only have fragments in most cases. Now, there's a magnificent fragment by Archilochus in which there is simply a description of a girl walking, with her hair about her shoulders. I wouldn't want to see her compared to a hind or whatever. I think that frequently images cloud understanding rather than illuminate it. Of course, I use images too. If something good comes along, fine. But I still think that reviewer's statement was pertinent.

Q. Well, perhaps we can talk specifically about your own poetry. Much of your earlier and some of your later work seems to contain a haikuesque simplicity and turn of thought. For example—just one out of many—is the little poem that reads, "What are you doing in our street among the automobiles, /horse? /How are your cousins, the centaur and the unicorn?" [By the Waters of Manhattan, p. 25]. It says a great deal about the sensibility of the speaker, who looks upon a horse as being so unusual that it has become a fabulous creature.

A. That's just what I intended. A Japanese boy came up to me once, after a reading that included that poem, and asked me what the last line was doing there. He would have left it out. After reading a lot of haiku, I realized that's exactly the way they're written in Japan. Most of them seemed to be just a simple statement that is expected to suggest a particular mood or feeling. But if I had left the last line out, my whole meaning would have been lost.

I may add this about my writing that kind of poem: I showed a friend who had been studying Shakespeare with Kittredge at Harvard two of my pieces that Harriet Monroe had accepted for *Poetry*. He began to read them the way Kittredge read Shakespeare, analyzing every word in minute detail. He tore my verse apart, and his comments were hardly complimentary. I was enormously gratified. I had just spent four years studying law, reading cases closely for the meaning of every word, and had thought those years completely wasted. And here I suddenly saw that all this machinery that I thought had to be junked was actually useful. I could analyze my poems as my friend did, in my own way, and I was often left with two or three lines. The rest seemed, by Kittredge's standards, negligible or superfluous; three or so lines—if that many—were all that had to be said. I suppose that's the way I reached the *haiku* style.

Q. I think it's really your medium and I'm happy Kittredge influenced you. I'd like to go on, if we can, to your poems on Jewish themes. These poems seem to emphasize the endurance of the Jews as a people, and yet the poet is alienated from Jewish traditions. I'm thinking in particular of the poem in which you write, "My parents were of a great company/that went together, hand in hand;/but I must make my way alone/over waves and barren land" [*BWM*, p. 106]. And the poem called "Russia: Anno 1905" [*BWM*, p. 36] seems to sum up the dilemma of the modern Jew.

A. Perhaps it represents a situation that is—and has been—common among Jews. Even in early times, many Jews were attracted to cultures they thought to be superior, like Hellenism. I was only expressing the way I felt. But one changes as one grows older and sees more reason for ritual—more value in it. I wasn't taught any Hebrew at all; I began picking it up in my thirties. The tendency is, on the one hand, to be assimilated and, on the other, to be yourself. Some people accentuate one or the other, but assimilation has historically been common among Jews. It's in one's nature to become part of the surrounding community.

Q. But in your poems assimilation does not seem to be the primary theme. There's a poem in *Jerusalem the Golden* that reads in part, "I have married and married the speech of strangers;/none are like you, Shulamite" [*BWM*, p. 19]. There seems to be a personal sense of isolation or exile here.

A. I don't think "isolation" is the word. I don't feel isolated in English; it's just that I'm missing a lot in not knowing Hebrew. Incidentally, Havelock Ellis in one of his books, as I remember it, points out the tendency in a writer to use characteristics of the speech of his ancestors, even a speech he no longer knows. For example, Ellis says that Addison ends sentences with a preposition, although this is not usual in English, because Addison was of Danish stock and the Danes end sentences with prepositions. This is only one of his examples among a number. I don't know how sound all this is but it may be worth going into.

Speaking of Jewish endurance, one of the poems I like is based on a situation that occurred when I was in high school. There was a boy in my class from Persia—an Aryan if there ever was one—but the non-Jews would have nothing to do with him and he would have nothing to do with the Jews. He was completely isolated and eventually, I was told, committed suicide. That greatly impressed me. In that poem I have it that Jews don't find such isolation poison.

Q. "Scorn/shall be your meat/instead of praise;/you shall eat and eat of it/all your days,/and grow strong on it . . . Jew" ["Glosses," BWM, p. 55].

A. "And live long on it."

Q. In any case, it seems that the true values in your poetry are sensitivity and an inner spiritual strength. And these values seem to be prevalent in your verse plays as well. It doesn't matter who the people are, their strength against an antagonistic society makes them the heroes or martyrs they become.

A. They question. Let me refer to The Apocalyptic Ezra [BWM, p. 94]. Ezra is a minor Job. His position is this: "Look, why is Babylon treated so well? Are they so good?" And the angel replies by asking him questions like, can he weigh fire or measure the wind? If he can't do even these things, how can he expect to know the ways of God? The theme is the limitation of human knowledge. Actually the work was stimulated by the treatment of the Jews under the Romans.

Q. One has the feeling in your poetry that Judaism is a state of mind rather than a faith.

A. I think it's a kind of discipline too. One may not accept all aspects of that discipline, but the one he must accept is that he be himself, although he may conform to his environment in minor ways. These are the Jews who survive as Jews.

Q. Survive spiritually, though they might eventually lose their lives, as does Miriamne in your verse play, *Captive Israel*.

A. I must confess that many of those plays began with my irritation with the current theater. *Uriel Acosta* started with my dissatisfaction with a German play by that name. It was very romantic; the hero wasn't bothered by any theological questions except incidentally—he was in love. That explained all his troubles. As for *Captive Israel*, there was a play, written by an Englishman on the same subject, that bothered me; so I went back to Josephus. What actually happened was this: Miriamne was married to Herod, who was apparently a professing Jew but also a tool of Rome. He married Miriamne because she represented the ancient royal family. Like any other politician of his time, he used assassination to get rid of her brother, who was the legitimate heir to the throne.

Q. But the point of the play really seemed to concern Miriamne and what she endured simply by being true to her principles—by not conforming.

A. Of course, I felt sympathetic toward her. But let me say this about the plays: they are really libretti and should be accompanied by music. They really require staging and dancing. When I wrote them, I was very much under the influence of German expressionist drama, particularly that of Georg Kaiser. I was also interested in *The Dybbuk*, which had a lot of music and dancing.

Q. Then your verse plays were meant to be performed?

A. Yes, but they never were and probably never will be.

Q. Well, I was much interested in the mode in which these plays were presented. The scenes were presented almost "imagistically," without any transitions between them.

A. That's true. That's the expressionist influence. In one of Kaiser's best plays, as I recall, a bank clerk throws up his job and goes through one experience after another. There's really no relation among them except that the man is trying to find himself. I think what I did in the plays is exactly what I tried to do in my other verse: cut out everything that wasn't interesting in the hope that what was left would be.

Q. So you were writing *haikuesque* plays as well as poems.

A. Yes, I think one does the same thing over and over again.

_Q_. That brings us to the question of _Testimony: The United States, 1885–1890_, a work that doesn't seem at all to be in the mainstream of your poetry.

A.   _Testimony_ may be explained by T. S. Eliot's "objective correlative," as I understand it. Something happens and it expresses something that you feel, not necessarily because of _those_ facts, but because of entirely different facts that give you the same kind of feeling. Now, in reading law, if the cases state any facts, they're just a sentence or two; but, occasionally, you'll find the facts gone into in detail, sometimes to explain or defend the judge's position. Still the facts have a function of their own—psychological, sociological, and perhaps even poetical. In _Testimony_ the speakers whose words I use are all giving testimony about what they actually lived through. The testimony is that of a witness in court—not a statement of what he felt, but of what he saw or heard. What I wanted to do was to create, by selection, arrangement, and the rhythm of the words used as a mood or feeling. I could have picked any period because the same thing is happening today that was happening in 1885. For example, in the volume I'm working on now there's a description of a Negro riot in St. Louis around 1900. A reviewer wrote that when he read _Testimony_ a second time he saw a world of horror and violence. I didn't invent the world, but I felt it.

_Q_.   But doesn't testimony as such come out as simply a transcription of reality?

A.   But I throw out an awful lot to achieve my purpose. It's not a complete picture of the United States at any time, by any means. It's only a part of what happened, a reality that I felt as a reader and could not portray adequately in any other way. But I will tell you, if it's any satisfaction, that _Testimony_ had very little sale.

_Q_.   That's certainly no satisfaction.

A.   This discussion about testimony and events being lived through brings me to a warning I'd like to make. I suppose I'm an "objectivist" and I have my own "formula" for writing, but no formula can be a guarantee of good writing. I think behind any poem there's a background of experience and emotion that explains its moving quality. Sometimes even the poet himself may have forgotten the background. It's a mystery.

LOUIS ZUKOFSKY

Q. I know that "objectivism" was short-lived as a movement, if it ever existed at all, but your essay in the February 1931 issue of *Poetry* does seem to suggest a particular way of looking at reality. In fact, you actually use the term nominalism in connection with André Salmon. Wouldn't you say that your own poems from the beginning attempted to get away from normal generalization and theme to present an experience of the object or of nature directly?

A. Well, I don't want to get involved in philosophy. I might as well say that *Bottom: on Shakespeare* was written to do away with all philosophy. Naturally you can't do it without getting involved in their blasted terminology. In the first place, objectivism . . . I never used the word; I used the word "objectivist," and the only reason for using it was Harriet Monroe's insistence when I edited the "Objectivist" number of *Poetry*. Pound was after her; he thought the old rag, as he called it, was senile, and so on. He had had his fights with her; he couldn't get across the people he wanted, and in one of his vituperative letters he told old Harriet the magazine would come to nothing, that there was this youngster who was one of the best critics in America . . . well, I'm reminiscing. In any case, Harriet was fond of Pound and after all she was enterprising. Well, she told me, "You must have a movement." I said, "No, some of us are writing to say things simply so that they will affect us as new again." "Well, give it a name." Well, there were pre-Raphaelitism, and dadaism, and expressionism, and futurism—I don't like any of those *isms*. I mean, as soon as you do that, you start becoming a balloon instead of a person. And it swells and a lot of mad people go chasing it. Another

Interview conducted by L. S. Dembo on May 16, 1968, in Madison, Wisconsin. Quotations are from *All, the Collected Short Poems, 1923–1958* (W. W. Norton & Co., New York, 1965) and *All, the Collected Short Poems, 1956–1964* (W. W. Norton & Co., New York, 1966), by permission of the publisher.

216

word I don't want to use is "reality." I try to avoid it; I use it in Bottom, I think, only because I had to quote some text. Occasionally, a really profound man—a Cardinal Newman, for example—can use the word; there isn't any word you can't use if you have enough body to make something of it. Anyway, I told Harriet, "All right, let's call it 'Objectivists,'" and I wrote the essay on sincerity and objectification. I wouldn't do it today. (I've sworn off criticism after Bottom, after nineteen years of going through all that.) In any case I wouldn't use the same terminology anymore. But looking back at that essay, and as it was revised in Prepositions . . . what I did in this volume of criticism was to get it down to the bare bone. Granted that there are certain infelicities of style in the original. Actually, I don't think I changed ten words in editing the collected criticism. I omitted a great deal though, and that made all the difference.

But let me explain what I meant by "sincerity" and "objectification." Any artist lives with the things as they exist. I won't go into the theory of knowledge. I don't care how you think about things, whether you think they are there outside of you, even if you disappear, or if they exist only because you think of them. In either case you live with things as they exist. Berkeley's table that exists only in the mind, Plato's table that couldn't exist without the idea of a table, or Aristotle's table that was a table because you started with wood and had a purpose to make something for the good of society—you're still talking about a table. The theory of knowledge becomes terribly dull to me unless somebody like Wittgenstein, who really saw what the word game was, writes about it. Then it becomes very moving, because of the life, the fact, that goes on in your head no matter how evaporated the body becomes, no matter how much "gravity" you have (what Laurence Sterne defined as the mysterious carriage of the body to betray the defects of the mind).

But getting back to sincerity and objectification: thinking with the things as they exist. I come into a room and I see a table. Obviously, I can't make it eat grass. I have delimited this thing, in a sense. I call it a table and I want to keep the word for its denotative sense —as solid as possible. The only way it will define itself further will be in a context. In a way it's like grammar; only grammar is more abstract. In traditional grammar, you start with a subject. "I'm going to talk about that," says Aristotle. "What are you going to say about it?" "Well, what can I say about it?" says Aristotle: "It is, it exists, or it acts, or sometimes you hit it on the head and it seeks an action, a change in voices as we call it. Grammar is that kind of thing. The object is. Now what objects aren't?"

To the human being with five senses. . . . (How many more is he going to get when he goes up there beyond gravity? Probably lose them all.) Some senses are more important to some people than to others. To the cook, I suppose taste and smell are the most important; to the musician, hearing (the ear); to the poet, all the senses, but chiefly, sight (the eye)—Pound said we live with certain landscapes. And because of the eye's movement, something is imparted to or through the physical movement of your body and you express yourself as a voice.

Let's say you start with a body, the way a kid does when it's born, and it cries almost immediately. It takes a long time for its eyes to focus, a month I suppose. But anyway, the eye concerns the poet; the ear concerns the poet because he hears noises, and like the kid he's affected. And you can do all sorts of things with the noises. You can imitate natural things, and so forth. I like to keep the noises as close to the body as possible, so that (I don't know how you'd express it mathematically) the eye is a function of the ear and the ear of the eye; maybe with that you might feel a sense of smell, of taste even. So much of the word is a physiological thing. I know all of the linguists will say I'm crazy. In fact I think there's a close relationship between families of languages, in this physiological sense. Something must have led the Greeks to say *hudor* and us to say *water*.

But the word is so much of a physiological thing that its articulation, as against that of other words, will make an "object." Now you can make an object that is in a sense purely image and, unless you're a great poet, it can get too heavy. You will become one of those painter-poets who are, really, too frivolous; they exist in every generation. You know, they look at something and they immediately want to write a poem. That's not the way to make an image; it ought to be involved in the cadence—something very few people realize. What I mean is the kind of thing you get in Chapman's "the unspeakable good liquor there." Obviously, the man who wrote that knew what it was to gargle something down his throat. So body, voice, in handling words—*that* concerns the poet.

The last thing would be, since we're dealing with organs, the brain or intellect. That's very abstract. The parallel in physics would be the gaseous state. Now gas exists, but it is awfully hard to write the gas-stuff unless you have a very clear mind.

The objectivist, then, is one person, not a group, and as I define him he is interested in living with things as they exist, and as a "wordsman," he is a craftsman who puts words together into an object.

I tried in *A Test of Poetry* to show what I meant by giving examples of different poets writing—colloquially, not philosophically speaking—on the same subject. People are free to construct whatever table they want, but if it's going to be art, you had better have some standards. I at least want a table that I can write on and put to whatever use a table usually has. Well, this is all the answer to one question, and I don't really like to discuss these things. . . .

Q. Please go on.

A. Well, I'd prefer a poem that embodied all I have said here, a poem which said them for me, rather than the criticism. They say my poetry is difficult. I don't know—I try to be as simple as possible. Anyway, I have a poem that shows what I've been talking about, "The Old Poet Moves to a New Apartment 14 Times" [*All, 1956–1964,* p. 78]. Let me read some of it:

> The old poet
> moves
> to a new apartment
> 14 times

> 1
> "The old radical"
> or surd—

> 2
> *I's* (pronounced eyes)
> the title of his last
>
> followed by *After I's.*
> "After"—*later* or
> chasing?

> 3
> All the questions are answered with their own words. . .

[Interrupting:] What was your question?

Q. "All the questions are answered with their own words." Why don't you continue?

A. All you have to do is say "yes" or "no." That's about all we have ever done as far as action is concerned. The trouble is most people just won't be that definite. [Continues reading:]

All the questions are answered with their own words
intellect the way of a body a degree "before"
soughed into them

[Commenting:] I'm thinking of boiling off water so that it becomes vapor.

if the words say silence suffers less
they suffer silence
or the toy of a paradox
a worth less worth
than that shall will be said
as it is

[Commenting:] There is something that exists and the "shall," well, I don't know; it's up to the scheme that seems to be running everything, God, whatever you want to call it.

4

Aleatorical indeterminate

[Commenting:] Are we determined or not determined?

to be lucky and free and original
we might well be afraid to think
we know beforehand exactly
what we're doing

[Commenting:] It sometimes helps not to know "exactly," and no one knows exactly. How can he know "exactly"? I think we might as well be honest about that.

rather let it happen

but the 'illogical' anticipation,

music, has always been explicit
as silence and sound have

[Commenting:] What have you? What does this art consist of? Well, with poetry as with music, I go on, with silence and sound, "how long is a rest to rest." All right, according to John Cage, sometimes it's all silence. You want it that way? Doesn't make very much sense to me. I don't see why you should call it music. Maybe it is. That's the intellect part of it. John Cage is an intellect; I think that's the trouble with him. Otherwise, he's very wonderful, does some marvelous "things" to evoke silence.

> in the question
> how long is a rest to rest.

> In the 'old' metered poetry
> the Augustan proud of himself
> jingle poet as he says it

> freedom also happens
> tho a tradition precounts

[Commenting:] He may think he's writing a line in iambic penta-meter, but is he? Does he control every bit of it? It's a question: are you going to write by chance? Are you going to be absolutely rational about it? All conventional poetry . . . poets have the idea that they're in complete control of what they're doing. Sometimes it happens that the jingle poet has a marvelously metrical line that somebody else may do consciously for that effect. Or he can't help himself; it's in the language that two stressed syllables will come together. He's al-ready determined by the speech that exists. It's one of the functions that the poet, if he is entirely honest, will realize.

> freedom also happens
> tho a tradition precounts

> but someone before him
> is counting for him
> unless it happens

> that the instant has him
> completely absorbed in that someone:

[Commenting:] Sometimes you may like Shakespeare so much you may, as Emerson says, turn out to be as good as Shakespeare for a minute.

> a voice not a meter

[Commenting:] That's what I'm emphasizing.

> a voice not a meter

> but sometime a meter's a voice.

[Commenting:] Sometimes you discover what you think is a *measure* and it's the same as that objectivist voice. And it's nothing "new"— that is, hankering for the *new* in the sense of *novelty*. I'd say this of Chaucer, of Wyatt at his best. You can't carry the poetic object away or put it in your pocket, but there is a use of words where one word in context defines the other and enriches it so that what is put over is somebody's reaction to existence. That's all I was going to say.

Q.   What about the relation between "sincerity" and "objectification"?

A.   Sincerity is the care for the detail. Before the legs of the table are made, you can see a nice top or a nice grain in the wood, its potential, anyway, to be the complete table. Objectification is the structure. I like to think of it as rest, but you can call it movement. I cut out things from the original essay because I wanted to avoid all the philosophical jargon. Actually, looking back at it, it wasn't bad for a guy of twenty-five or twenty-six; it's certainly clearer than parts of Whitehead. I don't mean the mathematical Whitehead; I couldn't even kiss his toe there. I don't know whether it was as good as Peirce. . . .

Q.   Concerning this phrase, "thinking with the things as they exist," doesn't one man make them different from another, or doesn't what existence means to one man differ from what it means to another?

A.   That's true. But I'm thinking of only one person, the poet. Anyway, there's a certain amount you've got to get across to the next man or there's no sense in talking about art—we'll have bedlam. If you're talking about art, you want to give it to at least one person—that's your audience. Otherwise, unless you're talking to yourself, you probably set up a person. I mean, if we can't agree that this is a table, then, all right, you can use it to sleep on, but you're messing up uses. I'd say the business of writing is to see as much as you can, to hear as much as you can, and if you think at all to think without clutter; then as you put the things together, try to be concise.

Q.   What is involved in thinking without clutter?   I don't think it's as simple as it seems to be.

A.   It depends on how long or how deeply you've lived; after all, it's thinking or, if you wish, sensing with the things as they exist. I said in the essay—perhaps it isn't explicit—that it depends on the depth of the person. Everybody, some time in his life, wants to write poetry for reasons that have nothing to do with poetry. A kid falls in love and he wants to write a poem; it might turn out to be a good one simply because he's so innocent. But it's not likely. That is, if you want to be a good carpenter, you either know something about your craft or you don't. Each poem is in a sense its own law; I mean the good poem always is and there's no other like it. But if you're talking about at least a minimum of human value, humane value, you better have some kind of standard, especially if you're going to be true to your language, if you really want to affect people, and so on.

Q.   Still, doesn't the "clear physical eye" see in a different way from the eye working with the brain or influenced by abstractions? For example, there's a poem in *All* that goes:

> Not much more than being,
> Thoughts of isolate, beautiful
> Being at evening, to expect
>   at a river-front:
>
> A shaft dims
> With a turning wheel;
>
> Men work on a jetty
> By a broken wagon;
>
> Leopard, glowing-spotted,
>   The summer river—
> Under: The Dragon: [*All*, 1923–1958, p. 24]

It seemed to me the poet here was seeing as an objectivist, in terms of particularities rather than wholes. He seems to be literally thinking with things as they exist and not making abstractions out of them.

A.   But the abstract idea is particular, too. Every general word is particular, *as against another*—glass, table, shoe, arm, head . . . "reality," if you wish. Individually they're all, apart from their sound, abstract words. I'd like to keep them so that you don't clutter them with extra adjectives, extra adverbs; the rest is just good speaking. It might turn out to be crabbed rather than being glib, but if you're good, maybe you'll be blessed by some grace. But this poem is an example of what happens if you deal mostly with sight and a bit of intellect.

_Q_. Yes, that's what I meant. And doesn't this mean that the poet sees in terms of individual details—with "sincerity," in your sense?

A. But it all mounts up. I suppose there's a general statement: "Not much more than being," whatever that is. The opposite would be non-being. And then I go ahead and say a little more about it; that being becomes isolate being, a beautiful being. These are all assertions. Where is this? That's the first tangible thing, a river-front; the one I saw was probably the Hudson or the East River. But the point is that the river-front becomes more solid as against the general flow of intellect in the beginning. The first part is intellective, "gaseous"; the second part would resemble the "solid" state.

Now what kind of being? There is a shaft with a turning wheel; there are men on the jetty, and a broken wagon. It could have been a good wagon, but I wanted it to be broken. And above this, the sky. So actually I suppose the guy who was doing this was trying to get the whole picture, instead of saying as a "romantic" poet, "Now I'm seeing, now I'm being; I see the jetty; this wagon was once pretty."

What really concerned me in these early poems was trying to get away from that kind of thing—trying to get away from sounding like everybody else. We are all dealing with the same things. Someone makes a table, a bad one; someone makes one that is new and hopefully not to be thrown out the next day.

_Q_. Where do the leopard and the dragon fit in?

A. That's the constellation. "Leopard, glowing-spotted,/The summer river—/Under: The Dragon:"

_Q_. Why do you refer to the constellation?

A. There I'm . . . I'm not for metaphor, unless, as Aristotle says, you bring together unlikes that have never existed before. But they're in words; they're in verbs: "the sun rises." My statements are often very, very clipped.

_Q_. Well, the colon in the last line after "Under" would seem to imply that the dragon is under the river.

A. "Summer river—/Under: . . . ." There is a question of movement and enough rest; notice the space after "Under." The dragon is also reflected in the river—inverted. Of course, that kind of thing has already been done by Mallarmé—not that I knew as much Mallarmé then as I do now.

Q. Well, to continue this matter of seeing, it seems that many of your poems—for example, "Immature Pebbles"—are based on "the unsealing of the eyes bare," as you put it in "her soil's birth." Isn't this kind of vision associated with what you have called the "spontaneous idea," which seems to be the mental activity that corresponds to "thinking with the things as they exist"?

A.   Yes. I would hope so. All poetry is that. Suddenly you see something. But what was I doing in "Immature Pebbles"? [Thumbing to the page and looking at it. *All, 1923–1958*, p. 46:] I start with a quote from Veblen. "*An Imponderable is an article of make-believe which has become axiomatic by force of settled habit. It can accordingly cease to be an Imponderable by a course of unsettling habit.*" Well, this was Veblen's way of writing; it amuses me sometimes. But it was always very difficult. Actually, Veblen was the kind of man who'd give you a bag of bees and walk off. All right, I started out with that: an imponderable is an article of make-believe and it's associated with settled habit, the ordinary, the mundane, and so on. The only thing is to unsettle it. This particular spring, in the poem, happens to be the kind of thing that you see on any beach, but I observed certain very particular things. Notice that the spring is still too brisk for water suds, and I've even defined it, "bather's dirt."

(All you can say about this poem is . . . it doesn't even have to be me, but the person will result from the poem. That's why I think it's useless to try to explain one's poetry. Better that it explain itself after the poet is gone. One way of its explaining itself is by your reading what's there: $2 + 2 = 4$ does not say $2 + 2 = 5$. Now where the difficulty may come in is that sometimes you get an equation that is so condensed, it is good only for the finer mathematician. I don't say that to compliment myself, but, you know, mathematicians have standards of fineness; the more condensed the equation, the "nicer" it is.)

Well, to go on, "ripples/make for . . . An observer's irrelevancy/ of April." May follows. Obviously, he's not very happy about it because it is "objectless/of inconsequence" and brings "the expected to the accustomed/in this place." How happy can it be? Obviously, this man who is looking at the "shivering" bathing suits and "the mandrill's blue and crimson/secret parts" is looking at things the "wrong" way and he wants to get away from the scene. But at the same time he has rendered it. "In our day, impatience/ handles such matters of photography/more pertinently from a train window." I

think you can gather that the man who wrote this poem isn't interested in photographing people bathing on a beach. That's it.

All right, is it as good as Seurat's painting? It may have rendered
as much as Seurat in words. Obviously, Seurat was happier with his
points of paint than I was with my words. But I've certainly rendered
much of these "immature pebbles," in the sense that one may give
another the (perhaps undesirable) gift of a *table*. These kids are
pebbles; they're a part of nature, they're "nice," but I'd rather see
them through a train window. I didn't want to make a photograph
and yet I did. It's an ironic poem, but irony is one of the ways of
saying things. I prefer singing to this type of thing, but there it is.

Q. I wonder whether you'd mind also commenting on "Mantis,"
and the poem interpreting it [*All, 1923–1958*, pp. 73–80]. You seem
to be concerned here with the sestina as the ideal expression of the
"battle of diverse thoughts" or associations arising in the poet's mind
upon his encounter with a mantis.

A. I never said it was the *ideal* form of expression. You have to be
careful with this sapless guy, you know. Actually, I was trying to explain why I use the sestina, and there are a lot of old forms used.
I suppose there are two types of natures. One is aware of the two-
hundred-year-old oak, and it's still alive and it's going to have some
use to him; the other one is going to say cut it down and build a
supermarket. I'm not inclined to be the latter, nor do I want to imitate a traditional form, but if that thing has lasted for two hundred
years and has some merit in it, it is possible I can use it and somehow
in transferring it into words—as I said in *"Aleatorical indeterminate"*
—make something new of it. And the same for the form of the sestina. Musicians have done that with fugues; there are some today who
try to do counterpoint or traditional harmony, but most won't even
talk in that terminology. Ultimately it'll come down to silence or
sound, words or no words. And where are you going to get them?
Where does language come from? Are you just going to make it out of
a mouthful of air? Sometimes, but most of the time you don't; there's
a world already there; it might be a poetic form that is still useful.

Now the so-called "modern" will say you cannot write a sestina
anymore, that Dante did it and it's dead and gone. But every time I
read Dante, it's not dead. The poet is dead, but if the work is good,
it's contemporary. There's no use in writing the same sestina as Dante,
because in the first place, you couldn't do it, except by copying it word

for word and believing it's yours—an extreme case. What is possible is that L. Z. or somebody else could write something as good as it. Well, Williams came along and said, "No, we've got to get a new poetic foot," and while he did wonderful things instinctively, I wish he had omitted some of the theory. Pound was more sensible. What kind of meters can you have? Well, what we've had throughout the history of poetry: you can count syllables, or your language is stressed and so you will count accents, or else you have a musical ear and know when so much sound approximates so much sound and there's a regularity of time. You want to vary the time or have no time signatures . . . whatever the case, it'll have to hold together. So there's no reason why I shouldn't use this "old" form if I thought I could make something new.

" 'Mantis,' An Interpretation" is an argument against people who are dogmatic. On the other hand, I point out that as it was written in the nineteenth century (and some "contemporaries" are nineteenth century), the sestina was absolutely useless. It was just a facility—like that of Sunday painters, who learn to smear a bit of oil on canvas. They're not Picasso; Picasso has used every form you can think of, whether it came from Greece, Crete, or Africa. But what I'm saying in " 'Mantis,' An Interpretation" is not that the sestina is the ideal form; rather that it's still possible. Williams said it was impossible to write sonnets. I don't know whether anybody has been careful about it. I wrote five hundred sonnets when I was young and threw them away. Then I wrote A-7 and a canzone, which is quite different from the sonnet, as Pound pointed out. A very intricate form.

Q.   I didn't mean to imply that the sestina was the ideal form of expression per se. I thought that for the particular experience that the poet was having with the mantis on a subway, his undergoing a process of "thought's torsion," the sestina was most appropriate.

A.   Someone else might have done it differently, but for me that's what it led to. I have that kind of mind. Somehow, you know, the thing can become kind of horrible—to connect a thing with everything. But how can you avoid it? And it's not that I want to be long-winded; I want to be very concise. And when I've done it the long way, as in Bottom: on Shakespeare or A, which is unfinished, then I want to make it very short. For anybody who is interested in the theory of knowledge, which is done away with in Bottom, here is the short way of doing it:

I's (pronounced eyes)
Hi, Kuh,

those
gold'n bees
are I's,

eyes,

skyscrapers. [All, 1956–1964, p. 71]

A man can't help himself, any more than Shakespeare could
help himself, from saying the same things over and over. The idea
is to say them so that people always think you're saying something
new. Not that I'm always conscious that I'm doing it. It isn't that
I have this concept in my head, that I must say this. God knows, when
I was through with doing away with epistemology in Bottom. . . .
(And I don't see why Wallace Stevens ruined a great deal of his
work by speaking vaguely about the imagination and reality and so on.
He can be a wonderful poet, but so much of it is a bore, bad philosophy.) I was trying to do away with all the things the Hindus avoid
by saying, as in A-12: "Before the void there was neither/Being nor
non-being/Desire, came warmth,/Or which first?/Until the sages
looked in their hearts/For the kinship of what is in what is not."
They had no trouble with non-being, you see.

I said solid state, liquid, gas; as a matter of fact you can word it
sense, essence, non-sense. As to the handling of words, there are
the words of sense. Then, there are words that generalize and say
"without this that thing can't be essence." So you have words like
truth and reality. The "real" is bad enough, but at least it's a voice,
a kid saying, "For real?" But then the philosopher adds the "i-t-y"
and you start playing all kinds of word games and that's non-sense.
You can get lost, really lost. But the Hindu knew that all these things
existed. They do exist and sometimes you want to record it. So much
for epistemology. When I'm sick of it, thoroughly sick of it, I handle
it this way. It was enough that I wrote five hundred pages of Bottom.

Q. What do you mean, you got rid of epistemology in Bottom? The
work seems to me to be all epistemology.

A. "The questions are their own answers." You want to say "yes,"
say "yes"; you want to say "no," say "no." It's a useless argument.
Well, Wittgenstein . . . he was the kind that wondered why anybody

should bother to read him. As at the beginning of "I's (pronounced eyes) . . ." the haiku—everybody's writing haiku. You remember Elsie, Borden's cow? That's what I meant, and I greeted her up on the sign there: "Hi, Kuh." "Those/ gold'n bees/ are I's." Obviously some apparition or vision. She's up there anyway and the golden bees . . . I don't know, she makes honey. The bees are also "eyes." You were wondering which "eyes" see. On the other hand, suppose, without my glasses, I look out at the tower—"those/gold'n bees/are I's,/ eyes,/skyscrapers": all I see is Christmas crystallography. It's wonderful, but absolutely astigmatic.

All right, the epistemological question? *I* see this? Yes. The eyes see it? But there's also an object out there. All right, whichever way you want.

Q.   Where does the idea of love fit in? It seems to be the chief theme of *Bottom*.

A.   Well, it's like my horses. If you're good enough to run or feel like running, you run. If you want to live, you love; if you don't want to live, you hate, that's all. It's as simple as that. It's like being and non-being again—just different words for states of existence.

Q.   The horses in A-7 don't have any manes.

A.   Oh, those particular horses are sawhorses. They don't have any manes. Oh, I see what you're after. I don't think that way, though. When I say they don't have any manes, that's all I mean. It's like the old song, "Yes, We Have No Bananas."

Q.   But you say these sawhorses are also words—so they're not just sawhorses.

A.   Then if I say that, they are words. I use words for them; how can I get them across except in words? I say "sawhorse"; otherwise they'd better speak for themselves. That's a case of objectification. There are these sawhorses. All right, somebody can look at them and not bother with them. They interested me. But I wanted to get them into movement because I'm interested in the sound of words. So I got them into movement. Of course, in A-7 I have also talked about words, what to do with words.

A is written at various times in my life when the life compels it. That also means that my eye is compelling something or my ear is compelling something; the intellect is always working with words.

Being a certain creature with my own bloodstream, etc., I will probably, unless I discover something new to interest me or something
worthwhile to write about, probably repeat many things. All art is
made, I think, out of recurrence. The point is to have recurrence so
that it isn't mere repetition, like Poe's "Bells, bells, bells, bells." The
idea is to have these recurrences so that they will always turn up as new,
"just" different. Something has happened to the movement or you see
the thing "differently." Now this business of words occurs in the first
movement, A-1, and though I'd like to forget it, I must say this: I
think that too much of our literature is about the craft of literature.
Two great faults I'd like to avoid, but unfortunately I'm among men—
I live in my times. . . . The other fault is pretension to learning. How
can they all know so many things? By the time I'm eighty I hope to
be very simple, if I haven't shut up.

Q.   Yet there is a great deal of erudition in *Bottom*, isn't there?

A.   I never looked at it as erudition. These were the things I read,
and I've probably read very little compared to most people. I don't
consider myself a scholar. These are the things I've read, the things
I've loved. You've asked about love before. I suppose love means if
you do something, that's love; otherwise you don't do anything. There
can be, I suppose, a purely passive kind of love. I'm certainly not proud
of the erudition. On the other hand, notice that much of the citation
of Shakespeare is edited, not because of presumption, but because I
wanted to show off the good things.

Q.   [Student:] I've been reading the French poet, Ponge, who's extremely interested in words and objects, too. And Sartre, in a little
essay on Ponge called "Les Mots et les choses," mentions that he
feels Ponge participated in a kind of crisis of language between 1918
and 1930, and that he was trying to make a word an object like the
objects he saw. I was wondering whether you felt that you also participated in a crisis of language, a kind of devaluation of words.

A.   Well, things happen, you know, in one's time. I've read some of
Ponge and recently Cid Corman printed a good deal of him, at any
rate a notebook. He's trying to write a poem in the old-fashioned style
about pines, so that it will turn out to be like something by Valéry
or Hérédia—the Parnassians or the post-Parnassians, something like
that. And no, he felt these *things*; they were, of course, botanical
things. (Incidentally, I wish that instead of studying philosophy I

had studied some botany.) One of the nice statements Ponge makes is that the poet who falsifies the object is an assassin; instead of calling the object what it is, this kind of poet develops grand metaphors and all the "baroque" curlicues. Well, I suppose you get to a time where worlds apart two people might be doing similar things. The work itself, of course, is different. Ponge is consistently concerned with botanical objects, just to describe pine needles, for instance. On the other hand, will they—the pine needles—help him? The one line about pine needles in the *Cantos*—the feeling of the redness of the pine needle in the sun—does what Ponge didn't succeed in doing in that notebook at all, though I admire what he is after. It's certainly more worthwhile than attempting another imitation of Baudelaire. I mean either you show that you're alive in this world, in making something, or you're not.

Q.   Would you mind commenting on *A*? Do you conceive of the poem as having an overall structure?

A.   I don't know about the structure of *A*. I don't care how you consider it, whether as a suite of musical movements, or as something by a man who said I want to write *this* as I thought I saw the "curve" of it in twenty-four movements, and lived long enough to do so. I don't know, how would you consider Mahler's *Song of the Earth* or something like that? No, I didn't think of Mahler. I simply want the reader to find the poem not dull. As I said on another occasion, not anxious to say it then: "Written in one's time or place and referring to other times and places, as one grows, whatever ways one grows, takes in, and hopes to survive them, say like Bach's music." Maybe you get that out of it; maybe it will make its music. I feel a curve or something like that. But in working it out . . . it's the detail that should interest you all the time.

I feel that life makes the curve. That's why Williams kept adding to *Paterson*; he found he had more and more to say and that it was all part of the poem. (You know, the poet is insatiable. I could go on talking forever.) Otherwise, you get down to the old argument, there is no such thing as a long poem; there are some good lines, and so forth. Maybe, I don't know. A long poem is merely more of a good thing, shall I put it that way? So the nice thing is, for instance, that Pound's *Cantos* are still coming out. I hope he isn't crazy devoting so much time to the idea that they charged six-percent interest in Pisa, and how wonderful it was. No—rather "Imperial power is/and to us what is it?/The fourth; the dimension of stillness." That's the great Pound. Or in a very late canto, "When one's friends hate each other/how can there be peace in the world?" And with that I leave you.

GWENDOLYN BROOKS

Q. You've written in the poem "The Chicago Picasso," which appears in your latest book, *In the Mecca*, that "we must cook ourselves and style ourselves for Art, who/is a requiring courtesan." And in an earlier poem, "The Egg Boiler," the speaker says that the poet creates his poems "out of air . . . And sometimes weightlessness is much to bear." Let me ask you to comment on these passages. Are they fair statements of your feelings about art and the position of the poet?

A. Well, in "The Chicago Picasso," first of all I was asked to write a poem by the mayor of Chicago about that statue, and I hadn't seen it. I had only seen pictures of it, and the pictures looked very foolish, with those two little eyes and the long nose. And I don't know a great deal about art myself; I haven't studied it. So I really didn't feel qualified to discuss what Picasso was doing or had intended to do. So I decided to handle the situation from the standpoint of how most of us who are not art fanciers or well educated in things artistic respond to just the word "art" and to its manifestations. And I decided that most of us do not feel cozy with art, that it's not a thing you easily and chummily throw your arms around, that it's not a huggable

Interview conducted by George Stavros on March 28, 1969, in Madison, Wisconsin. Unless otherwise acknowledged, quotations are from the following books of verse: *A Street in Bronzeville* (1945); *Annie Allen* (1949; for which Miss Brooks received the Pulitzer Prize for Poetry); *The Bean Eaters* (1960); *Selected Poems* (1963); and *In the Mecca* (1968; nominated for the National Book Award in 1969). A novel, *Maud Martha*, was published in 1953 (reissued in 1967), and *Bronzeville Boys and Girls* (for children) appeared in 1956. "We Real Cool" is from *The World of Gwendolyn Brooks*, by Gwendolyn Brooks Blakely, copyright © 1959 by Gwendolyn Brooks.

233

thing, as I said here: "Does man love Art? Man visits Art . . . ." And we visit it, we pay special, nice, precise little calls on it. But those of us who have not grown up with or to it perhaps squirm a little in its presence. We feel that something is required of us that perhaps we aren't altogether able to give. And it's just a way of saying, "Art hurts." Art is not an old shoe; it's something that you have to work in the presence of. It urges voyages. You just can't stay in your comfortable old grooves. You have to extend yourself. And it's easier to stay at home and drink beer.

Q. Were you satirizing those people who do stay at home and drink beer?

A. No. No, I'm not satirizing them, because I'm too close to them to do that. I "stay at home" (mostly) and drink Pepsi-Cola. I can't poke fun at them. But I do urge them—because after I saw the Picasso I admired it, and I'm glad it's in Chicago—I do ask them to look at that statue or any other piece of art that might seem perplexing and consider it as we might consider flowers. We don't ask a flower to give us any special reasons for its existence. We look at it and we are able to accept it as being something different, and different from ourselves. Who can explain a flower? But there it is. . . .

Q. I wonder if what you're saying applies to the poet or what poetry is? Is poetry like a flower that one must look at and perhaps not explain but just accept because it is there?

A. I think a little more should be required of the poet than perhaps is required of the sculptor or the painter. The poet deals in words with which everyone is familiar. We all handle words. And I think the poet, if he wants to speak to anyone, is constrained to do something with those words so that they will (I hate to use the word) mean something, will be something that a reader may touch.

Q. Let me quote a passage from a statement you made in 1950 and see whether you think it is still valid.

A. Almost certainly not.

Q. You wrote, "But no real artist is going to be content with offering raw materials. The Negro poet's most urgent duty, at present, is to polish his technique, his way of presenting his truths and his beauties, that these may be more insinuating and, therefore, more overwhelming."[1]

A.   I still do feel that a poet has a duty to words, and that words can do wonderful things, and it's too bad to just let them lie there without doing anything with and for them. But let's see, I said something there about it being the Negro poet, and that's no longer the acceptable word; black is the word. [Reads:] "The Negro poet's most urgent duty, at present, is to polish his technique, his way of presenting his truths and his beauties . . ."—1950. You know, the world has just turned over since then, and at that time I felt that most strongly, most strongly—I was very impatient with black poets who just put down anything off the tops of their heads and left it there. But something different is happening now. Black poets today—when I say black poets I mean something different from that old phrase "Negro poets"—black poets are becoming increasingly aware of themselves and their blackness, as they would say, are interested in speaking to black people, and especially do they want to reach those people who would never go into a bookstore and buy a $4.95 volume of poetry written by anyone. And I think this is very important, what they're doing. I didn't bring a new little book just off the press called *Don't Cry, Scream*, by Don Lee. Don Lee is an exception. He is changing all the time and is interested very much in what words can do, but there is also a brief to be put forward for those who are just very much excited about what is going on today and are determined to get that rich life and urgency down on paper. And I don't think we can turn our backs on those people and say airily, "That is not good poetry," because for one thing the whole concept of what "good poetry" is is changing today, thank goodness. I think it's a very healthy thing.

Q.   Would you feel then that technique and traditional form mean less to black poets writing today?

A.   I think form should be considered after I speak about technique, because I believe that later on—who knows, ten years or twenty years from now—what I said back there in 1950 will again be justifiable; by then the rawness will have come to some maturation. Hopefully

---

[1] *Phylon*, XI (1950), 312.

something will have been decided, and the poets will then have time to play more with their art.

Q. You mentioned Don Lee. Who else do you think is promising? I know you are very interested in encouraging the work of new poets.

A. Yes, there are some very interesting ones. James Cunningham, who is teaching, incidentally, at the University of Wisconsin-Milwaukee, is very good and desperately improving himself. Etheridge Knight. Walter Bradford (Poems From Prison) is another comer in this thing; Don Lee, whom I've mentioned. Carolyn Rodgers has put out one little book very much respected by the younger poets, those who know her, and is about to bring out another one. Jewel Latimore is about to bring out a third little book. Ebon Dooley. These are people who are very well known in Chicago, and their poetry is almost adored. I went to a reading of a little group of poets just a couple of weeks ago in the Afro-Arts Theater in Chicago, and it was packed with young people chiefly, who had come to hear poetry. This was unheard of a few years ago.

Q. How about poets who are more widely known? How do you fit LeRoi Jones among these writers?

A. Oh, he is their hero! He's their semi-model, the one they worship. I personally feel that he is one of the very good poets of today, and people hearing this who have no real knowledge of his work, but have just seen a couple of "inflammatory" passages in the newspapers, might say, "Well, what in the world do you mean? That's no poet." But he is a most talented person. His work works.

Q. What do you feel makes Jones the voice of his generation?

A. Well, first of all he speaks to black people. They appreciate that. And he's uncompromising in his belief that the black people must subscribe to black solidarity and black self-consciousness.

Q. Is it his message or a poetic method that makes his poetry appeal particularly to blacks?

A. If it is a "method," it comes just from the sincere interest in his own people and in his desire to reach them, to speak to them of what he believes is right.

Q. Is he employing any traditional forms, would you say, that may be associated with blacks, say, jazz rhythms . . . ?

A. Yes, he and a number of the other black poets such as Larry Neal are interested in supplying black poetry with some strains of black music which they feel is the true art of the black people. They worship Coltrane and Ornette Coleman, and whenever they can they try to push such music into their work. Sometimes the poetry seems to grow out of the music.

Q. You've said that poetry is an entirely different thing now from what it was twenty years ago. Do you feel, as some readers of yours have said, that your own poetry has abandoned its lyrical simplicity for an angrier, more polemical public voice?

A. Those are the things that people say who have absolutely no understanding of what's going on and no desire to understand. No, I have not abandoned beauty, or lyricism, and I certainly don't consider myself a polemical poet. I'm just a black poet, and I write about what I see, what interests me, and I'm seeing new things. Many things that I'm seeing now I was absolutely blind to before, but I don't sit down at the table and say, "Lyricism is out." No, I just continue to write about what confronts me . . . . I get an idea or an impression or I become very excited about something and I can hardly wait till the time comes when I can get to the paper. In the meantime I take notes, little bits of the idea I put down on paper, and when I'm ready to write I write as urgently and directly as I possibly can. And I don't go back to mythology or my little textbooks. I know about the textbooks, but I'm not concerned with them during the act of poetry-writing.

Q. In one of the "Sermons on the Warpland," you quote Ron Karenga to the effect that blackness "is our ultimate reality."

A. I firmly believe it.

Q. Then am I right in saying these "Sermons" are almost apocalyptic or prophetic? They seem rather . . . .

A.   They're little addresses to black people, that's all.

Q.   The last poem in the group ("The time/cracks into furious flower . . .") suggests that there will be a rebirth.

A.   Yes. . . . There's something I'd like to say about my intent as a poet that you touched upon a moment ago and which has some connection with that business of abandoning lyricism, et cetera. Changes in my work—there *is* something different that I want to do. I want to write poems that will be non-compromising. I don't want to stop a concern with words doing good jobs, which has always been a concern of mine, but I want to write poems that will be meaningful to those people I described a while ago, things that will touch them.

Let me tell you about an experience I had in Chicago. I went around with a few of these poets that I've just mentioned. They go to housing projects and out in the parks sometimes, and just start reading their poetry; and right around the corner—across the street from the Wall in Chicago, the Wall of Respect. . . .

Q.   That's the one you write about in "The Wall."

A.   Yes. Well, right across the street is a tavern, and one Sunday afternoon, some of the poets decided to go in there and read poetry to just whoever was there. I went with them. One of them went to the front of the tavern and said, "Say, folks, we're going to lay some poetry on you." And there had been a couple of fights in there, people drinking, and all kinds of exciting things going on; and some of us wondered how they were going to respond to poetry. But the poets started reading their poetry, and before we knew it, people had turned around on their bar stools, with their drinks behind them, and were listening. Then they applauded. And I thought that was a wonderful thing, something new to me. I want to write poetry—and it won't be Ezra Pound poetry, as you can imagine—that will be exciting to such people. And I don't see why it can't be "good" poetry, putting quotes around "good."

Q.   Are you suggesting that poetry should be restored to one of its original forms, that of the voice of the prophet, speaker to the people . . . ?

A.   I don't want to be a prophet.

Q. . . . Or a social voice, a voice that can be heard. Do you think that poetry as it's now being written and heard by the people is becoming a social force?

A. Some of these people do want their poems to become "social forces"; others haven't, I believe, really thought of such a thing. And I am not writing poems with the idea that they are to become social forces. I don't feel that I care to direct myself in that way. I don't care to proceed from that intention.

Q. Let me ask you about the character portraits in your poetry and in your novel, Maud Martha. In the Mecca, your most recent volume, portrays life in a large city apartment building. A Street in Bronzeville gave similar vignettes of people in the city. The same, I think, can be said for all your work.

A. It's a fascination of mine to write about ghetto people there.

Q. Are your characters literally true to your experience or do you set out to change experience?

A. Some of them are invented and some of them are very real people. The people in a little poem called "The Vacant Lot" really existed and really did those things. For example: "Mrs. Coley's three-flat brick/Isn't here any more./All done with seeing her fat little form/Burst out of the basement door . . . ." Really happened! That lot is still vacant on the street where I was raised. (My mother still lives on the street.) "Matthew Cole" is based on a man who roomed with my husband's aunt. And I remember him so well, I feel he really came through in the poem. "The Murder" really happened except for the fact that I said the boy's mother was gossiping down the street. She was working. (I guess I did her an injustice there.) "Obituary for a Living Lady" is based on a person I once knew very well.

Q. What about the characters in Maud Martha? I'm thinking of Clement Lewy, a boy who comes home every day to prepare his own meal while his mother is at work. Or the character of the young truck driver who finds that he cannot any longer abide his home life and one day simply abandons his family.

A. Again, not based on any specific persons.

Q.   There is a quality of pathos about all of your characters and compassion in your treatment of them. Many of them make a pitiful
attempt to be what they cannot be.

A.   Some of them. Not all of them; some of them are very much
interested in just the general events of their own lives.

Q.   Let me suggest one of the frequently anthologized poems, "A
Song in the Front Yard," about a girl who "gets sick of a rose" and
decides she'd like to leave the comfort and pleasure of the front yard
to see what life would be like in the back.

A.   Or out in the alley, where.the charity children play, based on my
own resentment when I was a little girl, having to come inside the
front gate after nine—oh, earlier than that in my case.

Q.   Isn't there a yearning to get away in many such portraits?

A.   I wouldn't attach any heavy significance to that particular poem,
because that was the lightest kind of a little poem.

Q.   How about a poem like "Sadie and Maud," a little lyric, I think
in quatrains, contrasting Maud, who turns out to be a lonely brown
"mouse," and Sadie, who "scraped life/With a fine tooth comb"?

A.   Those are imaginary characters, purely imaginary.

Q.   What about "The Sundays of Satin-Legs Smith," where the
hero spends much of his morning in his lavender bath. . . .

A.   . . . and in his closet, among his perfume bottles.

Q.   And his neckties and umbrellas which are like "banners for some
gathering war"?

A.   Not his umbrellas; I think I called it hats "like bright umbrellas,"
which implies that he is protecting himself under that fancy wideness
. . . . You probably don't remember the zoot-suiters; they were still
around in the forties, in the early forties. They were not only black
men but Puerto Ricans, too, who would wear these suits with the
wide shoulders, and the pants did balloon out and then come down

to tapering ends, and they wore chains—perhaps you've seen them in the movies every once in a while. That's the kind of person I was writing about in "The Sundays of Satin-Legs Smith."

_Q_. You write about young men in other poems perhaps like that. "Patent Leather" was an early poem describing a character who talks about his "cool chick down on Calumet," and he wears patent leather. Then there's "Bronzeville Man with a Belt in the Back," and more recently, "We Real Cool."

A. In "Patent Leather," a young woman is admiring a man (and that admiration is no longer popular) who slicks back his hair, so that it looks like it's smooth as patent leather, and shiny. "Bronzeville Man with a Belt in the Back"—"belt in the back" was a popular style for men some years ago; and this man feels dapper and equal to the fight that he must constantly wage when he puts on such a suit.

_Q_. How about the seven pool players in the poem "We Real Cool"?

A. They have no pretensions to any glamor. They are supposedly dropouts, or at least they're in the poolroom when they should possibly be in school, since they're probably young enough, or at least those I saw were when I looked in a poolroom, and they . . . . First of all, let me tell you how that's supposed to be said, because there's a reason why I set it out as I did. These are people who are essentially saying, "Kilroy is here. We are." But they're a little uncertain of the strength of their identity. [Reads:]

> We real cool. We
> Left school. We
>
> Lurk late. We
> Strike straight. We
>
> Sing sin. We
> Thin gin. We
>
> Jazz June. We
> Die soon.

The "We"—you're supposed to stop after the "We" and think about their validity, and of course there's no way for you to tell whether it should be said softly or not, I suppose, but I say it rather softly because I want to represent their basic uncertainty, which they don't bother to question every day, of course.

Q. Are you saying that the form of this poem, then, was determined by the colloquial rhythm you were trying to catch?

A. No, determined by my feeling about these boys, these young men.

Q. These short lines, then, are your own invention at this point? You don't have any literary model in mind; you're not thinking of Eliot or Pound or anybody in particular. . . ?

A. My gosh, no! I don't even admire Pound, but I do like, for instance, Eliot's "Prufrock" and The Waste Land, "Portrait of a Lady," and some others of those earlier poems. But nothing of the sort ever entered my mind. When I start writing a poem, I don't think about models or about what anybody else in the world has done.

Q. Let me ask you about some of your poems that are in specific forms, however—sonnets . . . .

A. I like to refer to that series of soldier sonnets.

Q. "Gay Chaps at the Bar."

A. A sonnet series in off-rhyme, because I felt it was an off-rhyme situation—I did think of that. I first wrote the one sonnet, without thinking of extensions. I wrote it because of a letter I got from a soldier who included that title in what he was telling me; and then I said, there are other things to say about what's going on at the front and all, and I'll write more poems, some of them based on the stuff of letters that I was getting from several soldiers, and I felt it would be good to have them all in the same form, because it would serve my purposes throughout.

Q. Then you find it challenging to write in a particular form, like the sonnet, when the occasion seems to lend itself?

A. I really haven't written extensively in many forms. I've written a little blank verse, and I have written many more sonnets than I'm sure I'll be writing in the future, although I still think there are things colloquial and contemporary that can be done with the sonnet form. And, let's see, free verse of course I'll be continuing to experiment with, dotting a little rhyme here and there sometimes as I did in part of In the Mecca. But I'm really not form-conscious. I don't worship villanelles, for instance.

Q. But then you have written formally, as you say, with sonnets, quatrains, the literary ballad, the folk ballad, "The Ballad of Rudolph Reed." Have you given up writing ballads?

A. I don't know. I might write other ballads, but they would be very different from those that I have written so far. I see myself chiefly writing free verse, experimenting with it as much as I can. The next book, I'm pretty sure, will be a book of small pieces of free verse.

Q. Do you consider the opening lines of In the Mecca as being typical of what you're trying to do in that poem? "Sit where the light corrupts your face./Miës Van der Rohe retires from grace./And the fair fables fall. . ."—and continuing. They're rather irregular free verse lines.

A. Sometimes I shall perhaps do something on that order. (You are, of course, speaking of the lines that follow those three.) But then I can't guarantee it. Suppose I thought of a poem that was free verse but didn't have such a variety of lengths of line; that would still be all right.

Q. A much-admired poem from Annie Allen is the one beginning "A light and diplomatic bird/Is lenient in my window tree./A quick dilemma of the leaves/Discloses twist and tact to me." Do you feel this is representative of your lyrical expression?

A. No, I wouldn't say that this is a representative poem, a poem that represents my usual sort of expression. This is to be considered as part of the story of Annie Allen. She's unhappy here, and she's looking out of the window at a tree near the window, and she sees a little bird, and she envies this bird because, of course, who knows?, the bird might have been as miserable as she was; but for all that she can tell he is able to absorb his own grief, and she has a little fancy conceit here: she's saying that he's singing out of pity for her. "He can afford his sine die./He can afford to pity me . . . ." Tell me how to be well balanced; tell me how to "bleach" (sic) away the impurities. It's really a very simple little thing that has no comparison, say, to a poem like "kitchenette building." I believe I have written more "kitchenette building"-type poems than I have written about birds singing and feeling sorry for a girl who's temporarily overwhelmed by grief.

Q. What was behind the title, "The Anniad," in the first place? Is this a classical reference?

A. Well, the girl's name was Annie, and it was my little pompous pleasure to raise her to a height that she probably did not have, and I thought of the *Iliad* and said, I'll call this "The Anniad." At first, interestingly enough, I called her Hester Allen, and I wanted then to say "The Hesteriad," but I forget why I changed it to Annie . . . . I was fascinated by what words might do there in the poem. You can tell that it's labored, a poem that's very interested in the mysteries and magic of technique.

Q. Technique—you've written, for example, seven-line stanzas. Is there any reason for that?

A. Lucky seven, I guess. I like the number seven. That really is probably not the reason; I really can't remember exactly, but I imagine I finished one stanza, then decided that the rest of them would be just like that.

Q. I think the seventh stanza is typical of not only the meter but the imagery and symbolism: "And a man of tan engages/For the springtime of her pride,/Eats the green by easy stages,/Nibbles at the root beneath/With intimidating teeth./But no ravishment enrages./No dominion is defied."

A. What a pleasure it was to write that poem!

Q. Was what you're trying to do in a stanza like that different from what you had done up until that time, and why was it such a pleasure? The writing in general seems to differ from the earlier writing because it is more cryptic, more compressed. Is there any sense in which you feel you were trying something totally new here in the poem?

A.   No, not something new. I was just very conscious of every word; I wanted every phrase to be beautiful, and yet to contribute sanely to the whole, to the whole effect.

Q.   Taking this as a typical stanza, you have indications of spring-time again, growth—greenery, "nibbles at the root beneath"; I imagine this is the root of their love . . . .

A.   Yes, you understand how the young man is courting her, and it's a—really, I could have said what I wanted to say in two lines, you know; I could have said, well, he came and he pursued her, but she was all ready for the outcome, in fact, eagerly awaiting it.

Q.   I was just suggesting that the stanza seems closely and carefully textured.

A.   Yes, and so was every stanza in that poem; every one was worked on and revised, tenderly cared for. More so than anything else I've written, and it is not a wild success; some of it just doesn't come off. But it was enjoyable.

Q.   Can you tell me what you're doing next?

A.   I'm very excited about what I'll be doing in the immediate future, and I'm retiring from teaching so that I can give my real attention to working with poetry . . . . I imagine the future poems will seem more like some of the poems in A Street in Bronzeville.

Q.   Please go on.

A.   They'll deal with people, that I know; and I won't be trying to prove something as I write. I want them to be pictures of black life as I see it today. This of course would include people who do not think they're thinking about the great fight that's going on.

Q.   From what you say about how you want your poetry not to teach anything but to stand on its own . . . .

A. Well, I don't say that I don't want it to teach anything; I'd merely say that when I write it, I don't have preaching in mind.

Q. Perhaps you agree with Ellison and Baldwin, who have attacked Wright's use of the protest novel, and believe that the protest novel should be replaced by something less social. Ellison said that the novelist ought to write on "the full range of American Negro humanity."[2]

A. No, I don't feel that way at all. I feel that the poet should write out of his own milieu. Now, I'm not "full-range" qualified, I less than some others perhaps, less than a poet like Margaret Walker, who knows much more than I do about everything. But I am in the black community; I see what's going on there. I talk with these people. I know how many of them feel. I am not in the banker's community. I'm not acquainted, that I know of, with any Wall Street high influences—people who run the country, as they say. So therefore I would not attempt to write about them. Perhaps Ralph Ellison is acquainted with every aspect of American life; I can merely say that I'm not, so therefore I can't write about America inclusively. But that's all right—I'm not sorry. You know, William Faulkner felt that if he just stayed with Yoknapatawpha County he was all right, and that in just concentrating on that single area—and that single multiplicity!—of life, that that would be "general" enough for his purposes.

I started out talking about Bronzeville, but Bronzeville's almost meaningless by now, I suppose, since Bronzeville has spread and spread and spread all over. Bronzeville, incidentally, was not my own title. That was invented by the *Chicago Defender* long, long ago to refer to the then black area.

Q. Is it still called that?

A. Once in a while you'll see on a store "Bronzeville Tailor Shop" or something like that, but almost nobody talks about Bronzeville.

Q. It's not a term as specific as Harlem in New York City, for example.

A. No.

---

[2] *Shadow and Act*, quoted in Seymour L. Gross and John Edward Hardy, eds., *Images of the Negro in American Literature* (Chicago, 1966), p. 20.

Q. I know you've been living in Chicago most of your life and consider yourself a Chicago native, so there's a great feeling of place in
your poetry—in *Maud Martha*, too. Do you try to evoke place in your
work?

A. No, I start with the people. For instance, Maud Martha goes to
the Regal Theater, which is almost dead now, but had a great history
in Chicago. She looks at the people; she looks at the star; she looks at
the people coming out of the theater. But suffice it to say that I
don't start with the landmarks.

Q. A number of your poems, too, reflect your family life, certainly
your mother, and you have written poems about motherhood. "The
Motherhood" is part of the "Annie Allen" series. It's extremely effective, I think. Do you feel that there is much of your experience as
a mother which has gone into those poems?

A. Chiefly my experience, not my own mother's experience.

Q. Your own experience as a mother, yes. I'm thinking of poems
such as those beginning "People who have no children can be hard"
or "What shall I give my children? who are poor,/Who are adjudged
the leastwise of the land,/. . . my sweetest lepers" or ". . . shall I
prime my children, pray, to pray?"

A. Yes, all questions I would ask of myself. My mother certainly
wouldn't ask such a question of herself, that last one. She feels firmly
that you must pray, and that only good can come of it.

Q. What of religion in your poems? I noticed that two or three
of your references to men of the church are at least uncomplimentary.
For example, there's Prophet Williams in *In the Mecca*—a faith
healer.

A. Yes, he was based on an actual man that I worked for in the
Mecca building. Haven't I told that story? Well, when I was nineteen, and had just gotten out of junior college, I went to the Illinois
State Employment Service to get a job. They sent me to the Mecca
building to a spiritual adviser, and he had a fantastic practice, very
lucrative. He had us bottling medicine as well as answering letters.
Not real medicine, but love charms and stuff like that he called it,

and I delivered it through the building; that was my introduction to the Mecca building. You've probably heard of the Mecca. John Bartlow Martin has written about it.

Q. Let me ask another question about your novel. It's been described as poetic prose. What did you set out to do in writing *Maud Martha*?

A. Well, I wanted to give a picture of a girl growing up—a black girl growing up in Chicago, and of course much of it is wrenched from my own life and twisted. But about its being poetic in parts: I suppose that could hardly be avoided, if it is a thing to be avoided, because even in writing prose I find myself weighing the possibilities of every word just as I do in a poem. This was true when I used to write reviews, too.

Q. Did you have any form in mind? I'd like to know how you decided upon the form of the novel—the small chapters, about thirty-four of them, the small prose sections fitting together into something like a mosaic.

A. Well, I had first written a few tiny stories, and I felt that they would mesh, and I centered them and the others around one character. If there is a form I would say it was imposed, at least in the beginning, when I started with those segments, or vignettes.

Q. Would it then be fair to say that the unity of the novel is simply the central point of view of Maud Martha herself as she grows up?

A. Yes, certainly.

Q. Have you given any thought to writing another novel?

A. No, because I don't feel that that is my category. No.

Q. Have you given any thought to writing a play?

A. Yes, small verse plays that will not be acted at all, but will just be published as poems, really. That doesn't mean that I've begun them, but they're in my mind. I do want to do that someday.

Q. Do you feel that writing in this form will help you develop different themes?

A. Well, if I can be said to be "using themes," I believe that the small verse plays would concern themselves with those same themes. I see no reason why the form should dictate different subjects. No, I believe I'll go right on writing about black people as people, and not "polemically," either.

Q. I meant to suggest that perhaps a more explicit social theme than you're willing to impose upon your poetry could be presented in, say, the drama. I'm thinking of the plays of Jones and Baldwin.

A. Well, that would depend, I believe, upon the climate of America —if it changes, well, we all have to respond to the changes; that's what black people are doing now.

Q. How do you feel about that climate in regard to what the black writer is doing now? Do you think his task is becoming easier, more difficult, more important?

A. I think it is the task or job or responsibility or pleasure or pride of any writer to respond to his climate. You write about what is in the world. I think I would be silly, and so would LeRoi Jones, to sit down now under the trees and write about the Victorian age, un- less there's some special reference we could make to what's going on now.

Q. Then your poems about Malcolm X and Medgar Evers, for example, are part of a continuing interest in poetry that involved you with matters of the day. Is that correct?

A. No, I didn't involve myself with Medgar Evers' assassination—I merely reacted to it, and I described what he had done, the effects he had had on the assaulting elements of his society, and I ended, most beautifully, I thought: "People said that /he was holding clean globes in his hands."

Q. What did you mean when you said he had departed from "Old styles, old tempos, all the engagement of/the day—the sedate, the regulated fray . . ."?

A. [Reads:] ". . . the antique light, the Moral rose, old gusts,/tight whistlings from the past, the mothballs/in the Love at last our man forswore." He just up and decided he wasn't going to have anything else to do with the stale traditions of the past and the hindrances and restrictions that American response to horrors had been concerned with.

Q. In other words, an impatience with injustice and continuing oppression.

A. Yes, he decided he would just "have none" of it anymore and would do something about righting things for his people.

Q. In your poem "The Wall," which accompanies the other dedication, "The Chicago Picasso," you write about "legislatures/of ploy and scruple and practical gelatin." Can you explain what you meant by that?

A. [Reads:] "On Forty-third and Langley/black furnaces resent ancient/legislatures"—first of all, the "black furnaces" are the very excited people that were out there in the street that day, and they resented the restrictions and the injustices—legal injustices, too—that had been visited upon them through centuries, hence "ancient." "Ploy"; "scruple"; "practical gelatin"—*that* is the injustice of a gelatinous nature that we are exposed to and for which we are told, in effect, that this is just something that has to be: "You can see that, can't you, folks? It's the practical way of doing things." Expert deceit.

Q. Is there a controlled anger in the way you characterize the legislature?

A. Yes, I believe there's a controlled anger here! "Legislatures," however, does *not* refer to Washington men or Springfield men! (Perhaps you would have liked it better if I'd said "legislatings.")

Q. I'm trying to press the point that your poetry in its most recent form is more socially aware than in the earlier work.

A. Yes, although many people hated *The Bean Eaters*; such people as would accuse me of forsaking lyricism for polemics, despised *The Bean Eaters* because they said that it was "getting too social. Watch it, Miss Brooks!" [Laughs] They didn't like "The Lovers of the Poor"; they didn't like "The Chicago Defender Sends a Man to Little Rock: Fall, 1957," which I don't care too much about—or at least I'd like to remove that last line ["The loveliest lynchee was our Lord"].

Q. How do you feel about some of your other poems, now that you've mentioned those with specific social commentary? Is it fair to classify them in the same way—for example, the "Beverley Hills, Chicago" poem or "A Bronzeville Mother Loiters in Mississippi. Meanwhile, a Mississippi Mother Burns Bacon"?

A. I couldn't put these poems in a second little book, under the title "Social Poems," "Social Speech." I just feel that they're poems. I think that the wonderment or resentment is inside the person who is making the accusation, if it is an accusation, and usually when people talk about the social content of the poems, they are accusing you of doing something dastardly.

Q. I didn't mean to do that. But one more point. You wrote in 1950 that poetry must do double duty: "At the present time, poets who happen also to be Negroes are twice-tried. They have to write poetry, and they have to remember that they are Negroes." Then several lines later: "They are likely to find significances in those subjects not instantly obvious to their fairer fellows. The raindrop may seem to them to represent racial tears . . . . The golden sun might remind them that they are burning."[3]

A. That's carrying it a stretch too far, as poets will do, I suppose; but at least in Chicago we have had spirited conversations about whether a black poet has the right to deal with trees, to concern himself with trees. And one of the things that I've always said was, certainly, certainly a black poet may be involved in a concern for trees, if only because when he looks at one he thinks of how his ancestors have been lynched thereon. Well, that's a way of saying that in the black experience everything is important just as it is in the white experience.

---

[3] Langston Hughes, ed., New Negro Poets U.S.A. (Bloomington, Ind., 1964), p. 13.

Q.   And it can be important in its own right, can't it? It is, of course, possible for anyone to look at a tree and see just a tree, or . . . ?

A.   It is possible, but if a black person looks long enough, he just might think of other things that a white person might not . . . especially if you've seen some of the pictures in *Jet* magazine of what has happened on some of those trees—horrific.

Q.   This comes around to what we were talking about at the beginning, that the black writer has more to see because perhaps more has happened to him.

A.   That's probably true. He has the American experience and he also has the black experience; so he's very rich.

GEORGE BARKER

Q. Many of your poems—from "Narcissus I" in the 1930s to work in *The Golden Chains* [1968]—take up the problem of solipsism. Would you say that the poem is a means of escape from solipsism?

A. Well, I would think that it is a means of escape from absolutely anything one didn't like. I believe that when one's in the presence of things that are very painful, the sensible thing to do is to escape. I don't think that the poem is a solution to anything except a very temporary state of affairs; it is not an escape from what is, in fact, an intellectual trouble. Solipsism is not a problem, it's a trouble. The poem's a solution just as long as one is engaged in the writing of it, and not afterwards.

Q. How about in the reading of it?

A. I read poems solely for pleasure. Poetry, I imagine, could have some kind of moral, some kind of even spiritual signification, but that's merely part of the operations that give one pleasure.

Q. If poetry is only a temporary escape, does it give you any flash of insight that goes beyond the temporary moment? Or is that insight itself a transcendence?

A. I believe with Goethe that if a man in the process of writing a poem could withdraw and observe his own processes, he'd split down the middle and go quite mad. I don't think it's possible, therefore, to speak as an unconditioned observer about the writing of the poem. Actually,

Interview conducted by Cyrena N. Pondrom on September 9, 1970, at Mr. Barker's home in Aylsham, Norfolk, England.

253

I think everyone's far too concerned with how poems get written. They get written largely with pens and paper and things like that. It's simply impossible to examine the processes that go on in the mind, when one is writing a poem, without some kind of act of partial withdrawal which stops the poem from being, at that moment, the complete act of dedication it should be; i.e., one then becomes a conditioned observer.

Q. But many of your poems are, in fact, about the state of being divided.

A. Yes. I think that what one tries to do in writing about the division that exists in the average human being—my poems about myself, certainly—is to present a kind of simple Manichean view of things: black and white are very pretty when put together. By "pretty," now, I mean just that. The inevitability for me of the schizoid feeling is so great that it's not unnatural or perverse at all, but perfectly natural. I can't visualize anyone, in other words, not having a sense of his own duality. I remember being fascinated once when I tried to write a play—I found that the central character had to split into two, to become a pair of twins, and I wondered why. I found, after I had written it, that it was out of this simple sense of the natural marriage of things: you cannot have a marriage without having the oppositions.

Q. So you wouldn't even see the oppositions as paradoxes?

A. Oh, by no means. Paradox would seem to mean to me precisely the reverse.

Q. I see. So it is a simple juxtaposition of antitheses that will not resolve.

A. Yes, yes. That are resolved, I think, in some kind of ultimate act of something like faith. And there you might get the resolution of purely intellectual paradoxes that would worry one, as a presumably thinking man. But the essential paradox that lies at the heart of human beings—I believe there is one—I don't think that's resolvable intellectually or consciously at all. Because of the passion of perversity that animates any truly human being, when any given proposition converts any rational, responsible man, instantly the possibility of its own obverse presents itself, with its possible justification.

Q. Is it possible for the poem to be a kind of revelation of faith . . . ?

A. Oh yes. It is very, very much an act of faith. And for this reason it's fascinating. I myself think an intellectual examination of a poem is a bore. The whole semantical thing to me is really utter drivel, because it doesn't get into the matter of how a poem aspires—in theory—to a condition like that of the prayer. In other words, all poems are ultimately not only religious statements, they also aspire to the condition of the prayer: they are praise. For instance, the oldest poem we have is a poem called the *Rig-Veda*. It actually signifies by its title "The Poem of Praise." This seems to me to contain the heart of the whole thing. There's an act of faith in praising that I think resolves—seems to resolve—all those oppositions of lines in one's consciousness.

Q.   You see life then as unresolved antitheses which find some kind of union in an act of revelation or an act of faith, and the poem itself can be such an act.

A.   I don't think that's an unfair representation of what I think—but then I don't think it very clearly at all, because I'm absolutely unsure of any of these matters; if I were sure I'm doubly certain I'd give up writing verse.

Q.   And why is that?

A.   Because I think what one's aspiring to is a condition not of knowledge but of faith. If one's got the faith. . . . Well, let me put it more simply. You remember that Saint Augustine defined faith as the pursuit of faith.

Q.   Yes. The poem is the pursuit of faith?

A.   Yes, yes, that kind of thing. Not an intellectual faith; perhaps I should say spiritual faith. I certainly mean something that transcends all intellectual predilections. I mean, it's demonstrable—is it not?—that by intellectual processes it's absolutely impossible to arrive at an act of faith, and it's also impossible to arrive there by any other means. If we knew the processes of acquiring the convictions of faith, we'd all dash to them.

Q.   Do you see all poems as such an act of praise?

A.   Yes. Yes, I do. Even those poems which seem to castigate the state of affairs . . .

Q.   For example, your "True Confession . . ."?

A.   Oh, most certainly. I think that's why there's a sort of pseudo-religious title there. One praises a process just as much by apparently satirizing it and castigating it as one does by the ostensible act of praise.

Q.   You talk as though we can't fail to praise, the world being what it is. We either praise negatively or positively . . . .

A.   Yes, I think so. In a certain sphere of, I suppose the word is "artistic," work, one either praises or does nothing at all. I'm thinking, for instance, of men entirely obsessed with technicalities and the craft. From the poems of such men I personally would get a conviction of things perfectly dead. I'm thinking specifically now of, say, a man like Bridges in *The Testament of Beauty.* I mean here's a man utterly obsessed—whether one likes the work or not, or admires it or not, is not the point. The point is that he was utterly obsessed with the technique of a certain kind of versification. The whole thing is stillborn, I think, because he wasn't in fact setting around, no matter how unconsciously, he wasn't setting around the business of praising anything really, right at the heart of the man. He was really praising the technique of verse.

Q.   Would you put some of the very contemporary poets who are trying to strip language of specific verbal meaning in the same category? . . . Someone like Zukofsky?

A.   Yes. I think it's an absurd thing to try to do, just as it's an absurd thing to try to remove, say, the skin of a human being, or to remove the conditions in which anything exists. The conditions are part of the delight, part of the fact that it is marvellous; you strip language of its meaning and what, precisely, have you got left?

Q.   Well, you have music left, you have sound . . . .

A.   You've got music without stripping it of meaning. I think the privilege of language is it not only has lovely sounds, but it has lovely meanings too. I can't see the point, quite, of depriving it of one of those conditions which make it, to me, superior to the art of music. I mean, the fact that one can convey, through words, things which one can convey through no other art, makes it very serious and very beautiful. I don't think the meaning is all that important, but it's one of the difficulties that make the writing of the language as fascinating as it is.

Q.   Now what do you mean when you say, "I don't think the meaning is all that important"?

A.   Well, as I say, because I think the intellectual specifications of a poem are part of the machinery by which an act of seduction of the reader is performed, and part of the process of praise by which the poet himself fulfills his true responsibility, which is ultimately that, I think, of making up something that competes with the prayer. It seems to me sad that so many prayers are quite out of the question insofar as they're so silly, so bad, so awful. And I think people like poems, if they like them at all, because there's a certain response in them to the inevitability and the necessity of the act of praise or prayer. Prayer is the formal word describing the purely theological praise of things of God. The word "praise" is the secular variation of it.

Q.   This means that you would reject the notion of the poem as a thing-in-itself, as an artifact or object, and see it always as something pointing to God.

A.   Oh yes. I don't have any conception of what it could mean to say that the poem exists by itself. Because obviously things don't exist in themselves and in themselves only. That seems to me a contradiction in terms. They are part of the body of things.

Q.   You're an admirer of Pound, I think; am I correct in that?

A.   I'm a most devoted admirer.

Q.   How would you link what you just said with Pound's notion of the creation of a poem that was a form, a beautiful object in itself? Would you go along with him on that?

A.   No, no, of course I wouldn't. I admire Pound's poetry in spite of disagreeing with him on almost everything he says. I think it's one of the lovely things about the art of poetry, or any decent art, that one can like all kinds of things with which one disagrees. I passionately disagree with what I believe was the over-intellectualization of Mr. Eliot's poems. I find masses of his poems entirely seductive; I wish they'd been done another way. But you are in the presence of a man who says the top of Parnassus is flat; there is room enough for us both. That's why I don't agree with what Ezra said about these things, but I adore some of his poetry. It's not rolling logs; it doesn't want one to believe in it—it's superior to that, as I see it.

Q.   Let's come back to something you said just a moment earlier. If you treat the poem as praise, is this a position you feel you have held throughout your poetic career, or have you come to this somewhere in mid-course?

A.   No, it's something which I think I began to try and understand, mentally, when I was about twenty-five. It first occurred to me that one might think what the hell was one doing, and what the hell was one doing it for, and then, in those moments when I wasn't drunk, it occurred to me that perhaps there was some point in the first poem we have being called *Rig-Veda* or "The Poem of Praise." The point was not just a historical taste for souvenirs or coincidences.

The idea of praise has been around in the poem for so long; I traced and followed this idea, through several historical antecedents, coming up, finally, to the man who said it most clearly, who is Rilke. It is there. And it seems to me that when you get several very serious and very beautiful poems agreeing on one particular matter, then what they say can be taken very, very seriously. And also, I think that if one happens to have any kind of, even pseudo-religious, mania, the idea of the poem as praise fits in very beautifully with that religious mania.

Q.   You have put your interest in this idea about 1940. Did this coincide with your adopting the Catholic faith, or . . . .

A.   Oh no, no. I was born a Catholic.

Q.   You were? This doesn't, then, represent a change but, really, the working out of a poetic view.

A.   Yes, to put it quite simply. It is the working out, or rather the rationalizing of what, in fact, can't really be rationalized. I think, for instance, that if I say the purpose of the poem is to praise, I'm still only getting at part of the purpose of the poem. I don't think it's simply to praise; I think there are lots of other impulses behind it. But this is the one which fascinates me, or rather, it's one of the ones that fascinate me.

Q.   Well, this takes me back to your early poetry. I know you've excluded quite a lot of it from your collected edition. Why? Does it have to do with content?

A.   No, no, I just couldn't find it. I've lost nearly as many poems as I've written. That book of essays contains just about a third of the stuff I've done. The rest is lost.

Q. I think you've left out, perhaps, most of the poems in *Thirty Preliminary Poems.*

A. Oh yes. Those were left out quite deliberately.

Q. Why?

A. I don't think they're very good.

Q. You just didn't like them? Does it have to do with the, perhaps, predominantly negative quality of vision in them?

A. Ah, no. Because to tell you the absolute truth, I wouldn't know what that was. I just thought they were badly written. You know they were written by someone trying to find out about the language. And now, that's amusing, but . . . .

Q. You were using language very differently then.

A. One would hope so.

Q. To what extent did you come under the impact of the surrealist movement?

A. Oh, very much. Because the best friend I had at that time, or one of the best friends, was David Gascoyne. And so we would kick this idea around—and anyhow, for any chap of my time, the surrealist idea was certainly the most exciting idea around then. For me it was infinitely more exciting than Marxism. Because politics has always rather bored me. I mean bored me in the sense that one is cynical, and has always been cynical, about it. All politicians are skullduggers and that's that. But the poems written by Breton and Eluard: there was a lovely series of poems in *transition* called "Simulations of Paralysis Essayed." These are terribly beautiful. You know they used language and ideas with an irresponsibility which was so heavenly to one at that time when one was overcome with a sense of responsibility, because one was new to the game. Oh God! one took oneself very seriously. It was lovely to see men playing around with ideas in apparently the service of a very beautiful idea: i.e., these poems were called, what were they? *Some Surrealist Poems in the Service of the Revolution.* So, what one was happy to believe in was that one was not only obsessed with aesthetics, but one was also doing a little political thinking at the same time. But even apart from that, the absolute destruction of all categories was an idea which of course excited us at that time.

Q. To what extent have you rejected the kind of technique that surrealism perhaps led you into for a few years? Your very recent poems are very formal, very pared . . . .

A. I don't think that that's a rejection at all. I think one begins with the use of words as a means of self-expression and I think that one proceeds to the use of manipulation of words as an art. And I would hope that I can now manipulate words as an art and not use them any more as a means of self-expression. And this is what I have against a great many young American poets—they seem never to contemplate the possibility of the manipulation of words as an art, but invariably and boringly use them as a means of self-expression.

Q. Precisely the accidental nature of the surrealist poem, then, would be the kind of thing that you are completely, now, rejecting?

A. If I reject anything—I would hate the idea of rejection—it is simply the ultimate personal irresponsibility involved in the surrealist idea. To me now the fascinating thing about things is to try to find out if they have a heart. If they do, I'd like to find out what it's saying. This seems to me an idea in contradiction to a surrealist idea. I believe in the essential comedy or tragedy of things, or both, preferably both; and one would like to listen to it talking, to them talking.

Q. Right after that, the New Apocalypse came along, and I've noticed that many of the statements about the New Apocalypse treat your work as an influence or a source. What was your connection with the New Apocalypse?

A. It was simply that I was the first chap who had the gumption to use the word "apocalypse," that was all.

Q. When was that and where?

A. That was about two years before the war. I wrote a bit of prose somewhere or other about how nature seems to have become apocalyptic, and suddenly this word. . . . You see many of us wouldn't have used a word like that, they were afraid, afraid. . . .

Q. Except perhaps Thomas.

A. Yes, but even he was too much of a puritan at heart. The word is too rumpty-dumpty, it's too Roman Catholic! You see it is absolutely a Bernini/Rome word. All the great tapestries, altars—and suddenly the word "apocalypse" entered the language. And this was absolutely all I knew about it. Then I went to Japan and when I got back to England several years later I discovered that the apocalyptic movement had not only got born and happened, but had already died.

Q.   That was 1939?

A.   Yes.

Q.   Did you know Henry Treece?

A.   No, no.

Q.   You didn't know him at all? Or G. S. Fraser?

A.   Fraser . . . had had the pleasure of meeting me several times.

Q.   I see, yes. They borrowed your word and that was all there was to it.

A.   Well, I do think there was a certain . . . there was, between Dylan Thomas and me, a friendship, which was not only a friendship of, you know, chaps who liked drinking. It was also that, I think, we were the first ones who hadn't any real care about politics at all. I'm thinking of how the atmosphere in London at that time was so full of political ideas and political passions, and one was *aware*—you were aware, you weren't alive, you were just politically self-conscious. But neither Dylan Thomas nor I had any care about such matters. This was one thing we had in common. Another thing, we used to go to the same place to drink. All that kind of thing. And also that Dylan was Welsh, in a way in which I liked to think I was Irish. We also hated the over-intellectualization of Mr. Eliot, and an evening's conversation between such men as were his friends, himself, me, and such men as were my friends, would have made no references whatsoever to the art of poetry, ever.

Q.   How did Herbert Read fit into this?

A.   He didn't fit in at all.

Q.   Didn't he perhaps share some of the attitudes toward poetry that you held?

A.   I don't know of his attitudes. I find him an unreadable man. I think he's so boring. His prose is gray and thin, like soup, and, I think, he has no passion. For me, Read is a man who was a lovely human being, but at the moment he began to write, whatever impulses he as a man delighted in seem to have gone. I speak quite personally. In other words, no, Herbert Read had nothing to do with us.

Q. I was thinking of his book on surrealism, and I had wondered if it had any significance for you.

A. Absolutely none, no. Not that—David's [Gascoyne] book on surrealism meant nothing. It was David's conversation about his friends in Paris, and his showing one and reading one some of the poems of Eluard, and translating them. Because, since I can't speak French, obviously I couldn't read the poems, so he would read them to us. I think too, though, that the whole disintegration thing was in the air. The surrealist disintegrations merely formalized it. I think it was all there, some kind of dreadful anticipation of the outbreak of the war. The total absence of any kind of true conviction, not only about politics, or spiritual matters, but even the technology of verse. Even there one felt, "well, this doesn't matter."

Q. When you are distinguishing yourself, then, from the poets who are political and who are concerned with the art of verse, you're primarily thinking of the Auden circle, is that right?

A. Yes, I suppose primarily I do, yes. Because these were the men who had preceded, say, Gascoyne, Dylan Thomas, and myself. These men were some four or five or six years older; they had all been to the universities; they had acquired, at the universities, the political awareness that they were bellyaching about. This was something which I personally rather despised because to me it was like wearing old school ties, you know. You were only allowed to be politically acute if you'd been through the proper universities, the proper schools, and so on.

Q. Though you were a close friend of MacNeice, weren't you?

A. No, not then, MacNeice wasn't published until I'd left London. I knew MacNeice the last five years of his life.

Q. I'd like to shift now and talk some about specific poems if I could. Let's begin with the "Daedalus," one of the early poems that you preserved in the collected edition. The specter in "Daedalus"—there've been quite a few speculations about it. Who was the specter?

A. Be damned if I know. It was probably my grandmother. I really simply don't know.

Q. Is it fair to see the specter perhaps as suggesting the whole body of attitudes connected with the loss of innocence, the loss of self-confidence, the fall in a kind of archetypal way?

A. I think that's perfectly fair. Just as I believe it's perfectly fair for any reader to put upon a poem any interpretation he wants to, that seems to him to hold water. I mean that's assuming that he's honest to himself and to the verse he's reading.

Q. What I was going to ask specifically is this: one critic has limited the meaning of that specter to fear itself. . . .

A. That would be unfair, quite frankly. That element is totally there, just as the poem says it's about fear. But it's a fear that—when you turn it round—is precisely its own opposite again. That's why the poem got itself called "Daedalus." I mean by that that the act of flying is also very courageous, trying to get to the sun and so on. The specter there is like the one at the Pharanoic family feast. It's just something to remind one of the terrible possibilities behind any act. . . .

Q. If it's fair to do that, then perhaps it's fair to go beyond the myth that you're working with and see Icarus as suggestive of the world of innocence in its larger sense. Is that possible?

A. That's perfectly possible.

Q. In one way, to oversimplify perhaps, you have the prelapsarian and the postlapsarian worlds.

A. Yes, yes, I think that's fair. Mark you, any imposition of purely conscious categories. . . . I only go on insisting on this because the whole point of what I would like to say about the reason poems aren't prose statements—they are not prose statements—is partly that they do not define and categorize.

Q. Does that help to explain some seemingly deliberately difficult passages in "Daedalus"? There is one section in which the syntax doesn't seem to resolve.

A. Oh yes. Though I don't think there's a single conscious idea in my mind that got into that poem, although it was written so long ago that I've almost forgotten all about it. But I do remember the thing didn't take longer than twenty minutes to write. I wrote that entire book of poems in about a month. Yes, I'd written that one and I sent it to Walter de la Mare, and he said, "Send this poem to Eliot." I sent it to Eliot and Eliot liked it and said, "When you've got a book of poems, we'll publish it." So of course I was delighted and I sat down and wrote the book of poems. That's really how it happened.

Q.   As I looked through the poem it struck me there were times in which you were using language, the sound of language, as a kind of metaphor itself. I wondered about this line, if you would comment: "I mourn him. Him I mourn, from morn to morning."[1]

A.   Oh yes, I think that that's the beginning of a simple passion for puns; in another sense it's a passion for getting the twin thing into one word. In other words it's a love of the ambivalence. I think also it's a thing that's been with me ever since. . . . Well, you see, my mother was born in the mountains of Mourne. She was born on top of a mourning. The word "mourning" has alway obsessed me. You'll find it in that poem I wrote to my mother, which finishes up with the line "That she will move from mourning into morning" [C.P. 121]. It's just this word, this one word. It goes back to my mother's birthplace. And there's really no more to it than that. There may be, but I don't know as I remember.

Q.   So there are at times biographical keys or details that also actuate puns.

A.   Oh yes, yes. In fact I would have thought that many poems are written only because they respond to some necessity for an act of auto-biography. They clear up a mess in one's life, in a lovely way, like creating a jewel about it. Certainly I think that's why that particular line and those particular words got used, insofar as I know anything about them—and I would think that I must know about sixty per cent of what they're all about, and no more.

Q.   It seemed to me, despite the fundamental suggestion of innocence in "Daedalus," that another theme or concern slipped in and has been returning again and again in your poetry. For example, you also say:

> Where wander those once known herons
> Or rabbits here

---

[1] George Barker, "Daedalus," *Collected Poems* (New York: October House, Inc., 1965), p. 4. Further references to this collection will be abbreviated C. P. and will be placed within the text.

could see them for what they were, without necessarily putting upon them what I had up to then thought in a fashion entirely narcissistic: world, myself, ego, the whole thing confused. The image of Narcissus was not quite right because I didn't even see the water. And then, this long poem ["Calamiterror"] was occasioned when a sporting accident happened and I blinded my brother in one of his eyes. The whole thing, then, blew up on me, and I don't think it was entirely by accident. I don't think the thing itself was an accident; it was one of those ghastly things . . . —a very close friend of mine, a poet by the name of Charles Madge, came up to me when he learned what had happened and said, "For God's sakes, now I know you are a poet." I could have hit him, but I knew the truth of what he was saying. My brother then became a very good painter. And I think the shift in these years was to do with that. . . . You see, I took my brother to the hospital and they said that had the sword entered his head by so much as about another sixteenth of an inch, he would have been insane for the rest of his life. And then I read about two days later that either Holbein or Dürer had spent two years constructing an instrument so he could see things as though he had two eyes. All these images got together at the same time, and they're all to do with the act of observing the objective world. That's how I see it now.

Q.   Even the poem "Allegory of the Adolescent and the Adult" written at that time emphasizes something you seem to me, now, to stress: "I look from my hill with the woods behind,/And Time, a sea's chaos, below" [C.P. 43]. This suggests a perception of the infinite in the phenomenal world, in the finite.

A.   Yes, yes. The line at that time signified: "Now, you simply don't know anything at all. The whole thing is as confusing as a sea and as beautiful. And as mysterious as the sea."

Q.   And Time? below?

A.   Precisely. There the image can be played on either hand. One saw time as confusing, and as beautiful, as experience. Often one imposes, with all one's hindsight, things on words. . . . There's a great deal of that in so much of what Churchill used to call gobbledygook. There's so much American poetry and American prose full of this inflation of language, to make it seem as though it were saying more than in fact it does.

Q.   Well, you're trying to say a lot in "Epistle II." I wonder if we can talk about it in some detail. It begins, "Time is not quick enough, space is not far enough,/But I can hit it with the point of my hand." And it goes on:

> Now as you sit by a window and watch the bough
> Struggling to catch your eye in America, I
> Move my right hand, and that is it in England.
> The kin of things is deeper and stranger than species:
> Kind calls to more than kind. . . . [C.P. 65]

A.   That seems fairly clear, doesn't it?

Q.   I wonder to what extent here you're speaking as the poet himself: "the point of my hand"?

A.   Yes. The whole stanza is simply trying to say, "Watch, I'm now going to write a poem about our friendship, so get ready"—that sort of thing.

Q.   In the course of that, you suggest some intuitive understanding. . . . Something very close to mystic communication.

A.   Yes, very much so. It was written to someone who had just written a book about *Moby Dick*, and there's a lot of Melville in it; I don't mean stylistically—not at all—I mean the influence of Melville. You know, the lovely sort of "paternal" thing that one often gets from the great poets.

Q.   When you talk about a kind of instantaneous communication . . . do you mean it?

A.   I believe it to be possible, even physiologically. I think it's perfectly possible that there could conceivably be such a thing as communication occurring in a sphere where temporal judgments and temporal rules didn't operate. This would be as near as I can get to talking about instantaneous communication, which is presumably something that has nothing to do with stop-watches.

Q.   "Whatever my message is, that I cannot write,/Things signify. . . ."

A.   That's "Whatever my message is, *that* I cannot write." *That* refers to the message. Whatever the message is, that message I cannot write. The word "message": "idea" I suppose would be clearer.

Q.   I see. "Things signify, that speak in the code of life/Not to a tongue translated." What do you mean here by the "code of life"?

A. I mean there some communication, I suppose ultimately some kind of animal magnetism, that occurs both under and above language. I mean finally, I suppose, what the word "empathy" intellectually is supposed to convey. I mean some kind of sympathy.

Q. As the metaphor develops, the person to whom you're addressing the poem becomes the west wind; and further along the narrator says: "I send to you/Not love, not love, but what's between us—space./Space greater than distances . . ." [C.P. 66]. I remember you once wrote that spaces between the lines are important, that the spaces are like Dante's love that moves the sun and the other stars. . . .[4]

A. That's what I was trying to get at there, you know. It's to do again with another line I remember writing, "A division exists only to prove who loves." It bears also upon that most incredible of all poems, "The Phoenix and the Turtle": the distance and the spaces. This is what one's trying to get at, the fact that the condition of love makes space both necessary and quite unnecessary—if that's clear. The Dante image is the clearer one.

Q. Are you also pointing to the underlying unity of things?

A. Unity if you wish, yes. It's the idea of all things being in a communion that renders space only there, so that they communicate over something and don't become identical. People would have no identities were it not for that, but they do have their identities. And this makes this kind of a communication both necessary and possible.

Q. This comes back to where we started, with the antitheses. . . . You go on in that same poem:

> . . . the space that makes
> Mountains and lakes and seas, the space that makes
> Sorrow and shadow by separation, makes
> Things like the bird that flies and falls from grace. [C.P. 67]

These lines, in many ways, bring together very disparate parts of your work. The bird, the fall from grace, and the love implicit in grace seem connected both with the fall of Icarus [*Poems*, 1935] and with the seagull in your 1950 novel.

---

[4] *Ibid.*, p. 177.

A. Well, that whole business of the idea of falling, you know, not only haunts the dreams of people in the Freudian sense, but haunted me too, because when I was a little boy, about six of us used to climb up to the top of the big building where we lived—a tenement. And there was a large architrave up at the top, not very wide and about seventy feet up in the air, and we used to slide down it—I suppose when I was about eight. All the terror that one could do nothing about when one was a little boy because one was along with other little boys, I think that's there.

Q. How about the seagull in your novel? The seagull falls dead at the man's feet. Are all these falls related in some archetypal way?

A. Well, I would imagine, myself, that it's because to me the word "fall" is one of the most ambiguous and beautiful words. It's my own passion for that kind of word, I mean words which are so full of a multiplicity of correspondences. The American word "fall" for autumn is so much more beautiful than "autumn," for this reason. It's an entirely marvellous word, because of the multiplicities of correspondences that meet in it—the implication, for instance, that whatever falls in fact occupied a height, such like that.

Q. We haven't yet touched on the gull. You speak also in "Epistle II" of "Love/Labouring like a gull in a gale" [C.P. 166], which again reminds me of the dead seagull and the link to love and fall. What about the gull image?

A. Well, that has to do with the fact that at that time I was living in a cottage on top of a cliff in Dorset. The gulls would come and sit on the window ledge. And I could look out; on days of great storms it was tremendously beautiful. These creatures were flying with a great deal of wildness, but they were flying at exactly the same height that I was sitting in my chair. That fascinated me. It was simply that this cottage was three hundred feet up; so were the gulls; the wind would be blowing them around and I would look up and see them.

Q. You link love with this image of the gull; and elsewhere, in "The True Confession"—to paraphrase it—you say "show me true love and I will show you that it's false." Are you playing on the word "gull"?

A. Most certainly. There's a single sentence in *The Dead Seagull* which simply says "Gull the bitch."[5]

---

[5] George Barker, *The Dead Seagull* (London: John Lehmann, 1950), p. 64.

Q. So the image of the gull, linked to the image of dead love, here, is precisely the play which is involved?

A. Yes, that was conscious, a deliberate thing.

Q. Together with the implications of the soaring possibilities of love?

A. Yes, indeed. And again this business of finding the seagull, which of course I did, you know, lying there on the shore, dead. It was the crossing of the images which made it seem to me so rich.[6] And because I think the word "seagull" is again such an extremely beautiful one.

Q. Is it fair to ask how much of that novel is based on autobiography?

A. Oh, I'd guess about a third. I had to get some money so I decided to write a novel. That novel was written in about a month, which wasn't long enough. It should have taken five weeks!

Q. Well, the gull returns us to "Epistle II." There are a few more things there that have struck me as basic to what you've been saying. "I dare give you nothing but the shapes I make/ . . . The tortured twistings of a headless hand." Nonetheless, these shapes are the most important things . . . perhaps being metaphorically "headless" is not so very important?

A. The idea there is the auspices of animals, and such like. I think it ties up with what I believe now, which is that poems say much more than the words in them.

Q. The poet as magician?

A. Yes, certainly. Yes. As seer, even.

Q. Would you go so far as to say that reason is inadequate for knowing in any profound way anything?

A. Oh most certainly I would. "The heart has its reasons which reason does not know," and so on.

Q. So in a way, the poem is a way of knowing.

A. Oh I am most sure of this. I'm sure it's one of the reasons why people still, in spite of all, take poetry seriously, and they do. You are still not allowed to put the word "poet" on your passport, you know.

---

[6] Cf. *The Dead Seagull*, p. 63.

Q. Really?

A. No, no. They cross it out and put "writer." In fact, it happened to me. An irritating chap put "writer" and when I got to Italy and showed my passport on one occasion—I had to in a restaurant to change some money—the man thought I was a waiter, because they had written the word "writer" so badly. The "r" looked like an "a"!

Q. This brings us to the next four poems that I'm particularly interested in: the first, "Turn on your side and bear the world to me . . . ."

A. Just a little love lyric.

Q. Yes. A marvellous lyric. . . . Do you feel that there's no way, apart from the birth of the child, to redeem the sexual experience? That seems to be one of the things you're getting at there.

A. Well, if you can tell me another one, I'd be deeply, deeply grateful.

Q. Apart from that, though, it remains caught in original sin, without intrinsic merit?

A. I think these matters are matters that are too difficult for me and for you.

Q. All right, fair enough. That may leave us in the same place with the sequence of poems called "The Bridal Nightmare."

A. Those were very horrible—at least they were very horrible for me. Someone I loved very deeply went through a process like that of dying. I can't be more specific about it because I would dishonour myself in speaking about it. I have written verses about it and I wish that I hadn't. But then I often have to be—sometimes writing poems is like the act of defecation; it's getting out of one's system, to put it simply, things that, if they stayed in, would turn one into a sort of gila monster, so that one was filled up with accumulated filth, and one would explode of it in the end. In other words, it's some kind of liberation of conscience. I speak now of the poem as a piece of mechanics, a piece of psychological mechanics. Those poems about "The Bridal Nightmare" were all tied up in a circumstantial situation that I knew was absolutely intolerable and that had to be gotten through. And the writing often was one way simply of placating both the Eumenides and my own conscience. I speak now of why I wrote them. I don't think they're difficult to understand.

Q.   Well, I don't know how difficult they may be. Perhaps there may be some criticism that's gone astray, and I may have misread them myself. Is it correct to say that the first of the three poems is spoken by the bride and the second and third by the man?

A.   Just give me the first lines. I remember how perfectly difficult it was to get the title for them. There's a pun in the title by the way—well, obviously.

Q.   Bridal, bridle? yes, right—as you pick up in the last several lines. The poem begins: "Nightmare in whose arctic wings/Lifelong I unmoving lie . . ." [C.P. 134].

A.   Oh yes, I remember. I do remember, too, the occasion, although I don't know whether it's amusing. The occasion was in Doré illustrations. I can remember that quite clearly, you know, those marvellous scenes in the illustrations for *The Divine Comedy,* those wonderful Doré drawings of angels and demons and such like. That's why I began to write those poems. Obviously the content was there, but Doré was what started me off. That's why that opening is what it is.

Q.   I am correct to read it as spoken by a woman?

A.   Oh yes, that's right. Yes, that whole poem is.

Q.   May I explain that one of your critics has said that there are two speakers in the poem, which I simply could not see.

A.   No, I don't think that's right.

Q.   Then next, though, in the following two poems, the speaker is the lover who abandons?

A.   Yes, that's right.

Q.   And the metaphor of crucifixion in the second poem is precisely that—metaphor, subordinate?

A.   Oh yes, that's precisely right. That one is simple. There are also some nice puns in that second one.

Q.   Yes, all the way through. There's also a very sustained metaphor of Christ on the tree.

A.   Yes.

Q. In fact, until one gets to the next to the last stanza, one isn't completely sure whether the subject is fundamentally religious or about a lost love.

A. The person about whom those poems were written was a passionate Catholic, very passionate, who would not have read the verses at all if they hadn't been interpretable in a formal Christian way. She would have simply said *"niente"*. . . . They were written to present one's excuses, in a way.

Q. Before we leave these poems, is there a sense in which you would parallel the guilt of irresponsible creation of a child with irresponsible creation of a poem?

A. I have never been able to take poems as seriously as I ought to.

Q. Oh. In short, no.

A. Yes, thank you, that's it!

Q. Now I'd like to shift completely to one of your last collections, *The Golden Chains.*

A. Oh yes. I always liked that one but no one else seems to . . . but there you are!

Q. The choice of form: you are consistently, through your life, moving to a more and more constrained form.

A. I would very much hope so, yes.

Q. With these two-stanza poems. . . .

A. I did it quite definitely there; but it seemed to me to be a very difficult thing to do, and therefore I tried to do it. I knew that to try to write in eight lines what one thinks about a given matter is very difficult, and to carry that on for some while without becoming either a bore or repetitious is both a technical and mental problem—and it is something that fascinated me.

Q. Am I correct to see in this poetry a greater reliance on an almost iconographic use of words, rather than on rhetoric?

A. Yes, that's precisely it. A distaste for formal rhetoric is something which very fortunately I have gone now, nearly, I hope, through. I was deeply in love with the whole baroque idea; for many years I adored it. I think I've worked my way through it, at least I hope I did. And now I prefer simple poems.

Q. With the kind of reference. . . .

A. Oh, I would hope they'd have lots of concealed meanings that would make them more amusing, more entertaining, even—God help us—more profound.

Q. Yes, that brings us to some statements that, though you say you abhor theory, are very close to theoretical statements about the role of the mask in a poem.[7]

A. Yes, it's a terrible bore, you know, to talk about theories, but one has to construct some in order—well, simply in order to maintain one's sanity about what one's doing. One has to make judgments and interpret to oneself why one is doing any given thing. Like writing poems . . . which seems to me to be an unpardonable occupation for a grown man, unless he's got to do it. Well, I found that I've got to do it in the same sense that I've got to defecate. I haven't been able to do anything else. Not that I can do that, I certainly can't do anything else. Therefore, I had to try to work out in my own mind what I thought the function of the poet, if he had a function, in fact, was, and is.

Q. And how does the mask come in?

A. The mask comes in quite simply: if one has found that it's necessary, physiologically necessary, to try to write poems, but one is in fact ashamed of doing so, then one invents a mask; this is how it begins. And when you find certain things you believe are things you'd rather not believe in, you invent a mask for that. A mask is a fascinating thing because no one ever knows what's behind it.

Q. In a sense you'd say reality wears a mask?

A. I would say that one doesn't know what reality is. One doesn't know whether the mask is real or what it conceals is real. Or whether both things are real. Because here language ceases to have any true responsibility; it simply doesn't say the kind of things that the mind is saying. Language often misrepresents what one thinks.

---

[7] See, for example, "St George and the Long-Snouted Allegory," *Essays,* p. 182.

Q. What is the mask in *The Golden Chains?*

A. There are about four of them. The first person singular in that poem is used in at least three or four different ways—sometimes to disguise that I'm writing a poem, sometimes to disguise the fact that the opinions being presented are not really mine, sometimes . . . all that kind of thing. The determination to show the first person singular in a poem is a pure formality; it's simply part of the architectonic, to show that it really has no relation whatsoever to the first person singular. Just that. In other words, it mustn't be believed. Do you remember that sentence of Mr. Eliot's, "The poet throws the meaning to the reader the way the burglar throws meat to a dog"?

Q. In some way we're supposed to understand something beyond the meaning?

A. Well yes. An act of ravishment is going on despite the fact that what is apparently being said is merely a few affirmations about whatever the subject of the poem is. At the same time an act of some kind of lovely ravishment is happening, as I see it. In other words, one is actually succeeding in convincing oneself and someone else that both the writer and the reader are joined in an act of praise.

Q. And this transforms the poet from magician really to priest?

A. Yes, well, precisely. The saint operates upward and the poet operates downwards.

Q. What do you mean by downwards?

A. The imagination of the poet, if he's a good one, observes things from the altitude of the imagination, downwards, looking at more things than, from the usual six feet, most of us can see. Just that. Do I make myself clear?

Q. Yes, I think so. This returns us then to the negative as well as positive praise.

A. Yes. I can only see the negative praise, myself, exemplified in such things as satirical poems. Everywhere else, even when one's castigating a condition that seems to be unpleasant, the mere fact of writing a poem about it transforms it from the complaint, which is sin, to an act of praise, which is merely recording as a natural fact, the fact that the condition has been observed.

Q. This is true even in a poem such as "Elegy II" in which, if I remember correctly, you're asking if it is not indeed a poison in the soul that one can view a world so monstrous and still see joy?

A.   Oh yes. And it would be true even if there were no joy. I'm thinking particularly of that speech in there about adultery—I tried to write about it somewhere or other—which exemplifies precisely what I mean: this speech is full of horror but behind the horror there's some kind of hideous delight at being able to say it. It's the domination, a kind of marvellous domination, that the imagination performs on the facts, and it doesn't really matter whether the facts are nice or nasty—some kind of transfiguration of them has been made.

Q.   And the poems of despair over death?

A.   Yes, they praise the fact of despair. That the creature can despair is an enormous privilege.

Q.   And a sin?

A.   Ah. Well. This is where one gets into theology. The exact nature of sin is sometimes so impersonal and sometimes so personal that unless one's a formal Catholic . . . and speaking as a formal Catholic, one wouldn't really know . . . I can't really be a formal Catholic . . . I disagree with . . . oh, blimey! . . . I do happen to see the Church as wrong in many many ways. Therefore I can't claim to have a classical Catholic sense of sin. Lots of things that the Church thinks of as sinful, I cannot see as such. I claim to be not a Catholic, but a renegade Catholic. I think the Church ideally should have a lot more renegades in it.

Q.   Perhaps we could end with a few specific questions about your life and what you have published. One thing that I haven't been able to find is *The Mortals*. Did that novel ever appear?

A.   It never got written.

Q.   And *Alanna Autumnal*: how do you regard it? As autobiography or what?

A.   Oh, it was a little novelina. And I suppose since it was the first novel I wrote (they tell me all first novels are autobiographical) that it must have been autobiographical. I went to see Middleton Murry and he said to me, "Have you written a book?" And I said, "Well, as a matter of fact, I've got some journals." He read them and said they'd make a nice novel. So I changed them around.

Q.   What are you working on now?

A.   I've just finished writing thirty-six political ballads. And they're funny. I got through with them last month. And I've just written three books of children's poems. That was really remarkable. I got a hundred-and-sixteen in about eight weeks. I know that it's terribly vulgar to talk like this, but I really do it in seizures, and then I just can't bear the sight of a piece of paper. Yes, I got three books of children's poems in not two months. And this last lot I finished about two days ago. I feel rather pleased with them because they're funny, and they rhyme!

Q.   Would you be willing to fill in a few details of biography?

A.   That depends very much on what they are.

Q.   Almost no information is available. I wonder if you could simply mention where you were born, where you were educated, and so on.

A.   Yes. I was born near Epping Forest. My father was a policeman and my mother was a lady who was born in an Irish village. She was the daughter of a pilot of Cork Harbour. They moved from where I was born when I was about two, and we went to a huge tenement in Chelsea. I went to the local school, which was an enormous place. It had fifteen hundred boys and girls; they were all horrid—they were marvellous, tremendous. I got a scholarship from there when I was about thirteen, and I met some Jesuit priests. I started writing poems—I think the first poem I wrote I wrote when I was seven. These priests knew that I wrote verses, you see, which was really quite extraordinary in this place. . . . Well, it was. You get a lot of chaps, you know, whose fathers were coal-men, and things like that, but not many who write verses. These priests came to my mother's . . . and so I used to go to the office of these two priests, who shouldn't have been there, but they were there, for their own reasons; I used to go there about three evenings a week. It was where I was really educated—these two Jesuits would tell me to read this and read that and read the other.

I was very physically precocious, and I was terribly in love. I was supposed to go to this school I'd got a scholarship at, and I went there for a year, but I got fed up with it. And I left school and got a job. I used to wear a long blue cloak down to my ankles, and an enormous Spanish sombrero, so I got the sack after about three days. I was supposed to have been an office boy. I used to take Milton with me—a few massive books—and I was called in by this very milk-soppy fellow, horrible little man, who said to me, "I refuse to employ someone who looks like an utter nihilist here, you're sacked." And so I had about twenty jobs between the time I was fifteen and the time I was eighteen, at least twenty. And when I was eighteen I got married. (My present wife I married in Italy, about six years ago.) And when I was eighteen too I sent this poem which I had written called "Daedalus" to Walter de la Mare, and that's how it all began. De la Mare in turn sent it to Eliot, as I told you. Then, I had no money, so Eliot did the most extraordinary thing: I never knew who they were, but he got five people to put ten shillings a week each into a bank and he gave me two pounds ten a week for years; that was what we lived on. I was given a cottage by a lady who was a friend of David Archer's, a cottage in Dorset, and my wife and I went down there. . . . And that's all.

CALENDAR OF INTERVIEWS

	Interviewer	Date of Interview	Publication in CL*
NOVELISTS			
John Hawkes	John J. Enck	March 20, 1964	VI, 2 (Summer, 1965)
John Barth	John J. Enck	April 17, 1964	VI, 1 (Winter–Spring, 1965)
Saul Bellow	John J. Enck	April 24, 1964	VI, 2 (Summer, 1965)
Vladimir Nabokov	Alfred Appel, Jr.	Sept. 25–29, 1966	VIII, 2 (Spring, 1967)
Isaac Bashevis Singer	Cyrena N. Pondrom	March 29 and April 9, 12, 1968	X, 1, 3 (Winter, Summer, 1969)
Jorge Luis Borges	L. S. Dembo	Nov. 21, 1969	XI, 3 (Summer, 1970)
Sara Lidman	L. S. Dembo	May 4, 1969	XII, 3 (Summer, 1971)
Per Olof Sundman	L. S. Dembo	May 8, 1969	XII, 3 (Summer, 1971)
POETS			
James Merrill	Donald Sheehan	May 23, 1967	IX, 1 (Winter, 1968)
Kenneth Rexroth	Cyrena N. Pondrom	March 23, 1968	X, 3 (Summer, 1969)
George Oppen	L. S. Dembo	April 25, 1968	X, 2 (Spring, 1969)
Carl Rakosi	L. S. Dembo	April 4, 1968	X, 2 (Spring, 1969)
Charles Reznikoff	L. S. Dembo	May 2, 1968	X, 2 (Spring, 1969)
Louis Zukofsky	L. S. Dembo	May 16, 1968	X, 2 (Spring, 1969)
Gwendolyn Brooks	George Stavros	March 28, 1969	XI, 1 (Winter, 1970)
George Barker	Cyrena N. Pondrom	Sept. 9, 1970	XII, 4 (Autumn, 1971)

* *Contemporary Literature* (before 1968, titled *Wisconsin Studies in Contemporary Literature*)

INDEX

absurd, concept of: 124–126 (Lidman)

Adam, Pierre: 184 (Oppen)

Agee, James: his A Death in the Family mentioned, 16 (Hawkes)

alchemy: 159, 162–163, 168, 171 (Rexroth)

Anderson, Sherwood: 32 (Bellow); 172 (Oppen)

angst: 118 (Borges)

animal magnetism: 269 (Barker)

Apollinaire, Guillaume: 143 (Merrill); 167 (Rexroth)

Archer, David: 279 (Barker)

Aristotle: 119 (Borges); 155 (Rexroth); 217, 224 (Zukofsky)

Assis, Machado de: 18, 19 (Barth)

Auden, W. H.: 142, 151 (Merrill); 262, 266 (Barker)

Auerbach, Erich: 33 (Bellow)

autobiography, use of, in their own works: 48 (Nabokov); 142 (Merrill); 254, 264, 271, 277 (Barker)

avant-garde, theory of: 4–6 (Hawkes)

Baldwin, James: 4 (Hawkes); 20, 21, 23 (Barth); 33 (Bellow); 246, 249 (Brooks)

—his Another Country mentioned, 21 (Barth)

Balzac, Honoré de: 20 (Barth)

Baraka, Imamu Amiri (LeRoi Jones): 236, 249 (Brooks)

Barker, George: on his passion for puns, xiv, 264; on choice of form, xiv, 274–275; on role of mask in poetry, xiv, 275–276; on solipsism, 253, 266; on composition of poems, 253–254; on division in human beings, 254; on paradox, 254; on the passion of perversity, 254; on the poem as act of faith, 254–255; on the poem as act of praise, 255–256, 257–258, 276; on meaning in poetry, 256–257; on his Catholicism, 258, 265, 277; on surrealism, 259–260, 262; on Auden circle, 262; on visions, 265; on image of Narcissus, 267; on blinding of brother, 267; on perception of infinite in phenomenal world, 267; on underlying unity of things, 269; on image of seagull, 269–271; on the poem as way of knowing, 271; on epistemology, inadequacy of reason, 271, 275; on negative praise, 276; works in progress, 278; biographical details, 278–279; mentioned, x, xiv

—works by: Alanna Autumnal, 277; "Allegory of the Adolescent and the Adult" (Collected Poems), 266, 267; "The Bridal Nightmare" (Collected Poems), 272–274; "Calamiterror" (Collected Poems), 266–267; "Daedalus" (Collected Poems), 262–265, 279; The Dead Seagull, 269, 270, 271n; "Elegy II" (Collected Poems), 277; "Epistle II" (Collected Poems), 267–269, 270, 271; The Golden Chains, 253, 274,